CHIT CHAT NORTHAMPTON

✳✳✳

A CLUB OF GENTLEMEN

Michael Toseland

This first edition is limited to thirty eight copies
This is number 24

First published in 2013 by Figaro Publishing
The Thatched Cottage, 20 Meadow Lane,
Little Houghton
Northampton NN7 1AH.

M A Toseland asserts the moral rights to be identified as the author of this work.

ISBN No. 978-0-9573754-1-3

Printed and bound by
MERLAND COPY & PRINT,
NORTHAMPTON

This book is dedicated to those pictured within and to my wife Janet whose idea it was in the first place and without whose continued prodding and encouragement it would never have come to fruition.

Characteristic device or smoky programme
by Tyrannus Jones 1896

Contents

Acknowledgements	vi
Foreward	vii
Illustrations	ix
Part 1. The Club	
1. Prologue	3
2. Early Days. May 1885 - May 1887	10
3. Greene Years. July 1887 - May 1892	23
4. Tyrannus III. July 1882 - February 1901	35
5. Browne Years. March 1901 - July 1923	57
6. Tyrannus V. September 1923 – 1949	70
7. Darker Days and Renaissance. Summer 1949 – 2012	86
Part 2. The Chatterers.	97
Northampton Chit Chat Members 1885-2012	100
8. Clergy	121
9. The Law	155
10. Doctors, Mad and Otherwise	197
11. Teachers	255
12. Others	272
Epilogue	306

Appendices

1. Guest Speakers	308
2. Rules	315
3. Tyranni	330
4. *Awake Northamptonshire*	331
Index	335

Acknowledgements

My thanks are to all those who have helped me to get this book together. The staff of Northamptonshire Libraries and Northamptonshire Record Office have put up with my ignorance of their filing systems and seemingly endless questions. Special thanks to Sally at Merland who has gently and expertly guided me through the printing and presentation processes. Above all it is the patience and memory of Chit Chat Club members, past and present that have made this volume possible.

Sources are referred to in chapter notes and their contributions have been gratefully received.

TYRANNUS ON GUARD

Foreword

When I became Club Tyrannus – Secretary, Treasurer and Chairman - in 2008 and began reading through past minute books and papers, I found myself becoming more and more deeply entrenched in the past life of the Club and its members. Sparks of genius and misdemeanours of Chatterers sprang vividly to life and I began to feel I knew these people who were inspired to start a Northampton Chit Chat club in 1885.

"Why don't you write about it, it would make a good read?" my wife suggested, doubtless bored with my endless regaling of hundred year old incidents so I did and I hope it is.

There was a great deal missing and past officials had hardly ever included many details such as dates of birth – or death. I then discovered the parent Club in Cambridge that had flourished from 1860 to 1897 and resolved to produce a magnum opus about both Clubs. This delayed my progress but hopefully now that it has been decided to divide the work into two parts both will be finished this year.

One problem was the soubriquet 'Club', rather than 'Society'. A Gentlemen's Club conjures up an image of silent be-whiskered cigar smoking men of a certain age lounging in deep leather chairs, waited upon by deferential lackeys providing never ending glasses of whisky and soda, all in good solid bricks and mortar. The Chit Chat was never that, there was and is no fixed abode, it moves around wherever the host of the evening shall decide. Members are essentially a group of friends, drawn together by a desire to discuss and probe past and current matters, subjects both bizarre and commonplace. Hence the book's title, a Club of Gentlemen, not for Gentlemen.

At an early stage it seemed there could be no better way than to let the past speak for itself with myself editing discretely in the wings and restraining for the most part any desire to comment.

Sometimes there was obviously a good story in the background and I indulged myself in bringing it forward. Any account of a Club, with so many names, could easily sink into a morass of dates and figures. I hope I have avoided this as much as possible.

Another problem was what to leave out and about half way through it looked as if all members should be mentioned, a course which meant dividing the book into two sections, the first broadly speaking a history of the Club and the second a roughly chronological story of members and their contributions. Whether this has become too complicated is left to readers to decide. Any omissions or errors are entirely my responsibility with my apologies in advance to the families of any Chatterers who may find stories or opinions even mildly offensive.

C.C.C.

TYRANNUS ON GUARD

Illustrations.

Canon Bury and Dr Richard Greene – Drawings by W B Shoosmith from *Our County* by Sir Ryland Adkins, 1893.

Three Chatterers in front of Northampton Grammar School – *Northampton in Old Picture Postcards* by Lou Warwick and Alan Burman 1986.

Images of C A Markham, School for Deaf and sketch of Sir Ryland Adkins by courtesy of Northamptonshire Record Office.

Images of Canon Sanders and M B Nettleton by courtesy of Northamptonshire Central Library.

Images of Rev. Tom, Rev. Beasley and 'young' Markham from *Northamptonshire Leaders, Social and Political* by Gaskell c. 1905.

Cameo portraits of Chatterers from *Northamptonshire in the Twentieth Century* by W T Pyke 1908.

Image of **Sir Basil Thomson**. A Getty image by courtesy of Gary Shaeffer, Popperfoto.

All other illustrations are taken from Club minute books and archives.

x

PART 1 – The Club

1
Prologue

It is May 1885. George Hooper drew up outside the headmaster's house. The journey from his Courteenhall rectory, though less than an hour had given him time for thought, most of which he'd spent admiring the view instead of concentrating on the meeting ahead. Down the uneven bridle path leading to the main London road, then turning right and enjoying smoother ground beneath the buggy's wheels, the horse had become less frisky, settling into a leisurely walk as he trotted towards Northampton. A short rise and the Nene valley vista opened before him. In the bright spring sunshine with a picture book blue sky overhead, the town revealed itself as a warm yellowish brown collection of houses with only a few churches breaking the roofline. Reddish blobs of brick signalled change from market town to industrialisation that the boot and shoe industry along with increased employment had brought. Down the southern slope of the valley the walls of Delapre Abbey loomed on the right of the London road and Hooper bowed his head towards the cross erected by Henry II in 1291 after bringing his dead queen from Harby, near Lincoln, to her eventual resting place in Westminster Abbey. Each night the cortege had stopped at an appropriate site where Eleanor's eviscerated and embalmed body could be prayed over and what could have been better than this nunnery of Delapre? George felt a feeling of wonder whenever he came this way at the devotion of a king who would erect crosses at each of twelve stopping places on the road to his capital city.

Crossing South Bridge the road became busier with traders' carts and pedestrians. George brought himself back to reality. Everything had started at Cambridge. Before that his childhood in Brighton was merely a mist, schooldays at Uppingham a haze. Sheltered within parental vicarage walls he'd experienced little of life but that had opened up in October 1870, demonstrating to the twenty year old student there was more at Emmanuel College than pure academic subjects when reading for the priesthood. He had never been at the forefront of student life, certainly not in the social strata of the more prominent public school sets, more of an observer. Everyone knew about the Apostles, that exclusive secret society whose reputation for unacceptable practices had not been helped by having Tennyson and Hallam, Alfred and Arthur, as members and where strange goings on were said to take place. No, the Chit Chat Club had presented George Hooper with a more practical goal, although one he had never attained, never been invited to join. It was not truly a Club, rather a Society for was not a Gentleman's Club a place to which one could retire and relax within an enveloping armchair and be waited upon with cigars and wine? The Chit Chat moved from room to room each Saturday night with the main intention of serious discussion but it was said there was sociable mixing from several colleges and divisions of society. George had heard about its various goings on, presentation of erudite papers and several internal wrangling sessions regarding rules. The idea intrigued him. One day he would start such a Club or Society if like-minded men could ever be found.

All this had been fifteen years or so ago but the possibility had never evaporated and today, yes today, the dream might well become reality. His first curacy in Northampton at the new church of St Edmund's had been followed by a welcome move into the countryside six years ago to the living of Courteenhall under the patronage of Sir Hereward Wake. Life was good, marriage to Annie the previous year completing his world. In spite of the distance

George had kept in touch with some of his town contacts, among them Sanders, headmaster of the Grammar School and curate of St Peter's Church, half a mile to the west of Northampton's centre. It had only been a month or so ago the two men found their memories of Cambridge included a desire to start a Chit Chat for themselves.

Sanders' recent journeys to Cambridge in connection with his Master's degree and forthcoming doctorate had sparked his enthusiasm. As headmaster he had instituted a debating Society that had surpassed his wildest hopes. It was a sort of parliament with himself as Speaker and other masters and boys as debaters. With characteristic common sense the subjects of religion and politics were banned but otherwise there was a broad base of discussion, heated at times, that brought staff and pupils together.

Having confessed their joint enthusiasm for a debating forum that would encompass all walks of life in the town, Sanders had called this first exploratory meeting, promising he would be careful who he invited, limiting numbers to friends and professionals for whom he could vouch. George felt slightly apprehensive however. The headmaster's last remark to him at their previous meeting had been somewhat ambiguous. When gripping George's arm he smiled and said "Don't worry, I think you'll make an excellent secretary!" George was not the best organiser in the world and hoped he could live up to the pedagogue's inference. So far there had been no mention of a structure to the Club, let alone any question of officials. Perhaps there would be someone else better qualified …. but the idea was not entirely unpleasant, you never know, he was used to writing after all, what about sermons, they seemed to slip off the pen fairly easily?

Up the rise from South Bridge and round the railed forecourt of All Saints' Church the horse now sensing that perhaps the journey was nearing its end, gathered speed. Travelling up broad Abington Street George came to a halt outside Number 81, the imposing double fronted School House, next door but one to the Ladies' Boarding School recently established by the Catholic Convent Sisters of Notre Dame.

Other guests had already arrived. Introductions were made over a welcoming glass of sherry. Bespectacled Mr John Eunson, the oldest member of the group at 52, now a consulting engineer to the recently 'municipalised' Northampton Water Company and manager of the Northampton Gas Company, was well known for his sharp mind and ability to speak both in public and at committees. Mr George, Tom to his friends, had recently become curator at the Northampton Museum as well as being Librarian down Guildhall Road. Hopefully he would find time to give the Club his experienced thoughts on both organisations. At 31 he was the youngest of the group rather to the relief of George Hooper, at 36 fearing he might be the infant at the meeting. Charles Hammond had come from his vicarage at Wootton, a village on George's way in and had he known this they might have joined forces for transport. The group was completed by Richard Scriven, a local historian who had already contributed papers to the Northamptonshire Natural History Society where he was a committee member.

Sanders had chosen well, the men blended ideally and soon got down to business. Persuasive as ever Sanders led the conversation. It was clear several guests were curious. Why Chit Chat? A short explanation regarding Cambridge origins did not satisfy and the question was rephrased as to why a name should be used that normally referred to gossip between women. With an apparent sudden surge of spontaneity Sanders presented the meeting with his thoughts.

"It is a clever twist on the Kit-Cat Club, that wonderful gathering of London's intelligentsia of the eighteenth century when such minds as Dryden, Addison and Steele ruled coffee houses across the capital". George smiled to himself, dragging half-forgotten memories from the back of his mind – were they not a set of rebellious Whigs? He kept his peace. Sanders continued.

"I like it but of course if any of you gentlemen have a better idea ....?" They had none. Discussion swiftly turned to other matters.

"I've found at school it's best to avoid religion of any sort and I am sure none of us wish to get involved with that, or politics, especially here in Northampton" George joined in the laughter, Charles Bradlaugh and his refusal to take the oath in Parliament had not improved Northampton's image. Sanders continued, "I would suggest we do not meet on Saturdays. Midweek would probably be best for all of us and for the time being perhaps just six times a year, possibly every other month." He paused again. There were no comments. "Alright then, we are agreed. Any other thoughts, gentlemen?"

"If we are to have chitchat at meetings," John Eunson commented, "then it will have to be about something or other specifically or else everyone will go off on his own, talking about his particular interest I mean. I've seen it so often in committees."

"Good point," Sanders came back immediately as if prompted, "I couldn't agree more. I take it we all think this should be a gathering where one of us should bring forward a specific topic - barring politics and religion of course."

"We all take it in turn at one another's house?" Eunson took off his glasses, gave them a wipe with his handkerchief and looked round for approval. All nodded. He continued "Not that I know anything about this Cambridge club of yours Sanders but is the meeting held in the home of the proposer of the evening's subject?"

Sanders looked across at George Hooper who gave a slight shrug of his shoulders, not wishing to interrupt the other's flow. "I believe the Cambridge Chit Chat met in the rooms of the host", the headmaster was on safe ground here, "but perhaps it would be better if we divided duties, then if anyone should not be able to fulfil his commitment things would be decidedly easier."

"And then?" Eunson was in full flood of organisation mode, "what do we do if the member introducing the matter for discussion is ill or just cannot attend?"

"He will have to appoint a substitute", Sanders responded somewhat tersely. There was a pause while the embryo club digested their mounting responsibilities. Hammond looked up. "Have you any thoughts as to the number of members in your, that is our club? Six of us are here and that seems to me very few. Especially if anyone falls by the wayside I mean".

Sanders had recovered. "Another good point. Perhaps we should have eight or nine, even ten."

Hammond smiled. "I was not suggesting quite so many, but I did think Gordon of St Mary's might be interested."

Tom George broke in. "And what about Thomas Green, the solicitor. I know he writes quite a lot, poems and books, that sort of thing."

"Any other nominations?" Sanders had clearly taken on the post of chairman. A little shuffling followed but no one spoke. "Right then, let us invite those two gentlemen. And may I suggest members may invite a friend along, if of course the member hosting agrees?"

"Excellent," Hooper felt he should say something; after all he *was* the other founder, "I expect we shall be looking around for new members eventually. What is more," he warmed to his subject," why don't we meet next at Courteenhall; I would be greatly honoured to host the first, that is the first proper meeting."

Tom George leant forward. "Thank you, on behalf of the Club! May I be the first to suggest a subject? How about Belemnites?" His enthusiasm was slightly dampened by blank looks all round. "Fossils you know, they are fascinating – once you get to know them."

"I'm sure". "Really?" "Of course". Polite muttering was followed by general conversation about the club and its future. George Hooper relaxed with the third or perhaps fourth cigar of the evening, chatting with Hammond about problems of village life when something Sanders was saying to Eunson thrust itself to the fore;

" …. and I said to him he would be the obvious choice …. has some good idea what's needed. You never know how we shall evolve and minutes are the best way of recording what has gone on, put some form of order into things."

"Quite so, and he agreed?"

"Yes, well he certainly raised no objection," Sanders turned to Hooper whose eavesdropping was now evident, "may I interrupt you George," the unusual use of his Christian name warned Hooper what was coming, "you don't have any objection to being our secretary, do you?"

Caught off guard Hooper could only reply "Well, if you think I would be …. that is if no one else …. I suppose I could for the time being …." Conversation had stopped, all looking hopefully in Hooper's direction, "Very well, I will give it a try." The grudging nature of his acceptance hit him. "Of course I am honoured to be asked."

And that is how the Chit Chat Club of Northampton started. Or at least it is how it may have done.

2
Early Days
May 1885 - May 1887

It was inevitable that among Cambridge Chit Chat Club members and their visitors someone would have sufficiently enjoyed the experience to start a similar Club in the outside world. In San Francisco, California a Chit Chat Club was established in 1874. It is a thriving society with records and publications both on paper and line but in spite of investigations by them and at Cambridge University Library there is no evidence of its founders having any connection with the University Club. In the English town of Northampton a Chit Chat Club was founded in 1885 and the following chapters will attempt to tell the history of the Club and its members, where possible in their own words.

It is not clear who was the initial mover in Northampton. Two Cambridge graduates were among the founders, one a grammar school headmaster, Canon Sanders, the other the Rev Hooper, Rector of Courteenhall, a hamlet five miles south of the town. Both were up at Cambridge during the University Chit Chat years and although neither is recorded as attending a meeting the probability is that one or both were well aware of the Club's activities. Similarities in the two societies are such that a leap of faith can be made – the Cambridge Club was the model for Northampton.

The senior man, Sanders, invited his fellow graduate and friends to the School House at 81 Abington Street, Northampton in the spring of 1885[1]. There has been a great deal of conjecture as to who was the initial instigator. Club Secretary Frederick Ince-Jones wrote in 1951 *Though Hooper was the founder of the Club, it is probable that Sanders was at first the moving spirit,*[2] a view that was probably influenced by a letter in 1917 from Richard Greene, early member and ex-secretary. There he says, with reference to the title Chit Chat.......*But the name had been given by Hooper who started the Club so it was left*.....[3]It is likely however the idea was a mutual one, thought up over a pipe or cigar, with memories of Cambridge in both their minds. It has always been assumed that since the meeting took place at Sanders', as host he would have been the prime mover but logic suggests a more practical reason, how much more sensible it was to meet in the town rather than everyone travelling five miles to Hooper's rectory at Courteenhall in the pre-automobile era. Sanders had been connected with Cambridge since his degree in law, taking a Master's and working for his doctorate and it is reasonable to assume he would have learned more about the Club, then in its most prominent era.

*

Samuel John Woodhouse Sanders was born at Hadnell, Shropshire on 15th February 1846, son of Samuel Sanders, minister. After attending Ludlow Grammar School he went up to St John's College Cambridge where he obtained his BA in 1865 and MA in 1868. The following year he took the post of Vice-Master and head of mathematical and scientific departments at Bedfordshire County School and becoming curate of Kempston village, having been ordained priest in 1871 by the Bishop of Ely. In 1872 Sanders moved to Northampton, appointed headmaster of the Grammar School, a position he held until 1893. In the year he took up his school appointment Sanders married Roberta Henrietta, daughter of Rev C J P Douet, rector of Metcalfe, Jamaica. Roberta died at Northampton in March 1891 aged only 39 and Sanders' second marriage in 1894 was to Annie Elizabeth Pegg, a widow of Leicester. He acquired his Doctorate in Law in 1886 and was always known locally as Dr Sanders. During his stay in Northampton Sanders held the post of Curate of St. Peter's, assistant clergyman at All Saints' Church and was made an honorary canon of Peterborough Cathedral by Bishop Magee shortly before the latter was translated to the see of York. After leaving Northampton Sanders moved to Leicestershire where he died on December 15th 1915 at Rothley Rectory.

At the time of the Chit Chat's founding the Grammar School had a busy social life. Christmas 1872 saw Sullivan's *Cox and Box* being produced, followed by two concerts and three plays, all in 1873. Summer outings were popular, as was the debating Society. This last was formed in 1880 and open to outsiders, meetings being held every week at a subscription of 6d, (2½p) a term. It was run on the lines of a mock Parliament with Dr Sanders as Speaker. One rule forbad the debating of religion or local politics, mirroring restrictions in the future Chit Chat Club. Dr Sanders had arrived at the school as numbers were in decline but rebuilt it to a record of 160 pupils by 1884. During his time a library and museum were started in 1875 and 1881 respectively. He had interesting views on education …. *Examinations have a deteriorating effect on the mind*[4] and dealt with examination boards in a cavalier fashion.

*

George Brereton Hooper was the younger Cambridge man, born in Brighton in September 1849. He attended Uppingham School and went up to Emmanuel College, obtaining his BA in 1874 and MA three years later. Ordained deacon in 1876 and priest in 1878 he came to Northampton in 1876 as Curate of St. Edmund's Church and moved to Courteenhall on being appointed Rector in 1879. After only eight years another move came in 1887, to Woolverstone in

Suffolk. His further career may not be completely relevant but does throw light upon his character....

A scholar of Emmanuel College Cambridge [Hooper] *came into the diocese* [Truro] *in 1889 as vicar of Herodsfoot and will be remembered by many as a diligent parish priest and an enthusiastic sportsman. Somewhat abrupt in manner and impatient of contradiction, he possessed the rare quality of admitting and apologising for any errors of judgement, which he had passed.*[5]

David Thomas, one of the archivists at Cornwall County Hall, Truro, comments:

He disliked Methodists and was a broad churchman, neither high nor low but taking from both. He did a lot of work for the poor, for example delivering coal to their houses secretly at night. He would not let anyone smoke in the Churchyard, although he was very fond of cigars. He would leave the Rectory smoking one and, when he reached the gates, he would put the cigar on the hedge [a Cornish hedge is similar to a granite wall], *go into the Church, take the service, and collect his cigar on the way home.*[6]

In 1893 Hooper became vicar of St Just in Penwith. The sexton, Mr E S Millet, kept a diary which has been transcribed by Fran Stewart and makes fascinating, if somewhat morbid, reading. He sometimes wrote to the Home Secretary for advice but more often in complaining mode and did not entirely share the general view of his priest. He had occasion to 'speak sharply' to Hooper in 1895 and in January 1898 makes an entry:

By this mornings Post received receipt from the Vicar for his Fee over the above burial [Maria Oats] *– it seems that he told Henry and Peter Olds "he did not know what became of the Fees, he never had any" a deliberate lie because I hold his receipt for all Fees paid him since he came to the place, our Worthy Vicar is a most dangerous* *man to have any business with, untruthful he is and dishonest I have found him.*[7] The sexton, who appears to have seen off several vicars in *his* parish, made no comments in his diary for 1900 when Hooper moved to Camborne in Cornwall where he remained for 36 years until his death. Hooper's first wife died and his second outlived him.

*

So, two strong characters, who better to start a Club? The first meeting took place in Spring 1885. The exact date was not recorded by the chronicler which is strange considering how meticulous Hooper was in other matters. Someone, from the writing it was likely to have been Richard Greene, the second Secretary, has pencilled in *? May 1885* above the entry. Along with Hooper, Sanders invited Mr John Eunson, Mr Tom George, the Rev Charles Hammond and Mr Richard Scriven. There is little detail to suggest what went on at this inaugural meeting. Presumably there was coffee or tea along with some spiritual help in the form of whisky or brandy, setting a routine for the future.

It is worth considering why a group such as the Chit Chat should need to have, or more correctly, choose to have, a secretary. In any official organisation a record or minutes of meetings is normally considered essential. The logic of this is clear when a public meeting or government department is concerned as reference may be made to the document in the future in order to refer back to rules or protocols adopted at that meeting. Responsibility for decisions and who agreed to what is then easily attributable and suitable punishments given out to those guilty of misdemeanours. In addition minutes provide a useful means of disseminating proceeds of meetings to members of the organisation, especially those who were absent or asleep during the meeting. Private clubs and

May 1885

At a meeting held at the house of the Rev. S. J. W. Sanders, present J. Emerson Esq, T. George Esq, Rev. C. S. Hammond, Rev. G. S. Hooper, Rev. S. J. Sanders, Richard G. Scriven Esq, it was resolved to form a club for the purpose of discussing subjects other than of a political or religious nature. In addition to those present it was resolved to ask the Rev. C. J. Gordon, & T. Green Esq. to become members.—

It was resolved to limit the number to Eight members for 6 months

It was resolved that each member be allowed to bring a friend to the meetings

It was resolved that each member in turn bring forward a subject for discussion

that the member appointed to open the discussion be permitted to choose a substitute

that all business be transacted before the discussion

that the meetings be held on the last Monday in January, March, May, July, September & November.

Northampton Chit Chat Club
Minutes of first meeting 1885
Hooper as Secretary

societies have less obvious reasons to be minuted unless matters of finance or the establishment of rules need to be recorded.

In the case of relatively informal gatherings, such as the Chit Chat Club it is possibly the vision, or rather hope, of founders that the society will grow over time with future members being curious as to why and how the society was established. A more pragmatic reason is that the founders wished to place the Club on a proper professional level with accompanying status.

George Hooper would appear to have assumed the role of Secretary although the term is not mentioned in the earliest records and there is no indication he was ever elected, perhaps due to no one else being willing to take the post or even seeing the necessity for it. More likely it was Hooper's vision of a vibrant Club, mirroring that in Cambridge and his determination it should run along similar lines. What is certain is the number of suggested rules he recorded at this business meeting, along with professed aim of the Club. From the first it is evident this was to be a club run on strict lines, motions proposed and seconded before being put to the vote, a rigid calendar structure and limitation of membership numbers. It must also have been decided that Hooper should act as chronicler. The writing is certainly in his hand continually until he left in July 1887.

The minutes of the May 1885 get together are quite terse, as if the meeting were merely a rubber stamping exercise. *It was resolved to form a club for the purpose of discussing subjects other than of a political or religious nature.* Other rather secondary resolutions were passed. There would only be eight members, at least for six months, members were allowed to bring a friend, each member in turn would bring forward a subject for discussion after any business had been transacted unless he chose to appoint a substitute speaker and meetings would be held in January, March, May, July, September and November. The ground rules had been laid down. In the last quarter of the nineteenth century it was sensible to limit meetings to six annually. Members had busy lives and the effort of travelling many miles between Chatterers' homes could not have been easy, especially at night. It says a lot for early Club members that they were willing to contemplate such an onerous, to modern eyes, regime for the sake of discussion. A change from Cambridge was having Reader and Host as different members. This must have been discussed and made sense, spreading the burden by separating the responsibility of hosting and catering from reading a paper.

*

The first meeting when *discussing subjects* took place was on July 29th 1885. In view of the proposed calendar, this is an added reason for supposing the first get-together had been in May. It was held at Courteenhall Rectory, where Hooper hosted and Tom George, Librarian and Archaeologist, gave a talk on *Belemnites …. of which he brought a great many specimens.* The minutes record *an interesting discussion followed.* It was many years before details were recorded regarding discussions, let alone papers, the former being characteristically *interesting, lively, well-sustained* or occasionally *desultory.* If anything can epitomise the frustration future generations would have with scanty early minutes it must be the final sentence … *It was asked whether a frog had three hearts and nobody knew.*

This early membership structure set the seal for generations to come, three clergymen, two solicitors, a headmaster, an amateur scientist and a town worthy with medical men being added four months later. The preponderance of church, medicine, law and a succession of School heads was to last for nearly a century. They were all well acquainted, if not already friends. Perhaps significantly Sanders' eldest daughter Millicent married Eunson's son George.

*

John Eunson was born at Kirkwall, Orkney in 1833 and is said to have remembered the accession of Queen Victoria to the throne in 1837. His father, who introduced gas, light and heating into Orkney took up the appointment of Manager of the Wolverhampton Gas Works when John, still a boy attended Wolverhampton Grammar School and later Queen's College, Cork. He worked alongside his father, now consultant engineer to Northampton Gas Company and was appointed Manager in 1854. In 1877 he became consulting Engineer to the Northampton Water Works Company and pioneered many of the town's water supply undertakings. It is claimed in his obituary that he had no hobbies but this is hard to believe in a man who was a JP, a high ranking Mason and an extensive traveller worldwide and not least a member of the Chit Chat Club.[8]

Charles Hammond M.A. graduated from Balliol College, Oxford and became Rector at the village of Wootton, three miles south of Northampton from 1882 until he resigned in 1887. Richard Scriven practised as a solicitor in Northampton with interests in history and archaeology taking up most of his spare time.

Tom George, born in 1854, was an excellent choice as a founder. At the age of thirty, already a Fellow of the Geographical Society and librarian at the Guildhall Road Library in Northampton, he was appointed Curator of the Northampton Museum. In the twenty one years of his Club membership he gave ten papers on local, general historical and archaeological subjects.

At the first meeting it was agreed to ask Mr Thomas Green and the Rev Charles Gordon to join the Club, conveniently bringing the total membership up to the target of eight.

Thomas Green, described as solicitor, poet and novelist in the minute book, was born in 1846 and after being awarded a BA at London University came to Northampton to practice law in the firm that became known as Becke, Green and Stops. His exploits as a novelist and poet are not documented but he did give a paper to the Club, *Ancient Copyhold Tenure,* in 1886. His membership lasted intermittently until 1899.

The Rev Charles Gordon did not remain in the Club for long. Born in 1853 he was a Pembroke College Cambridge graduate and having served as curate in various locations became vicar of St Mary's, Northampton in 1882. Gordon gave one paper*, Socialism*, in 1885. He successively became vicar of Nassington with Yarwell, Rushden and Abthorpe before leaving the county. He died in Lancashire on May 8th 1944.

In November 1885 it was decided to increase membership by another five, although only four names were put forward. Two of these, Dr Richard Greene and Dr Arthur Jones not only became secretaries but established a long tradition of medical men as members. Within a year the upper limit of membership had risen to eighteen, a figure never increased and sometimes difficult to maintain.

During the next year a degree of formality was introduced with rules, entrance fee and annual subscription. Election to the Club should be unanimous, 'one black ball excluding'. Within a year it became compulsory to attend all but two meetings each year 'unless excused on application'. Early in 1886 subscriptions were introduced, 2s (10p) a year, presumably to offset the cost of printing notice-of-meeting cards, intimation of attendance postcards and postage although there are no official accounts during Hooper's time. Papers were introduced and read at each meeting in turn.

One effort made to recruit a member for the Club deserves particular mention. At the time of the Club's inception Hooper was incumbent at the church of St Paul and St Peter, Courteenhall, nearly five miles south of Northampton. Courteenhall is a country house built in the neo classical style designed by the then unknown 34 year old budding architect, Samuel Saxton and commissioned in 1791 by Sir William Wake. The surrounding park was designed by Humphry Repton and the small village is largely owned by the estate. In the 1880s the 12th Baronet, Sir Hereward Wake, High Sheriff of Northamptonshire in 1879, would have been well acquainted with the Rector and Hooper invited him as visitor to the Chit Chat in September 1886. Sir Hereward addressed the club on *Instinct and Reason* as visiting speaker the following month. He was recorded as having been elected a member the following January. There is no further specific reference to Sir Hereward in Hooper's minutes as a member and it must be assumed he cancelled his membership fairly soon afterwards, possibly before the next meeting. His name is among a long list of 'proposed members' in 1892 when Greene was attempting to sort out membership details in his latter days as Secretary before resigning. The entry *Wake Sir H* is crossed through as *withdrawn* in spite of having been duly elected in 1887. It is likely the omission of Hooper in not recording Wake's resignation was embarrassment that the baronet had declined the 'honour' arranged by his religious advisor. Sir Hereward attended the dinner in May 1894 with other past members at the Grand Hotel in Gold Street, Northampton[9] and the comment by Greene, Secretary at the time, that *routine meetings had for long proved unattractive to those who once bore the names of Wake....* probably gives a good idea of why the baronet withdrew from the club seven years before. He was in good spirits at the dinner. As the chronicler put it:-

Then in his turn the Wake, arose the Club to toast.
He did not know the "Grand", but he was proud to boast
Of past connection with the Club. He said mischance
Had happened to him, but now his polished lance
Was ready for another fray o'er "instinct and reason"
Or whatsoever subject might well benefit the season
And please the Chatterers.

Sir Hereward's association with the club is last recorded at the Summer Meeting in 1894.

On the same day Wake was elected the Club welcomed E. Montague Browne. Browne occupied a solicitor's office in St Giles' Square, Northampton although living in Kingsthorpe, then a village to the north, just outside the town. He would become the fourth secretary.

The first great change in membership took place in July 1887 when Hooper announced his resignation due to taking the Curacy of Woolverstone in Suffolk. By unanimous consent Richard Greene was elected Secretary, a post he held for the next five years. Fortunately for posterity and readers of this book minutes became interesting.

NOTES

1. The School House at 81 Abington Street became *The Wedgwood Café* in the first half of the 20th century and subsequently a Berni Inn in 1988 and is now a trendy bar.
2. Ince-Jones F. *Short History of the Chit Chat Club,* (1951).
3. Greene R. Correspondence in Club archives 1917.
4. Lees T S. *A history of Northampton Grammar School.*
5. Burt A. *The parish church of Saint Just in Penwith, Cornwall*—Eglos, Lanuste, Kernow; Boleigh Press, Essex: 2003.
6. Thomas D. Correspondence 2010 to author.
7. St. Just in Penwith, *The diary of the sexton 1893-1902.* Written by E Millet of Bosavern, transcribed by Fran Stewart 2003.
8. Obit. *Northampton Independent* April 8th 1911.
9. The Grand Hotel in Gold Street is now a Travelodge.

3
Greene Years.
July 1887-May 1892

Richard Greene qualified as a medical practitioner at the University of Edinburgh in 1868. He developed an interest in construction and management of institutions for the insane along with their care and treatment. In 1878 he was appointed Medical Superintendent of the County Asylum at Berry Wood in Northampton and joined the Chit Chat Club in 1886.

When he took over the reins of office in July 1887 it was in Greene's minutes the term *Honorary Secretary* first appeared, referring to Hooper's announcement he would resign on leaving Northamptonshire. It became normal practice for the Secretary to manage the Club's financial affairs and gradually the meetings themselves were being definitely chaired by Greene, in effect he was now Chairman, Secretary and Treasurer. He soon brought his own stamp of authority to the Club. A letter from 1917 gives an insight into his mind thirty years before.

I never quite liked the name "Chit Chat Club". It seemed to me just a trifle frivolous; and moreover it savoured little, in Sound, of the old Political Club of Addison's day - The Kit-Kat [sic] *I mean.*[1]

As already noted he went on to say the name had been given by Hooper and as he had started the Club the title remained. Typically generous he adds with commendable foresight ... *and I venture to hope it will survive to a remote posterity.*

After Greene was elected Secretary....*A Committee, composed of Browne, Greene, Jones and Sanders, was appointed to arrange the details. This Committee met on the 28th July and a copy of the*

Regulations agreed to was subsequently sent to each member of the Club. This would appear to be somewhat high handed of the new Secretary, there is no explanation of the term *details* and members were given no opportunity to debate the committee's recommendations, they were presented as a fait accompli. In Greene's 1917 letter *Sanders, Jones and I had an informal meeting before the winter campaign began, and we then revised, or perhaps, arranged the Rules.* These were not strictly speaking Club Rules, just an addendum of times and dates of meetings ending with the important *Regulation.....5. 'That refreshments be limited to the following:- Sandwiches, Coffee, Tea, Jellies, and Fruit.*

Any two, but not more than two of the following wines:- Port, Sherry, Claret, Hock.

Brandy or Whisky and Aerated waters may be offered.

Greene recollects it was also agreed *no professional, courtesy or other titles were to be used at the meetings.* The following year in November 1888 a proposition was put by Jones and seconded by Sanders that when the Secretary introduced visitors they should be accorded their appropriate titles. R. A. Milligan, surgeon at the Northampton Infirmary and John Haviland, solicitor, both elected members in September 1887, gave notice they would oppose the resolution when a vote was taken at the next meeting. The motion was duly put in January 1889. Greene records:-

The Secretary was about to put an amendment relative to the use of the Professional and Courtesy titles of the Visitors present, but he found that neither Milligan the proposer nor Haviland the seconder was present (it being hinted that these members had gone on a primrosing expedition).

As they had not entrusted the Amendment to any other members the original motion was put and carried. 'Chickened out' would be the modern but less graceful way of summing up the situation, but gathering primroses seems a much more delicate, if perhaps ambiguous, phrase.

This tradition of using surnames only has remained right up to the present day, occasionally to the amusement and confusion of guests finding themselves the only ones present afforded their due title.

Greene brought freshness to his minutes with personalities of members beginning to creep in. Earlier, in November 1887 Richard Scriven, a senior solicitor in Northampton and Club founder, had proposed the Secretary should give ten days' notice of meetings and this was passed. He went on to propose that the notices of meetings should include the subject to be discussed. He had no seconder and Greene rather caustically writes '.... *the proposal dropped; but the Secretary undertook to name the subject on the Card to Scriven'.*

In February 1888 the meeting directed the Secretary to contact members who had not attended a minimum of two meetings, reminding them of the November 1886 resolution, now Rule 8.....*Any Member not attending at least two Meetings during the year ceases to be a Member of the Club, unless excused on application.* As a softening of this rule it was agreed *that the reading of a Paper to be held equivalent to two attendances.* Replies from Sir Hereward Wake and T Green were considered to be satisfactory but H W K Markham and the Rev Charles Gray did not reply. There is no mention of action being taken regarding Gray. He had read and hosted in the previous Club year and although there is no reference to it in the minutes his excuse would have been sound as he had been relocated as Vicar of Belgrave with Birstall, Leicestershire in 1887. At the meeting on July 14th 1888 *HWK Markham's name removed from the list of Members as he had attended no Meetings during the season.* His cousin Christopher Markham joined the Club the same year and unlike his namesake was a prolific writer and presented 22 papers, eight concerned with the county of Northampton.

One of Greene's hobby horses was the publication of club papers. In the 1917 letter already quoted he says:-

There was one thing I was very anxious to see carried out:- namely, that a Selection of Papers should be printed in a volume at intervals of a few years (see Minutes). If I remember rightly Jones was the only one who opposed the idea. [1]

Greene is correct that Jones was against the idea. In March 1888 there was a *desultory conversation* about the publication and:-

Some of the members seemed a little timid at the idea of appearing to the world in an Author's dress; but the majority evidently thought that their own Papers at least were worthy of preservation from decay and oblivion.

The subject was allowed to simmer for a month and in June, after due notice had been given, an amended resolution by Jones, joined by Baker, was put, *That the papers not be printed*. This was defeated and a compromise was arranged whereby authors might consent to publication and a small committee should be set up with Greene as editor. The subject lay on the table until November 1892 when, as newly elected Secretary Jones recorded *Greene then proposed that a Committee of Greene, Sanders and Jones consider what papers read before the Club should be printed and published and the manner of doing it. This was seconded and passed and Greene was asked to act as Editor.*

A handsomely bound copy was to be presented to the Editor as an expression of the Club's appreciation of his forbearance and all those other virtues he displayed during his five years' reign as Tyrannus. Jones, as Secretary, had let his thoughts run away with him, *appreciation* in the minute was originally *recompense* but wisely this was scored through.

The following month Sanders challenged *the minute recording the resolution to present Greene with a copy of the Transactions*, but the meeting voted him down. Jones, with apparent relish, notes *a member even alleged that Sanders proposed it.* The following year in September Greene complained his editorial duties were at a standstill as members had not sent in their papers. The matter seems to have been dropped after this, a loss to posterity as there are no papers extant from this period.

In June 1888 a 26 year old Ryland Adkins attended as visitor and just over a year later was admitted to membership, having been proposed by Sanders and seconded by Jones. The Club had acquired one of its most colourful members.

By June 1889 there was frustration at members who did not reply to 'intimation cards' signifying their attendance at the next meeting. These were sent out by the Secretary and replies were expected in the post. In May Canon Bury complained he did not know whether to expect three or thirty persons present including guests, known as 'visitors'. Browne gave notice he would propose a fine of 3d. (1½p) for those who did not answer the cards. Sanders agreed to second this. At the next meeting it was Adkins who proposed and Scriven who seconded the motion, that *Members not answering the Intimation Cards within Seven days be fined sixpence each*. Although the reply period has altered the fine still stands at sixpence, that is six old pence or 2½p. Since the demise of the ½p coin members are expected to pay with a 'real' 6d piece.

Berry Wood Lunatic Asylum established itself as a summer home for the Club. Greene first invited members to his house for an ordinary

Sir Ryland Adkins
Watercolour sketch for posthumous portrait

meeting on July 6th 1887, the day Hooper resigned as secretary and Greene became his successor. There is no reference to Summer Meetings being held in daytime until 1895 when the start time is 3.30 p.m. although it can be assumed an afternoon start was made before this date.

Weather permitting it would have been held outside in the garden. This was certainly the form and location for many years to come and in early days it was no different in nature from a normal meeting, with the paper read by a member. June meetings were held at Berry Wood for the next two years but although there was no official change in name Greene records the July 1890 meeting as being 'Summer'. This title was resumed in 1893 when the new secretary, Jones, records:

The Summer Meeting was held as usual at Greene's..... Greene's admirable arrangements for the comfort of the Club, together with the remarkably favourable weather contributed very largely to the success of the meeting.

The last Summer Meeting to be held at Berry Wood was in 1898, Harding, now in charge at the asylum, extending hospitality begun by Greene eleven years before. The tradition of a special meeting held in summer months had been established.

Minutes were brief until 1890 but after this several entries demonstrate the way Chatterers had developed into a group that could make fun of each other among more solemn proceedings. Greene recorded, after minuting a paper on March 20th about *The reign of Edward III* by The Rev. Edward Nicholls Tom, Rector of St. Peter's, Northampton,

A long and very interesting discussion followed in which Adkins, Faulkner and Sanders distinguished themselves.

The following month Adkins produced the first of his many good natured arguments with the Secretary. He objected to the word *distinguished* as being applied to himself ... *but on being assured that no other word so well expressed the Secretary's meaning he consented to allow it to stand as written*.

Greene noted with barely disguised sarcasm that Sanders was not at the meeting…..*but would probably not have raised any objection had he been present.* This was not the end of the matter. Greene sent humble apologies for absence at the next, extra, early summer May meeting when members present passed a motion of censure on the Secretary for *using such frivolous language in the minutes.* Greene's comments when he came to write a second hand account of the session were typical, using his skill as minute master to good effect.

It is evident that a mean advantage was taken of the absence of the Secretary to pass this vote .... This vote of censure was really a sort of stab in the back of the irresponsible Ruler – a stab unworthy of the great members of a great Club: but the Secretary hereby informs members that he bears them no malice. On the contrary he cherishes the warmest feelings towards them, and he feels sure that this return of good for evil will make the Proposer and Seconder of the vote hide their diminished heads in confusion and shame, as he does not think they are utterly lost to all the higher feelings of human nature.

Frederick Ince-Jones considered the word 'Ruler' was the moment when *out of this modest egg sprang the dragon of "Tyrannus"* [2] although this title for the Secretary did not appear until 1891.

Greene was in his element with the minutes, he writes about the senders of unsigned reply cards:-

As none of these cards are signed the Secretary cannot gibbet the delinquents: but he hopes they are in this room and that the consciousness of guilt will make them betray themselves by as deep a blush as ever reddened the cheek of the most innocent maiden, whoever she may happen to be.

The *frivolous language* of some minutes is in inverse proportion to the misery Greene must have seen in his post as Superintendent of a lunatic asylum.

At the meeting of October 1890 Greene, under 'members present', commented *Adkins, who had been "dining out" came in after the paper had been read, but in time to enliven the discussion.* Adkins rose to the bait and next month –

On the minutes of the previous meeting being read, it was pointed out by Adkins that the words "dining out" were not fitting as applied to him, and he moved that they be expunged. It cannot be wondered at that this motion, having no seconder, fell to the ground.

As usual the repartee continued:-

Haviland then proposed that the Secretary be complimented on the extreme appropriateness of the words "dining out". It is extremely odd that this motion also found no seconder.

Greene made sure he always had the last word, the privilege of a Club Secretary then as now.

Greene was not always easy going. In October 1891 a suggestion was made to move a meeting from the third to the fourth Thursday of November. It was ruled by him, as Secretary, that the rules were specific and could not be changed without a month's notice. He was not always so tyrannical but so it came to pass, as minutes of the day would have put it, that Greene became known as Tyrannus. Ever since then successive Secretaries have been known as Tyrannus, to be addressed as such and hold sway with what can only be described as a democratically dictatorial demeanour. To put the record straight Hooper was eventually and retrospectively known as Tyrannus I and Greene as Tyrannus II.

Meetings were not quite the *frivolous* occasions they may appear. Papers and discussions following were the object of meetings and any levity tended to be present only in the business session. Once business had been disposed of papers were read and although subjects were often biased towards the reader's occupation, variety was notable, from *Chaucer* to *A new Reading of Gulliver's Travels*, *The Human Voice* to *Vegetarianism* and *Poor Law* to *County Courts*. The clergy kept to the rules regarding religious subjects, certainly in the titles of their papers such as *The Reign of Edward III* and *Protection from Lightning* but occasionally became dangerously philosophical with *Some Tendencies of Modern Thought* and *The Forgotten Man*. It would seem there was a high degree of tolerance towards readers most of the time.

In May 1889 a paper was read by a non-member, Mr H. C. Burdett, on *Pre Christian Hospitals*. Members were not to know the reader would become Sir Henry Burdett K.C.B, who after an early career assisting hospitals and medical schools was appointed Administrator of Dreadnought Hospital and thence, by the logic of the day, Secretary of the Stock Exchange. He was later greatly concerned in the benefaction of hospitals and nursing institutions. He had a way with words that would have been appreciated by the Club. His best known comment, frequently quoted in modern times, is in connection with the sick poor …. *the object of the hospitals is to cure with the smallest number of beds the greatest number of cases in the quickest possible time,*[3] a comment that could well be made by hospital administrators in the twenty first century.

At the beginning of the 1891/2 session Greene announced his intention to resign but continued to record proceedings throughout that Club year. His last two meetings saw the start of Volume 2 of the Minutes. He summarised that year with ....*The Season of 1891-92 cannot be said to have been a good one*. Attendances were falling and several members had attended less than the prescribed number.

In May 1892, having minuted his resignation, Greene soliloquises:-

'Tis said that no one ever does anything for the Last time without regretting it, and while convinced that a younger and firmer hand must now take the helm, he feels the truth of the old saying; and he hereby wishes to retract any little personalities which may, inadvertently, have crept into the Minutes.

Although Greene vacated the post of Tyrannus he continued to attend meetings, presenting seven more papers until his last, *The ancient religion of Egypt*, in 1906.

Tyrannus III, Arthur Jones, took over the reins of office on July 23rd 1892.

NOTES

1. Greene R. Letter of 1917 in archives.
2. Ince-Jones F. *A Short History of the Chit Chat Club.* 1951
3. Burdett H C. *Hospitals and asylums of the world.* Vol. 3. London, J and A Churchill. 1893. pp. 889-90.

4
Tyrannus III
July 1892 - February 1901

Arthur Henry Jones was born on January 11th 1853 in south London, the son of a Grahamstown, South Africa, merchant. He received early private education under Dr Pinches in London but spent part of his boyhood in South Africa. With many relatives in the medical profession in London, it was hardly surprising he chose to train as a doctor at Guy's Hospital, qualifying as surgeon in 1874 and graduating with a London MB in 1876. Following a period as House-Surgeon at Northampton General Infirmary he obtained an MD in 1880 and Membership of The Royal College of Physicians in 1882. He then commenced private practice from 45 Sheep Street, Northampton and was elected Honorary Physician at the Infirmary. He founded the Northampton Centre of the St John Ambulance Association and actively participated in medically associated charities. When he arrived in Northampton Jones was a staunch non-conformist but ....*Dr. Jones made the acquaintance of the Rev Canon Sanders, who was then Head Master of the Northampton Grammar School, and it is said that influenced greatly by that gentleman in course of time he left Nonconformity and became a member of the Church of England. Be that as it may, deceased subsequently attached himself to the Church and congregation of All Saints, and up to the time of his death was a. staunch Churchman.*[1]

Jones, like Greene, took the art of minute writing seriously and continued the style of his predecessor. Having arrived ten minutes late for his first meeting, July 23rd 1892, due to *circumstances over which he had no control*, he found the Club, in his absence, had arranged *with an expedition hitherto unknown in its annals* that the day of meetings should be changed from the first Monday to the first Tuesday of the month. The minutes become terse, more a comment than a record of proceedings:

<u>Greene's resignation</u>

<u>accepted Greene's resignation</u>; *passed him a hearty* <u>vote of thanks</u>;
<u>Jones appointed secretary</u>

appointed <u>Jones Secretary</u> *in his place and passed 12 pages of minutes. Who did it all is not recorded Perhaps this is as well.*

He now goes on the offensive.

<u>Libel on Jones</u>

The New Secretary in accepting his portfolio first wishes to notify the Club that the 12 pages of minutes already referred to [Volume II of the minute book, already started by Greene] *contain a gross libel upon him, and he looks to the Club to vindicate him from the attacks of the retiring Secretary who accuses him of only having attended two meetings during last year, whereas his own minutes shew that he was present five times.*

<u>Day inconvenient to new secretary</u>

The second suggestion of the new officer is that the Club would do well to amend its hasty resolutions of July, and find either a day that suits its Secretary, or a Secretary that suits the day of meeting.

<u>Sequence of Papers</u>

Unless the Club expresses any special views on the order in which members are to read papers, or act as hosts, the new Secretary will do as he pleases, for he can make nothing of Greene's order except that it is arbitrary and irrespective of minutes or precedents.

The acid tone should not be taken seriously, the Club revelled in humorous word play and Greene as host for the evening doubtless took it in good part. At the next meeting, in September, a suitably chastened and red faced Greene moved that Mondays should be the day. This was passed. The new Secretary had started as he meant to go on.

Occasionally there is a paper whose title intrigues and research reveals an iconic attitude of the times which is worthy of further comment. No reason is given but in October 1892 a visitor, Dr Clifton, spoke on *Sir J Crichton Brown's Oration on Sex in Education*. The annual oration, given on this occasion by the Lord Chancellor's Visitor in Lunacy to the Medical Society of London was concerned not about sex education but the difference a pupil's sex could make in his or her education, with rather surprising conclusions.[2]

Sir James started with the premise that comparison of the sexes showed *In the mental sphere man is more wilful, enterprising, passionate and energetic (katabolic)* whereas woman *Is more receptive, tranquil, affectionate and constant (anabolic).*[2] By examination of 1600 lunatics dying in asylums he 'proved' that not only men's brains were larger than women's but the blood supply is superior and the density of grey matter is greater. This, he alleged, led to an increased tendency to react to 'overpressure' (stress) in girls at high school. He quoted figures for evening headaches in girls doing their homework. This in turn caused the increased amount of phthisis (pulmonary tuberculosis) and anaemia in young women in comparison to men of the same age. Stress also resulted in decreased attention and acquisition of facts as seen in apathetic dementia and other mental states and could lead to epilepsy. Other conditions cited were somnambulism (sleep walking) leading to hysteria, insomnia to insanity and anaemia to life-long debility. Warming to his subject Sir James explained that women's tranquil lives account for there being less general paralysis of the insane in women. *They experienced freedom from stress and strivings of professional and business life that so often leads up to it.* A cynic of today would point out the 'little woman at home' did not go around acquiring syphilis that in its tertiary form presented as this form of insanity.

Sir James concluded *The University of St Andrew's, in deciding …. to open all its classes in arts, sciences and theology to women as well as men, has taken, not a retrograde step …. but a downhill step towards confusion and disaster…. The essential difference between male and female cannot be obliterated by a sweep of the Senatus Academicus.* Dr Clifton's views and those of the Club upon this tirade against education of women were not recorded by Greene, apart from the enigmatic *A well maintained discussion followed, the historical genius of the Club as ever well to the fore.*

*

Secretary/Tyrannus baiting continued. At the February 1894 meeting Jones *was unavoidably absent but he found the following notes in the minute book when it returned from the meeting*

"Browne made some observations, more or less coherent, on Chancery.

Adkins (inter alia) remarked that in constructing the minutes of the last meeting, Jones displayed more than his usual incapacity. The acting secretary administered an appropriate rebuke" (sic) "*The acting secretary was regarded by all the more enlightened members of the Club as a very excellent substitute for the real thing, and discharged his duties in a manner which did credit alike to his head and to his heart.*"

Adkins had once again taken light hearted offence. The minutes were on January's paper by Cunningham about *Backsheesh,* with Jones including an enigmatic taunt at Adkins *It was a remarkable fact that all those present had experience on the subject from the givers point of view. The discussion was, however, saved from being one sided by Adkins, who accepted a brief on behalf of tipping, and drew forth high moral utterances from Beasley and Mr Church.* Jones, turning the matter to his advantage when he comes to transcribe the 'notes', continues......*The person described above as a "thing" in inscribing these "rude" notes in the minute book trusts that even the less enlightened members of the Club, (whoever they may be!) will accept them as the best report of the meeting he was able to obtain.* In the context it may be assumed the acting secretary was Browne.

In April Adkins, who it will be remembered had featured in an argument about 'dining', suggested a dinner should be held for present and past members of the Club. This was enthusiastically agreed to with the proviso that at least ten members should be present and that not only *swallow-tails be made de rigueur,* but the cost should not exceed 5s. 6d. (27½p)[3].

The dinner took place on May 10th 1894 at the Grand Hotel, Gold Street, Northampton. Jones, writes:

The Chair was taken by Greene, who has ever been known in the Club as "Tyrannus" now styled "Tyrannus I" in consequence of his resigned his portfolio ... to the present Secretary, whom the Club has honoured by the name of Tyrannus II – would that the mantle had really fallen on his shoulders!

Speeches were made and the event was recorded by a budding poet, almost certainly the Secretary:

The toast was drunk right heartily by every chatterer there,
And Roberts, rising solemnly, did thus address the chair:-
'To you, Sir, I would cordially for these past chatterers here
Return our thanks for compliments and for the excellent cheer."
And with many such like words sat down.

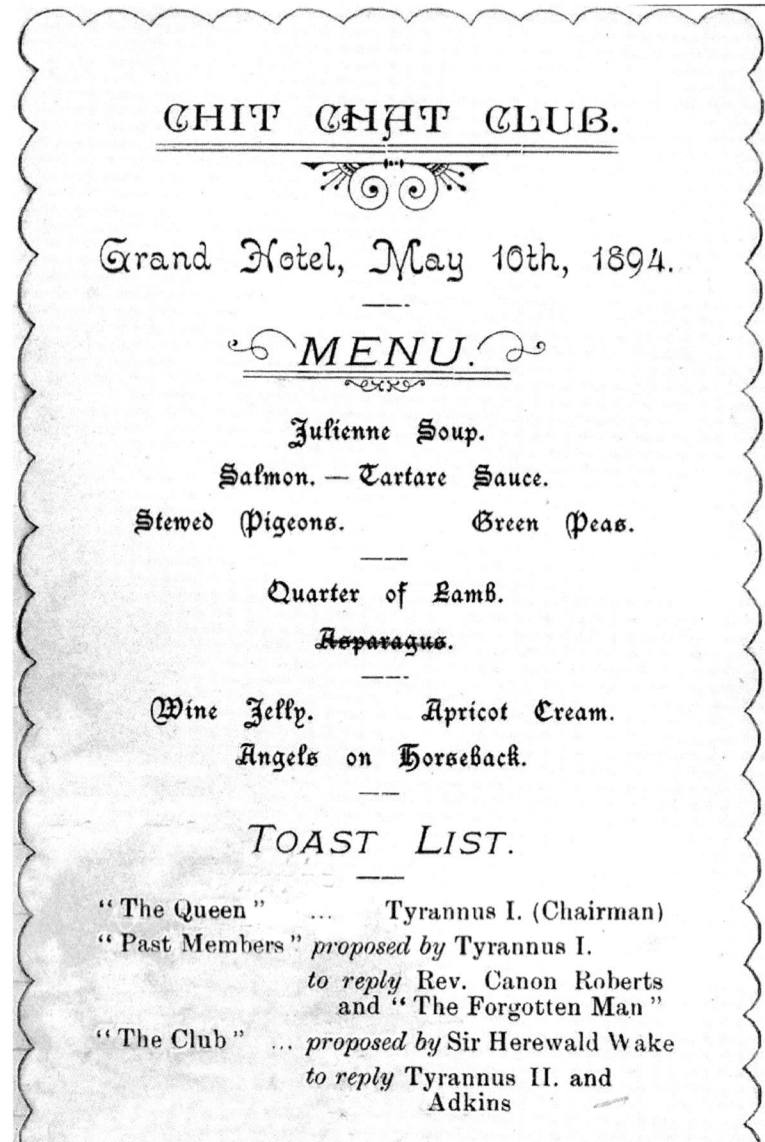

Menu Card for 1894 Dinner at the Grand Hotel

40

Then Bury, "the forgotten", murmuring at selection,
Which, said he, was anything but natural; in affection
Still laid claim to membership, grieving, however, much,
That matrimony had so terribly put him out of touch
With haunts of batchelorhood.

On Sundays now his lot to speak to those who would not hear,
On Thursdays to refuse, with grace, to aged poor good cheer
While chatterers classed him as forgotten.

Then in his turn the Wake, arose the Club to toast.
He did not know the "Grand", but he was proud to boast
Of past connection with the Club. He said mischance

Had happened to him, but that now his polished lance
Was ready for another fray o'er "instinct & reason"
Or whatsoever subject might well benefit the season
And please the Chatterers.

The Jones responding for the Club, its annals traced;
While Adkins stood, and with his energies well braced,
In well turned sentences, and with most dulcet tones
Reclothed in lifelike form the very driest bones
Of Chatterers lore

Then like a distant echo, on th'assembled Club there burst
The murmur of good wishes pledged sincerely at St. Just,
Where Hooper, founder of the Club in eighteen eighty five,
Rejoiced to hear that now so well his infant project thrived
And waxed exceeding strong.

So passed the feast with satisfaction unto all concerned.
And Adkins, in whose fertile brain the thought arose has earned
The hearty thanks of all the 6 times 3.

*

Jones adds *The only fault the Secretary heard found with the proceedings was that someone lit his cigar before the Queen's health was drunk.*

Papers continued on a variety of subjects, philosophical such as *Intellectual, not moral agencies the dominant factors in the progress of Society*, historical, for example *Reign of Elizabeth*, literary in the form of *Comparison and contrast of Taylor's "Dunstan" and Tennyson's "Beckett"* and those of local interest including *Whyte Melville, the Northamptonshire Novelist*, presented by Adkins on Friday October 15th 1897.

It was inevitable death should eventually touch members. The Rev. Charles Gray, Vicar of St Mary's, died in the winter of 1894/5, Mrs Scriven died in February 1895 and Mrs Percival in March.

On a lighter note Jones records that on two occasions he organised transport for some members and hoped they appreciated the arrangements but <u>some</u> *of them being afflicted with short memories left the secretary to pay their share of the expenses.*

A tongue in cheek paper of 1896 was *Gleanings or the Humours of a Mad House, by an inmate* by Harding which was *sometimes necessarily clothed in unparliamentarily language*. Medical men of Berry Wood Asylum, later St. Crispin's Hospital, were affectionately known in the Club as *The Mad Doctors* and will be considered later in more detail. Fortunately they had a sense of humour, a necessity for doctors in any age but certainly those resident in 'lunatic asylums'.

In March 1897 Jackson had escaped a fine on the grounds of being out of the county when he should have sent in his December apology. This minute aroused the ire of Adkins who *fearing the Club was losing its principles moved that the minute exonerating Jackson*

from a fine be rescinded. Markham seconded. The Club was so excited on the subject that the votes were equal till Jackson made a majority against the motion. The voting was two for, and three against, out of a total of ten members there present.
Faulkner then wished to move that Jackson be fined double, but as this involved alteration of a rule he was requested to give notice for the next meeting, and on legal advice the Secretary requested that the notice be in writing.

It is hardly surprising nothing further was heard of the matter. It would not have escaped the notice of the Club, certainly the Secretary, that Adkins was probably the member most fined and most liable to be late in paying those fines, if at all.

Jones continued a practice started by his predecessor of publishing attendance figures of members during the past year. This was considered necessary in view of the rule requiring two or more attendances annually, a paper being taken as two appearances. Over the years several members fell foul of this regulation and were recorded as their membership having 'elapsed' rather than the miscreant being expelled. In the 1897/8 year Greene, Green T and Harding were recorded as in peril. Greene had left the area, Harding was saved by the prospect of hosting the Summer Meeting in July and at that meeting *Green T was conspicuous by his absence and accordingly once more passed into the nebulous.*

The Club found Greene's imminent departure from Northampton in 1898 another reason for arranging a dinner. Eighteen past and present members assembled at the Grand Hotel in Gold Street, Northampton on February 21st 1898 with the Secretary having produced a most professional commemorative card. Jones, *in obedience to Club law, and as its oldest existing member took the Chair; Browne as next oldest member, and most faithful in his attendance supported him in the Vice Chair.* The minutes waxed lyrical, mirroring the previous dinner in 1894:

The Secretary having picked up the following anonymous lines on the floor after the dinner was over, begs to make them serve as minutes of the doings and sayings on that occasion.

   Twas the voice of old Greene
   I heard him declare
   I am going so soon
a *and I cannot say where.*

   So our Ryland D. Adkins
   Proposed we should dine
   And take Greene to the Grand
   And give him some good wine.

   one and all there assembled
   the board was well spread,
   Browne sat in the Vice Chair
   And old Jones at the head.

   Blyth came down from great London
   and with five others past,
   made the number eighteen,
   which was just like the last.

   Soon the feasters were merry,
   And drunk were the toasts,
   Jones first drank to the Queen,
b *Then smoke brought up the ghosts.*

   He next toasted old Greene, Sir,
   Our great Hercules,
c *Who had wrought labours twelve,*
   With such wonderful ease.

Farewell Dinner for Dr Richard Greene, Tyrannus from 1887-1892
Drawn by Arthur Jones

    To him Faulkner soon followed
    Who at Berry Wood,
    Had admired Greene's great paper
d Population and --- "food".

    From this shore like old Charon
    Next Haviland said,
    He – twice past – our Greene,
e To the nebulous led.

    Then our guest sadly rose up,
    And gave his reply,
    Which with epigram teeming
    Touched on time now passed by

    He then toasted the Club, and
    Blyth next had his say,
    Who by Adkins was followed,
    In his eloquent way.

    He reminded us Greene had
    At all times combined,
    The Social, Scientific
    And Literary mind.

    So then Browne gave "Tyrannus"
    Who briefly replied,
    And recited from Kipling
f How Kanal did ride.

    This led Adkins to speak of
    Lovers, Truth and the Well,
    Which is all of the dinner
    I can very well tell.

a. *Greene had not decided where to live*
b. *This refers to the Club frontispiece*
c. *Greene's eleven papers & the minute book*
d. *Population, **prafries** and production.*
e. *another reference to the frontispiece.*
f. *The song of the East and West.*

The frontispiece referred to is the cover for the 1896/7 programme, (see page iv) the original filed away in the minutes' book. A combination of the Club's interests, learning, books, drink and smoking, it was later used as a cover for Ince-Jones summary of papers in 1923.

In note *d*. Jones' handwriting, normally decipherable, is at odds with the minute of Greene's paper of 1894 on *Population, Pauperism and Production*, in no way can Jones' script be translated as 'paupers'.

*

Greene was elevated to the rank of Honorary Member in July 1898 and retired to the lovely Sussex town of Lewes where he proposed the following year to establish a Chit Chat Club and wrote to Tyrannus requesting a copy of the rules. Extensive trailing through the East Sussex archives has failed to find any reference to a Chit Chat Club in the area.[4] Whether there was insufficient enthusiasm for such an erudite society in the shadow of the South Downs must remain a matter of conjecture. Greene continued to attend as an Honorary Member and gave three more readings.

In October 1898 another good natured feud broke out between Jones and Adkins, when *the Secretary pressed by professional engagements entered the room at one minute five and 6/10 of a second past the half hour, he was greeted by Adkins in stentorian voice with an assertion that the Club had already in that brief space of time passed a resolution "censuring the secretary and fining him a shilling [12 pence, 5p today]". But such underhand and rushed proceedings were soon proved to be both irregular and discourteous, and when the Secretary with dignity as becomes the post of Tyrannus, repelled the vote as contrary to all precedent, and absolutely unsupported by the rules, the members one and all withdrew their attack and authorized the Secretary to pass over in silence an incident which in self-defence he begs to record.* Posterity is grateful to Jones for this....*But still further vote was made by the members to the effect "that a note be entered on the minutes of the embarrassing form of circular issued by the secretary with regard to the election of new members."*.....(Regrettably the circular has not survived)......*This was passed by a small majority so small that the secretary has failed to remember its number. Needless to say Adkins was the proposer of this censure, but alas Markham seconded it....... In order to shew that notwithstanding these attempts to reflect on the integrity of his character as Tyrannus, the secretary bears no malice he hereby tenders his deep regret that in minutes long past he so departed from the truth as to spell Adkins name with a T instead of a D. Henceforward he has determined that Adkins shall be D'd.*

At Berry Wood asylum in January 1899 a new member, Dr Francis Crookshank was hosting and the problem of non-notification of intent to attend once again reared its head. Harper had paid his fine in advance before being fined at the meeting, *altogether unprecedented*, Jones recorded. Percy Page, Northampton Borough Treasurer, had written to Tyrannus, not the host, in contravention of Club Rules, two other members, Adkins and Manfield, had not replied and *Beasley had actually addressed him as dear Sir*. Jones continued *The serious nature of these delinquencies was at once appreciated by the Club. Page, Beasley and Harper were sent summons to explain themselves at the next meeting.* This they did and *Beasley gave the Club an ample apology for his error, and solemnly promised not to so offend again. Page was informed of the nature of his delinquency and Harper proposed, which Browne seconded that he be heard. It was most satisfactory to the Club to find that Page had sinned in ignorance, and upon his tendering an ample apology, with a promise not to repeat the conduct complained of his offence was condoned.*

Harper also having partaken of the pie of Humility Crookshank proposed and Harper seconded a resolution to the effect that it was to be understood clearly in the Club that Harper's method of dealing with fines incurred was not to be regarded as a precedent. This was carried unanimously.

Some readers may consider the continual attention, even obsession with rules accompanied by petty arguments over minor points of procedure constitutes childish behaviour quite unbecoming in a club dedicated to erudition and learned discussion. During daytime hours in late Victorian and Edwardian England Chatterers would be playing their various roles in law, the Church, medicine, local government or education, not expected to be anything but bewhiskered pillars of society. It was only at Club meetings they could let their hair down in the company of like minded men in a manner that could well be deemed improper at work or even in their own homes. Tensions would be relaxed and humour associated with gentle banter be enjoyed, for inside every man there is a schoolboy waiting to tell a doubtful joke. Middle aged professionals were reliving their easy going student days. A more relaxed approach in public life came in post 1945 England that would not have been tolerated during these early Chit Chat years.

The variety and depth of papers presented, often unrelated to the reader's daytime occupation, may be considered as the counter, flip side in today's jargon, to any accusations of undue levity.

At the Summer Meeting of 1898 Jones, seconded by the Rev Sleight proposed *that Honorary Members be elected from among past members to shew recognition of distinguished services, but that such members should be asked to contribute a paper to the Club in person at least once in two years, as a condition of such honorary membership. This was carried unanimously.*

It was then proposed, seconded and carried unanimously that Greene be elected the first Honorary member. By introducing a new grade of membership the number of speakers available was increased and those who had moved away could be included in the Club 'family'. The Honorary title continued into the second half of the twentieth century and then lapsed until reinstated in 2011. The 1898 obligation to read every two years was not rigidly applied.

July 6th 1899 saw the Club holding its annual Summer Meeting in the grounds of the Court House, Kingsthorpe at the invitation of Browne. *Assembled at 4.30 the members immediately passed a resolution proposed by Tom that the meeting adjourn for half an hour for tea. That repast being ended a circle was formed under a leafy shade...*

One of those enigmatic moments in the Club's history followed:

For some reason or other Beasley proposed "that the Club should read more" and Markham seemed to find something to second in it. On being put these two members voted for it and Terry against it so they claim it was passed.....there were eight members at this meeting......No doubt the future annals will shew Beasley and Markham possessed of the greatest erudition, while Terry – who can say what will happen to him? As would have been said at the time, do not wonder more gentle reader, George Terry, solicitor and lay preacher, forsook his legal calling and after being ordained became Vicar of St Michael's Church, Northampton.

The next passage in these minutes is of importance in being the first time ladies' presence at a Summer Meeting is mentioned.

The members after a short discussion interrupted and enhanced by strawberries and cream <u>and the presence of the Ladies</u>, broke up amid the usual rejoicings- for the Holidays.

The underlining is by Jones, whether in approval or disapproval is not clear. It was not until seven years later ladies were specifically allowed as guests at these Summer Meetings.

Basil Thomson joined the Club on that July day. He hosted in November 1899 and only attended one other meeting, in October 1900, to read *Decay of Native Races*. This would have been his quota as he was soon to leave the town in 1901 and Thomson would have passed from Club annals without mention had it not been for his subsequent history.

Basil Thomson was born in Oxford on April 21st 1861, the son of William Thomson, then provost of Queen's College and later Archbishop of York. After attending Eton he went up to New College, Oxford but after two terms went down with a depressive illness, subsequently travelling to Iowa in the United States where he worked as a farmer. In 1883 the young man entered the Foreign Office, assisting the Governor of Fiji, Sir William Des Voeux. Following time as a stipendiary magistrate throughout the South Pacific islands Thomson was invalided back to England with malaria. After marrying in 1890 he returned to Fiji as commissioner of native lands and then to Tonga, becoming assistant premier to Siaosi U Tuku'aho, the island Chief. Three years later due to his wife's deteriorating health Thomson came back to England to write memoirs based on his experiences in the South Seas. Another change of career saw Thomson reading for the bar and being admitted to the Inner Temple in 1896. However a further shift of direction possibly due to personal acquaintance with Sir Evelyn Ruggles-Brise, Old Etonian and house guest back in Tonga, gave Thomson the opportunity of becoming deputy governor of HM Prison Liverpool and so to Northampton as governor of the prison there. He soon moved on to other prisons, Cardiff, Dartmoor and Wormwood Scrubs, having found time in 1899 to expedite the establishment of a British Protectorate over Tonga, given his acquaintance with the island. This duly happened in May 1900, despite Tongan resistance, sandwiched between Thomson hosting and reading for the Chit Chat.

This meteoric career continued with appointment as Assistant Commissioner "C" (Crime) Division of the Metropolitan Police in London, carrying with it the post of head of CID. Involved as he was in the Secret Service Bureau (later MI6) he was engaged in the cases of Margaretha Geertruida Zelle (Mata Hari) and later, Roger Casement. He was appointed CB in 1916 and KCB 1919, in which year he became Director of Intelligence at the Home Office. Two years later he fell out with Prime Minister David Lloyd George for reasons that never came to light and was asked to resign. Thomson's great friend, William Reginald Hall, took up his case in the House of Commons. On 3rd November 1921, Hall declared: *There is no man who has been a better friend of England than Sir Basil Thomson.*[5] He went on to argue that Sir Basil's downfall was due not merely to his *open enemies*, the Bolsheviks, the Russians and extremists but a secret plot that involved the Labour Party.

In 1920 R A Bennett, an anti-vice campaigner, showed Sir Basil a monthly publication, *The Link* [6], containing in its advertising pages sections headed *Ladies, Soldiers and Sailors* and *Civilians*, columns purporting to be requests for 'companions' and 'friends'. The women advertisers promised adventure with 'sporty' and 'jolly' girls, including one, a 'Bohemian Girl, 24' who was 'interested in most things' and wanted a 'man pal'. A male advertiser, 'intensely musical' was on the lookout for a 'manly Hercules' and 'Lothario, London West' desired 'cuddlesome girls'. The Assistant Commissioner was duly shocked and ordered the arrest of editor Alfred Barrett. Again this story would not be of great interest were it not for *The Hyde Park Incident*. In December 1925 Basil Thomson was arrested in Hyde Park, London and charged with *committing an act in violation of public decency*.[7] He appeared in Marlborough Police Court, London in January 1926, the officer who arrested him alleging he *was sitting on a park bench with his arms around the woman's neck .... and all that*. The policeman in question had to be ejected from the court because *he was smirking and making grimaces*. In spite of Sir Basil's protestations that he was collecting data regarding vice conditions in the West End, at first hand, he was convicted and fined £5.

Sir Basil wrote his entertaining memoirs, *Queer People,* in 1922.[8]

No later reference to Sir Basil was ever made in the records of the Club and he was merely cited by name as a celebrity in Ince-Jones' history of 1951; no details were given.

*

Eighteen ninety nine continued to provide nice points of order. In September *Adkins and Cox, or rather one of them failed to return his P.card*....[a printed postcard with spaces to fill in signifying the member's intentions regarding attendance].......*and the other did not sign it. The Secretary ventures to opine that the "Alas No" written on the unsigned card was in the handwriting and in the epigrammatic style of Adkins and therefore lays the fine on Cox's shoulder, but such a knotty point requires the consideration of the Club.*

This was duly considered in October, the meeting deciding to fine both members, *it being distinctly laid down that the Secretary was not expected to recognize handwriting.*

1900 produced a string of excellent papers, although with little comment from Tyrannus. Then in February 1901 there appeared

On Monday

The 11th day of February 1901

Markham

was to have read on "Some early Text Books", at Harpers

But on the same morning

Jones

Our friend and gentle Tyrannus

Left the Club for ever.

It is only in a letter to his widow signed by thirty four past and present members that the extent of affection in which the Club held Arthur Jones is brought to the surface. Typically it was Adkins who led the drafting of this tribute that is warm and caring:

.... He was devoted to the Chit Chat, and spared no effort or bother in promoting its interests ..... The continued success of the Club is principally owing to his efforts. He was a friend to all members, hospitable and kindly, and ever courteous ...... He embodied fully the spirit of the Club, its union of high mental aims with unaffected social life and a sense of true comradeship, and all members .... are the poorer by the withdrawal of his sunny nature and high souled influence.

The local press had this to say:

As member and presiding genius of the Northampton Chit-Chat Club (in which position he succeeded Dr Greene, formerly of Berry Wood), deceased stood high in the regard of the coterie of gentlemen of whom the Club consists, ruling with a light, but firm hand, and producing minutes of the proceedings in which bare formality often gives way to a keen and playful criticism, which was greatly relished. However, on this ground we fear we trespass, the Chit-Chat Club being an institution of a strictly private character.[9]

At the next meeting Browne was unanimously elected Tyrannus IV.

NOTES

1. Obituary. *Northampton Herald* 16 February 1902.
2. Crichton-Browne Sir J. *The Annual Oration on Sex in Education*. British Medical Journal May 7. 1892.
3. This would be about £12.50 in 2012. National Archives Currency Converter (to 2005).
4. Correspondence on file 2011. East Sussex Record Office.
5. Quoted by *Spartacus Educational* on its website. No reference found in Hansard.
6. Leafe D. *Mail Online*. 25 February 2009.
7. *Time* magazine 18 January 1926.
8. Thomson B. *Queer People* 1922. Reprint *Forgotten Books* 2012.
9. Obituary. *Northampton Herald* 16 February 1902.

5
Browne Years
March 1901-July 1923

In the family history of Tyrannus IV a certain Mr Browne was hanged, drawn and quartered in 1689 in Ireland for his Protestantism.

Edward Montague Browne was the son of the first vicar at St Edmund's Church, Wellingborough Road, Northampton and joined the Club in 1887. By 1901 he had read seven papers, at first limiting himself as all good Chatterers tend to do to subjects he knew best, in his case those related to law, then branching out on such as *Snake bites, Dawn of the 20th century* and *Illusion and hallucination*.

He had enjoyed a good relationship with Jones, after the February 1894 meeting he wrote the minutes as deputy Secretary and had proposed the toast of 'Tyrannus' at Greene's farewell dinner. It seemed logical to the Club to elect Browne, on March 11th 1901, to the post of Secretary or as that official will in future be called, Tyrannus.

While keeping to the general format of his predecessors Browne soon managed to add touches of his own. His main advance was to summarise papers in the minutes, at first sporadically and superficially but later in more detail and introducing a few comments from and about discussions.

It was not long before Adkins, now *one of the few coming men on the* [County] *Council*[1] continued his needling of Tyrannus, showing the office, not the officer, was the object of his barbs. In November 1901 he requested his 'Talk' be taken down in shorthand, which was duly done but by whom there is no record. This would imply 'readers' sometimes did not have 'papers', only notes to which they could refer. This may account for some papers being termed talks by Tyrannus.

The absence of Tyrannus a year later led Adkins to refuse to pay two fines to Markham, the acting Secretary, on the grounds he *felt doubtful of the fines reaching the proper quarter.* Two others, *of a more trusting disposition*, paid up. At the same meeting, on November 10th 1902 another member, Harding, complained he had been sent a postcard notifying him of a fine and this might *materially damage his credit in the neighbourhood.* Being delivered by a postman a postcard was considered to be 'within the public domain'.

More Tyrannus baiting came in February 1904. The weather had reduced the members present to three, Dixon, Jackson and Tom, when it is noted ….*Tyrannus incurs the displeasure of the Triumvirate.*

The next item on the agenda was "Apology for Tyrannus IV for absence". The leader of the coalition enquired if anyone wished to apologise for him – (Note by Tyrannus: "Just like his cheek") but no one volunteered. He therefore read Tyrannus' card which contained a very natural expression of regret, but in the opinion of the meeting …. no apology. So far from this, Tyrannus was found to have brazened out his offence by writing that he had to go out with Mrs. Tyrannus, and no doubt that was his first duty. In view of Tyrannus' frequent and solemn asseveration that attendance at the C. C. C. meetings was the first, if not the whole, duty of man, it was agreed that these words ought to be entered upon the minutes. (Tyrannus enters them accordingly, dropping a furtive tear over this record of frailty – for which the extreme youth of the Triumviris can alone excuse them)

Browne was again absent in 1906, returning late from Falmouth. The minutes of this meeting are scanty and end:

In playful humour Stuart and Hickson persuaded a few (-it is hoped, very few-) of the Club to commit themselves to some preposterous, monstrous, and unconstitutional proposal connected with the imposition of a fine of eighteen pence on the Honourable Tyrannus. It is much to be hoped that such frivolities will be heartily reprobated by the Senior and saner members of the Club. The last word, rightly so, rested with Tyrannus.

On September 13th 1904 Adkins resigned active membership and was elected an Honorary Member in October. He had not been a regular attender for some time and had run up a bill of fines of 4s (20p) which is not recorded as ever having been paid. He gave occasional papers, the last in December 1923 being *Scenery and the Soul*, reminiscing about his early life in the countryside around Northampton.

Hugh Neville Dixon attended a meeting in January 1901 as visitor, was proposed in March and elected to membership in June. Born on April 20th 1861 he obtained his M.A. at Christ's College, Cambridge in 1883 and became headmaster of a school for the profoundly deaf at St Paul's Road Northampton in 1884. By the time he joined the Club he had developed his love of botany and particularly the study of mosses, bryology, in which he became a world expert.

*

On February 1902 the long awaited, at least by those in the legal profession, joint meeting with "The Moot"[2] took place. How much or little of a success this was, is difficult to gauge. Whilst fourteen members of the Chit Chat Club attended at the Grand Hotel only seven representatives of the other club were there along with four visitors. Minutes are extremely cursory and the experiment was never repeated. Browne recorded *Mr Sidney Lee read a valuable and interesting paper on "Shakespeare' in Oral Tradition"* but to many this would have been the highlight of the season. Forty three year old Sidney Lee had graduated in modern history at Balliol College Oxford in 1882 and the following year became assistant editor of the Dictionary of National Biography. After becoming editor in 1891 he concentrated on Elizabethan writers and statesmen, contributing over 800 articles. His *Life of William Shakespeare*, 1897, reached its fifth edition in 1905, while in 1902 he edited the Oxford facsimile edition of Shakespeare's first folio. Perhaps Mr Lee's presentation method was not as interesting as his material for Browne to cast him off so lightly. Sir Sidney Lee, knighted in 1911, died in 1926.

1906 was significant for the minute *Summer Meeting on Wednesday June 13th to which ladies were invited*. This is strange as there are no reports of such a proposal ever having been debated and certainly if such a motion had been proposed, in the frequently used phrase of successive Secretaries, *an animated and well-sustained discussion* would have followed. It was evidently a popular decision, at least with the eleven ladies present. 1907 saw a return to an all-male Summer Meeting and the following year it was noted, almost as an afterthought, *(ladies welcome by special request)*. The only ladies on that occasion were the host Beasley's wife and daughter. It was not until 1912, again apparently without discussion of any nature, ladies appear on the Visitors' list. The nine ladies who attended that day started a tradition lasting to the present.

The casual reader of Tyrannus' minutes might be persuaded the two years prior to the First World War passed quietly, at least in the outside world. Significantly there were two events ideal for Club papers ignored by readers.

A cause for great grief throughout the kingdom was the liner Titanic striking an iceberg during the night of April 14/15 1912. This tragedy of 'too little too late' rescue attempts and wireless telegraphy failure was transmuted by press and public into a glorious example of British heroism with 'women and children first' and 'the band played on'. A perfect subject for a Club paper it might be thought.

Captain Robert Scott reached the South Pole on January 17th 1912 only to find Roald Amundsen had arrived five weeks earlier. On the return journey of the final expedition party all five members died, Scott on or about March 29th. Today it seems almost inconceivable the news did not break until February the following year, causing national mourning and a memorial service in St Paul's Cathedral on St Valentine's Day, February 14th 1913. Club speakers missed another great opportunity for a paper and it was 93 years before a paper was presented touching on the subject when Shaeffer told the story of Scott's photographer in *Beautiful tragedies*.

Back in 1913 W B Shoosmith found the subject of his paper on April 1st 1913 nearer home. Six weeks before, on February 13th suffragettes, as part of their militant escalation of activities, set fire to Chancellor of the Exchequer David Lloyd George's weekend house in the process of being built close to Walton Heath golf course in Surrey. Shoosmith talked on *The Tyranny of Man*, apparently giving a history lesson of domestic life from a woman's viewpoint then......*After a gradual evolution which culminated in the invention of a cooking pot, things steadily improved, until at the close of the last century, chiefly by the voluntary action of the ruder sex, woman became emancipated in almost every respect, save in regard to the questionable luxury of divorce......*

Shoosmith took the current male view *that an attempt to anticipate the natural growth of public opinion by violence and clamour would prove a failure, but that all things (within reasonable limits) would come to her who knows how to wait.*

Two months later on Wednesday June 4th forty year old Emily Wilding Davison walked in front of the King's horse *Anmer* at the Epsom Derby and died from her injuries the following Sunday. Whether this was an intentional attack or a failure of foresight when crossing the track will never be known for certain but suffragettes largely did not *know how to wait*.

It is interesting to speculate whether the parochial attitude to news shown by Club members mirrored that of many in England, tragedies abroad were indeed tragic but their impact on and relevance to life on this island was marginal.

It is tempting to look upon the summer of 1913 with rose tinted spectacles, a season of balmy days, parasols, boaters and picnics on river banks, the calm before clouds appeared in brilliant blue skies foretelling distant storms of war. The Rev Alfred Ewen, a member since 1901 had moved from 2 St Paul's Terrace, Northampton to Bedford and was responsible for invitations to the Summer Meeting:

C.C.C.

Thursday, 19th June, 1913,

AT 23, EMBANKMENT, BEDFORD.

20 minutes' walk from Midland.

Trains from Northampton :
    2.32 - - - - - via Olney.
    2.45 or 3.22 - - via Wellingborough.

Tea at 4.30.

Talk by Ewen on "Literature," followed by boating, swimming, &c., on and in the Ouse. (Members will please provide their own hydroplanes.)

Each member is invited to bring a friend—lady or gentleman.

Return trains leave at 6.5 and 7.43.

An answer is requested not later than the 17th.

It is to be greatly regretted there is no detailed account of this occasion apart from a tantalising....*most enjoyable trip up the Ouse in good steam launch Lodore concluded the day* owing to Tyrannus being in the Lake District. Acting Secretary Markham recorded nothing apart from Club business, thereby depriving future minute readers of any description of how eight members and five visitors, including four ladies employed their time between Ewen's talk and the boat trip. Whether any *swimming &c.* took place is open to speculation. Railway enthusiasts will note the use of a convenient train timetable by two routes from Northampton to Bedford, neither of which survived into the third quarter of the century.

November 1913 saw an entry in the minutes of a candidate being 'black-balled'. Blackballing, dating back to the seventeenth century was a method of maintaining the ethos and exclusivity of a club. When the election of a new member was arranged members would be given the opportunity of registering their approval with a white ball, or disapproval with a black, the chosen ball to be placed in a ballot box under cover of a cloth. When opened the presence of a black ball would signify rejection of the candidate. This system of anonymous veto has had its detractors who maintain that with informal advance notice of a candidate to members such humiliation would not be necessary. The Chit Chat adopted a black ball policy in 1887 and this remained until 2004 when the rules were amended so that preliminary enquiries by Tyrannus could be made and if any member objected to the candidate his sponsor would be given the opportunity to withdraw his sponsorship. In many clubs there was a tradition that if a candidate were blackballed the proposer and seconder would resign. There is no official record of this custom in the Chit Chat although it may have occurred in the last twenty years. The present system may appear more democratic and correct but still means in theory any member may have a veto. In practice discussion with Tyrannus hopefully solves any problem without rancour. On balance in such a small organisation as the Chit Chat it is reasonable that no member should be in the position of being unwelcome in the host's home.

Back in 1913 the Rev A. H. Birk and Frederick Ince Jones had been proposed for membership. Birk was blackballed and Jones elected. It was unfortunate for Birk but not for the Club as Ince-Jones became Tyrannus in September 1923 and one of its great leaders. At this November meeting William Walker had given a talk as guest on the Scout Movement which reinforced the Club's intention of recruiting him. Tyrannus announced Walker's eligibility for membership but the following month *A letter from Mr. W. A. Walker was read in which he stated, with regret, that owing to the mode of election, he must decline to be proposed for membership.* In spite of this Jackson proposed Walker the following February with the promise to use his powers of persuasion. These must have been successful as Walker became a member in June 1914. As a footnote, on 27th October Birk was again proposed and seconded but possibly wisely withdrew his nomination before the next meeting.

There was no Summer Meeting in 1914 but the tradition continued the following year. War impinged little on the Club's everyday running but inevitably some papers reflected concerns of those remaining at home. In January 1915 the Rev Basil Davies, an ex-member living at St Sepulchre's Vicarage in Northampton talked on *The War and After*, a philosophical review of the causes of conflict and the ways these might be changed. His was one of the early papers where readers provided a summary for the secretary to paste in the minutes' book. At the Summer Meeting in 1916 Ewen gave a paper on the unlikely wartime subject of *Death and After*.

The following January Bruce Muscott read *Questions to be faced after the War*, including Greater Production, Piece Work, Capital and Labour, and Agriculture. In 1917 Wagstaff, a doctor, talked on *The Work of the RAMC* and Sir Ryland Adkins, as ever merely referred to in the minutes by his surname, gave prophetic insight on *The Problem of Poland*. The Summer Meeting that year was the first at which a lady had addressed the club. Mrs Chamberlain spoke with feeling and at length on *Woman in the Home*. Tyrannus noted it was *Not wholly a "War Problem"*, and, tellingly, at the end of his summary noted *(one hour)*. The next February Shoosmith waxed lyrical on *German Psychology* with the discussion afterwards posing the question, apparently unanswered, *How far is the German Soul involved in the unprecedented Crime and Tragedy now being enacted?*. The last 'War' paper came in April when Jackson suggested, after advising universal disarmament that, in his paper *The only possible Settlement of the War* would be *a situation in which the attainment of the highest Christian ideal is the only true solution*. One member recorded as being directly involved in the conflict was Major Peverell Smythe Hichens MD, who had joined the Club in 1902 and after serving in the RAMC returned to Northampton but resigned from the Club in 1920. There is no direct mention of any members having lost one of their family in the War which is rather surprising considering their ages.

In the autumn of 1917 Browne as Secretary presented a paper *C. C. C. – 32 years and after* a copy of which he sent to previous members, among whom were the Rev George Hooper, a founder, now Rector in the Cornish parish of Camborne and Richard Greene, the second Tyrannus, living out his retirement in Jersey. Their replies are recorded in the minutes and it is this letter of Greene's quoted in the earlier chapter.

In the discussion following Browne's paper a clarification of one of the Club's basic rules was made *The practicability of greater freedom in the regions of religion and politics was discussed at some length. It was decided not to overhaul the rules or perpetrate any drastic reforms, but "it was to be understood that the word <u>Politics</u> means <u>Party Politics</u>, and the word <u>Religion</u>; <u>matters of Sectarian difference</u>"*. This relaxation of Sanders' original restrictions gave readers much greater latitude in choosing subjects for their papers. Never included in printed Club Rules until 1950 this proviso was strictly adhered to, being verbally carried down the years from one generation of Chatterers to another.

Browne, perhaps with the intention of curbing those members who let their tongues run on, had started to record the length of papers. These ranged from a marathon 90 minutes on *XIXth Century Memoirs* with numerous quotations by Hankinson in September 1917 to a brief 13 minutes by C Markham in 1923 on the appropriately titled *The Short Cut*. The average length seems to have been between about 30 and 50 minutes, giving members adequate time for discussion. Time was considered important as meetings started at 7.30 in the evening with a welcoming drink, followed by business. Then the paper and discussion, ending at 10.00, and refreshments lasting until close of meeting at 10.30. The rules at this time allowed members to stay chatting until midnight should the host allow it. It would appear that then as now times were not strictly adhered to.

Three papers given in 1920 illustrate the wide variety of subjects explored. W. W. Hadley, editor of the Northampton Mercury, read his maiden paper on *'What is wrong with the Middle Classes?* and came to the conclusion *a moral revival is badly needed*. In November Ince-Jones lectured the Club with *Some possibilities of*

Northampton that recommended a fairly drastic remodelling of the town centre and electing a super-citizen to manage the town's affairs. As a visitor Guy Muscott, son of Bruce Muscott, gave his experiences as a prisoner of war in three different camps, the last near Berlin.

Three years later at the April meeting when Guy Muscott was elected to membership of the Club Browne announced his intention to resign as Tyrannus, to *make room for a younger man*. He had been in the hot seat for about twenty two years and a member for thirty seven.

Voting cards were sent out with the result that at the Summer Meeting Dixon was declared favourite. He firmly declined with the result that a new postal ballot was proposed with *the intimation or warning that members should not vote any more for Dixon, he having proved himself unworthy of their confidence.* That this rather derogatory motion should have been carried was due entirely to Dixon, who, acting as Secretary, had written the words. *Anyhow,* Browne adds as a footnote *he has a sense of humour.*

On September 28th 1923 a new Tyrannus was announced, Frederick Ince Jones.

NOTES

1. Obituary, *Northamptonshire Mercury* January 1925.
2. *The Moot* was a Club or Society of legal persons in Northampton but so far there have been no traces found. Tyrannus V, Ince-Jones, in an address to the Club in 1935 refers to the Moot as *an inferior body of great pretensions, which died an early death.*

6
Tyrannus V
September 1923 - 1949

Frederick Ince-Jones, born in 1884 was called to the Bar at the Inner Temple but returned to his home town and taught at a school for the profoundly deaf in Cliftonville Northampton where he succeeded Hugh Dixon as headmaster in 1916. He had been elected to the Club two years previously and his history as a Chatterer will be considered in Chapter 9.

Ince-Jones' first task was to organise a presentation to commemorate Browne's time in the Tyrant's chair. The Rev. W. C. Hall, a member of only three years standing, having joined in 1918, wrote a short poem in terms that left no doubt as to members' feelings. Hall's poem was duly pasted into the minute book.

Now all the Club assembles: here are met
Good spirits of the past, and shades of men
Whom fate has driven apart, and they who yet
Forgather o' winter nights, maintaining then
The long tradition of rare fellowship;
And in the midst is one of gracious mien,
Benignant, courteous to a finger-tip,
The gentlest Tyrant earth has ever seen.

Dear Browne, if love can tell you what you are,
And troops of comrades speak their hearts aright,
Believe no word can come from near or far
That would not bless and honour you tonight,
And in your memory abide, and live
With prayers for all the good that life can give.
*   -William C. Hall*

At the meeting on February 29th 1924 fifteen past and present members assembled at Bruce Muscott's home in St George's Street Northampton when Markham as the longest standing member presented Browne with a solid silver rose bowl. Following Browne's death the inscribed bowl was donated to the Club and is still brought out on occasions such as Summer Meetings:

> Presented to E. Montague Browne Esq
> Tyrannus of the Chit Chat Club
> March 1901-July 1923
> by his loyal and affectionate subjects
> Northampton. July 1923.

A glowing tribute to Browne from Adkins, delayed in the post, was read the following month, praising his modesty, powers of persuasion and ability to have kept together a group of men so diverse in their ways. Browne continued as an active member until February 1925 when he expressed a desire to retire after 38 years membership, whereupon the Club unanimously elected him an Honorary Member and his son H. St John Browne as an ordinary member. E M Browne continued to attend an occasional meeting until his death in January 1928.

Keeping alive a tradition of having Northampton Grammar School headmasters as members, the Club elected W. C. C. Cooke in 1921, the year he became headmaster. Cooke revealed himself as a lover of humorous poetry as well as a well-read educationalist. He remained a member until September 1938 when he resigned, having been told by his doctor to cut down on evening engagements. He continued to attend Club meetings intermittently as a visitor. Cooke introduced several of his staff as visitors but only one joined the Club, Mr, later Dr, Field, a geographer. Field remained a member for only seven years, retiring due to pressure of work in June 1939. Doubtless the prospect of losing members of staff to the Armed Forces placed a great burden on the Grammar School.

Deaths of early members feature prominently in the minutes of the 1920s. January 1925 saw the death of Sir Ryland Adkins, a member for 36 years, after a short illness, from *gastric influenza and heart failure*.[1] He was only 62 and died at his home, Springfield, Cheyne Walk, Northampton. A resolution *recording the Club's great sense of loss* was passed and entered in the minutes.

Richard Greene, the second Tyrannus whose retirement from the Club was marked by the dinner of 1897 and the Rev William Blomefield Sleight both died in 1927, Greene on the island of Jersey and Sleight at Towcester near Northampton. The Rev Alfred Ewen, living in Cornwall, E. M. Browne and Dr R. A. Milligan, a retired member, elected September 1887 and colleague of Arthur Jones, the third Tyrannus, all died in 1928

At the same meeting as Adkins' death was reported Ince-Jones raised, not for the first time, the printing of a list of papers given to the Club over the years. This was approved and the listing of papers until the end of 1924, paid for by Club members, at a cost of 1s. 6d. (7½p) each, provided valuable material for future chroniclers.

The 1927 Summer Meeting at Dallington Vicarage was notable not only for wintry weather and a total of forty two Club members and guests but also the speaker. Fifty two year old Sir Edward Penton, educated at Rugby and Oxford, was head of a firm of leather manufacturers. After holding the position of mayor of Marylebone from 1912-13 he joined the Royal Army Clothing Department, later absorbed by the Royal Army Service Corps during the First World War. He was the driving force in persuading the British boot and shoe industry to use Indian leather and was knighted in 1918. His lifetime interest was the Royal Society for Asian Affairs in which he held the post of Secretary until becoming Treasurer in 1919. In 1903 he had travelled an overland route from India to Russia, inspired by efforts to open a trade route through Persia. By camel, horse and caravan he travelled across Afghanistan, landing up at the railway station of Askerbad on the Russian border. By all accounts this journey was infinitely safer than it would be in the 21st century and his story was well received by the Club. As a footnote Sir Edward acted as Chief Inspector of Clothing in World War II and received the Order of Leopold in Belgium. He died in 1967, a widower, leaving six children.

The Summer Meeting of 1929 would long be remembered for the falling from grace of Tyrannus. The Rev J P de Putron, vicar of Kingsthorpe was host on the only cold day in a heat wave which meant the meeting was held indoors. During the reading of a paper on *George Eliot* by the Rev T L Cartwright, Vicar at Christ Church, Northampton,

One of de Putron's best chairs, groaning too long beneath the weight of the venerated Tyrannus (Ince-Jones), *deposited him ruthlessly, but more or less peacefully upon the floor. Delighted smiles appeared upon every face: joy reigned with merriment; but whether their pleasure was caused by the fall of a tyrant, the neatness of the trick or relief at the providential escape from injury of the honoured chairman, it was impossible for him to say. Mrs de Putron was heard to murmur that she had long had doubts about that chair. She need have no further doubts, she knows all.*

Perhaps the most telling comment of the Secretary is *This event brightened the proceedings considerably and caused the ensuing discussion to be animated.*

In November 1929 reference was made to a 'Chit-Chat Club' of 1714. The senior member, Markham, sent an extract from *The Spectator* of that year as *an interesting communication* and Ince-Jones recorded it in its entirety, without comment. It would have been *interesting* to know whether members accepted the report as genuine.[2] This is one of the most debated episodes in Chit Chat lore. Addison and Steele, founders of *The Spectator* were both members of the Whig Kit-Cat Club at the end of the seventeenth century. Addison took over the paper in 1714 and published a letter in June purporting to come from a *pert young baggage,* a member of a female *Chit-Chat club*. This was a 'spoof' but in all probability gave rise to the Cambridge University club's name.

Papers around this time were as varied as ever. During the 20s and 30s the most frequent subjects were geographical, about 30 papers ranging from *A Summer Holiday within the Arctic Circle* to *The Valley of the Nene*. Philosophy was not neglected from *What makes for happiness* to *Belief'*, and contemporary matters such as *The Northampton Town Planning Scheme* and *Causes of Social Unrest in India*. The Arts were represented by several papers including *The Poet Cowper and Northampton* and *The Substance of Poetry* while medical matters embraced *Rejuvenation* and *Glands and Personality*. Two papers stand out as slightly unusual in these decades, *Whom ought we to kill?* and *Eugenic Sterilisation*.

1935 saw the Club's Jubilee and a good reason to hold another dinner, this time at The Northampton and County Club, known locally as the George Row Club, occupying the building once used as the Northampton Infirmary and adjacent to the old Town Gaol. Sixteen current members, three Honorary Members and twelve 'old' members attended along with nineteen visitors, including some who were *sons of honoured past members and others who, as visitors had given papers.*

Unfortunately the minutes are rather matter of fact, there being no wordsmith present who felt he could record the event in verse. There were four toasts, five replies including a 'short' history of the Club by Ince-Jones and five 'one-minute' speeches. The occasion was deemed *a great success*. The manuscript of Ince-Jones oration survives at the Northampton Record Office under the title of *History of the Chit Chat Club, Northampton*.[3] It is eloquent, amusing and clearly the work of a man with great love for the Club. His conclusion is worth quoting

It is not a mean achievement, in a somewhat prosaic provincial town, where things of the mind are none too prominent, for men of widely differing tastes, professions, political and religious views to have preserved in a comradely spirit for 50 years, a gathering for the discussion of intellectual matters.

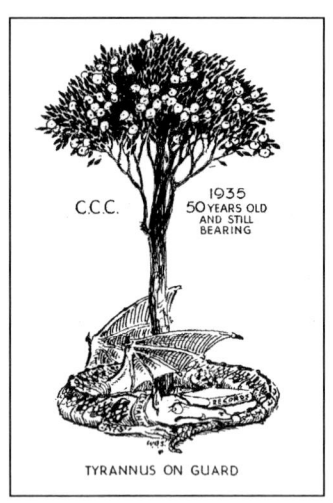

1935 Jubilee Dinner at Northampton Town and County Club
Menu Card – 'Tyrannus on Guard' designed by W. B. Shoosmith

Each early volume of Club minutes is prefaced by a list of past and present members, suitably edited by Tyrannus at the time, as Chatterers moved house, resigned or died. At the beginning of volume 6 Ince-Jones noted, for use in his speech;
36 clergy and ministers, 16 medical, 20 law, 6 business men, 4 bankers, 2 newspaper editors, 6 schoolmasters. 47 died. 90. Ince-Jones was to use this address later, in 1951, when he published a summary of the Club in its 68th year.

Two sons of E Montague Browne joined the Club. Born in 1882 Harold St John Browne followed his father into the firm of Browne and Wells, Solicitors and became a Chatterer in 1925. He contributed seven papers and died in 1947.

The younger brother Lawrence Edward, a Doctor of Divinity, joined the Club in 1936 when he was rector of Gayton in Northamptonshire. Laurence Browne brought a refreshing attitude towards religion into his papers. His first, *The Crusades as seen from the East* contrasted the squalor of *the greatest calamity in history* with its romantic side. Other papers will be considered later.

Another son, Eustace attended occasionally as visitor.

During the late 1930s the cloud of war hovered over members of the Club. Lt. Col. R M Raynsford DSO substituting for Hankinson in 1936 gave a paper, *Francophile or Francophobe?* and created a new 'first' by appearing in evening dress and giving his thesis whilst standing. He was elected a member the following year and in March 1938 talked about the Territorial Army during which he *discussed the function of the Territorials should another war break out and wondered whether they would do their work well.* The shadow of Munich must have been on all minds for in the September minutes Ince-Jones notes:- *In spite of the excitement caused by dramatic peace taking the place of almost certain war....* and in a paper on *'The Problem of Leisure* by the Rev T H Perry, another Dallington vicar:-

A day or two before....those assembled....had been faced by the prospect that the only leisure likely to be theirs would be enforced inactivity in a gas-proof cellar or trench.

1938 was not all gloom. At the end of the March 1938 meeting already mentioned *it was found that mysterious things had happened to the cars of Hankinson and Raynsford. Both of the same type, they seem to have changed places in different roads. With the assistance of the police they were discovered, but only after a prolonged search. Was it a poltergeist?*

Tyrannus, having left early, was subject to some undeserved suspicion.

The first meeting of the Second World War years, on September 29th 1939, took place at 4.30 in the afternoon at George's Parlour, a café in the town centre opposite All Saints' Church with tea and sherry. It was agreed that *the Club should continue in spite of the war* and meetings should start promptly at 7.30 with business but without the customary sherry and chat. Any refreshments should be after the paper or *at some suitable break*. Afternoon meetings were considered......*though it was felt by most that an evening meeting leads to a more convivial spirit and better Chit Chat*. In spite of this an afternoon start, between 4.30 and 5.00 was introduced in November 1940 and appears to have continued in winter months throughout the war.

Once war had started the Club took the attitude of when, rather than if, victory arrived. Early on in 1941 Raynsford discussed *The Future of England*.

During the war years Tyrannus' minutes give a fair representation of attitudes of the time and the conviction all would be well, victory would come, if not by Christmas then early next year. Fewer papers were presented on subjects connected with wartime than in the 1914-18 conflict but with 'blackout' and the prospect of air raids everyday life was affected more. Northampton escaped bombs apart from one that created a mess in Billing Road cemetery.

After a winter of snow and ice that lingered in the memory of many a member, Dixon gave *Reminiscences as a Would-be Octogenarian*, Parker talked on *The England of Defoe* and a visitor, Mr John Blakeman gave his views on *The Spiritual Basis of Life*. Shapland lightened the mood with *Food and Drink*, ... *a subject obviously dear to his heart and comforting to an organ rather lower in the body.*

For the 1940 Summer Meeting held at Dallington Vicarage by courtesy of Perry, Ince-Jones gave an 'impartial' talk on *The Weaker Sex*, juggling the merits of both sexes but *came out by the same door wherein he went.*

County Librarian Ellison suggested the Club could learn *Some lessons from Ancient Greece*. These concluded.......*Their history, which he illustrated suggestively from their three great wars, showed the supreme value of sea power. This comforted us all not a little.*

This was the time of the Atlantic blockade by German U-boats.

Following a paper by Stuart, the psychiatrist, on *Shakespeare and Medicine* where he *quoted....*inter alia.... *the dangers of night air and repression* the Club came down to earth with *The Church Chest* by Perry. 1940 had been a memorable year.

1941's papers struck a more sombre note, *Time the Tyrant, Changes in Religion* and *Trade and Liberty* being three.

There were a few minor irritations in those war years. At a meeting on Friday, October 30th *It was agreed that, in the present difficult times, a host should not be expected to provide the usual standard of refreshments. Cigars need not be supplied. Sherry and Port were luxuries. Whiskey and beer would be ample.* Food was rationed, alcohol was not, just hard to find.

1942 saw the first lady speaker for 24 years, Miss Joan Wake, sister of the then current Sir Hereward Wake. Joan established the Northamptonshire Record Society in 1920, leading to the County Record Office being the depository for all important county documents. She spoke at the Summer Meeting held in Gayton Rectory, the home of Lawrence Browne about *Great Northamptonshire Houses and Families - more nobles to the acre ... and more deer parks than any other county.*

Considering the situation in Europe a provocative title in October 1942 was *The unpopularity of the Jews* by Ince-Jones, ending with a plea for *more sympathy and understanding*. The *after talk* was not quite as serious as might be expected. During the discussion Hillaire Belloc's *How odd of God to choose the Jews* was capped by Hankinson with *Of course, why not, He knows what's what* and Raynsford told a story of having played bridge with Victor Gollanz, the publisher, who *professed not to know the game at all but went off richer by £2.*

In February 1943 the minutes read *At the last meeting Tyrannus had announced that he would have served the Club for twenty years if he continued until the summer..... and he felt he ought not to be regarded as 'The Old Man of the Sea'. He therefore proposed to tender his resignation in the summer.*

There are no minutes for January that year and November 1942 has no note of any such announcement. Was there a meeting in

January? Ince-Jones had probably decided what would be recorded in Club history, underlining the cynical assertion that history is only what is written in history books. He continues....

At the meeting of Feb 26th, the members met in solemn conclave without Tyrannus. On his return to the meeting, Jackson, the senior of the members, told him it was the unanimous hope of the members that he would continue in office and thanked him for his past service.

Tyrannus, who was much moved by the kind speech of Jackson, said that, as he seemed to have retained their confidence, he would carry on with great pleasure and expressed his warm appreciation.

It would appear to any suspicious mind there had been rumblings behind the scenes and Tyrannus was in effect asking for a vote of confidence.

Raynsford followed his 1941 talk on England's future with a rather complicated dissertation on *Leadership or Linoleum* in 1943 and the need for leaders in the future, involving a levelling of the classes. James Jackson, giving his 21st paper in 48 years as a Chatterer, spoke on *Post-war Reconstruction*. This at the age of 84 was to be his last reading. In 1944 Shaw, a consultant physician, raised the question *Was democracy damned?* in the course of a paper on *Possibilities* and provoked a brisk discussion.

One of the most popular programmes on the radio during wartime was the Brains Trust where a panel of learned individuals discussed various matters, an innovative entertainment at the time. Tyrannus took the chair, bombarding the Summer Meeting of 1944 with questions posed by members. Regrettably he only records the questions, not the answers although assuring posterity these were brilliant. Question 8 is a notable exception:

The discussion lasted for nearly two hours.

The following were the questions:-
1. What does "D" stand for in "D. Day"?
2. In view of the increasing difficulties of life, is the Brains' Trust of the opinion that it would be a good thing for it to be compulsory for every boy to have a 3 months' domestic training (as part of the school curriculum)?
3. On the balance of results, is the invention & perfection of the aeroplane a benefit or a curse to mankind?
4. If you had to live somewhere out of Britain, which place would you choose, and why?
5. Are Chain Stores a good thing?
6. In view of the small returns on invested capital coupled with high taxation, is the habit of saving, so much recommended in the past, an over-rated virtue?
7. Is it a fact that migraine is only to be found among people of a high standard of intelligence?
8. If it were within your power to become the greatest – soldier, statesman, musician, poet, cheesemonger or cricketer in the world, which would you choose?
(12 for statesman, 7 for musician, 6 for poet, 2 for cheesemonger)
9. Is it a good thing to have illusions?
10. Is it true that absence makes the heart grow fonder?
11. More women than men seem to attend church. Are women today more religious than men? Does this apply to other religions?
12. Which is the happiest period of life – childhood, youth, maturity or age?
13. Is the life of the people in fallen empires, or in countries which have never controlled empires any less worthy or happy than in great empires?

14. *In the animal kingdom males are usually more decorative than females. How is it that women are much more decorated than men?*

*

On Monday January 1945 *The absence of Ince-Jones on account of illness was the subject of special mention by several members and Browne (St.J.) was asked to write to him and express the sympathy of the Club.* It must be assumed Browne was Deputy Tyrannus on this occasion. He stood in for Ince-Jones in February, contributing excellent minutes but in March Tyrannus was back, thanking his deputy and members for their concern. He also *congratulated Raynsford on his appointment as High Sheriff, an honour which his family seemed to make a habit of deserving and Jackson* [James] *on having been a member of the Club for nearly fifty years: such persistence merited honour and celebration.* This was certainly an achievement, in his fifty years Jackson had read twenty one papers. He last attended the Summer Meeting of 1945 which consisted of a recital of the horrors associated with housing in England and the main suggestion of replacing the traditional open fire by a modern stove. The guest speaker was Dr J M Mackintosh, now Chief Medical Officer of Health in Edinburgh, returning to the Club. Reading between the lines members had to be *fortified by Raynsford's sherry* as the paper was not entirely well received, whether for its gloomy content or the reader's delivery is not certain. The minutes conclude: *The company broke up in an atmosphere of philanthropic energy tempered with philosophic calm in view of the inevitability of graduations in bettering existing conditions.*

Since April Shapland had been acting as Tyrannus. Although this is not minuted the writing is definitely his. At the January 1946 meeting Ince-Jones announced his retirement as Tyrannus after twenty three years in the post and the following month Shapland's position as Tyrannus was regularised. Three years later in April *Shapland expressed his intention of resigning the office of Tyrannus and the hope that Ince-Jones would resume it.* The minutes of October record Shapland as welcoming Ince-Jones *back to the chair again* although handwriting shows the returning Tyrannus had been minuting since April.

During Shapland's reign Club business is recorded only minimally and when Ince-Jones resumed papers are described in sparkling prose and great detail but of cut and thrust at meetings there is nothing. It may well be illness was taking its toll of Tyrannus, the spark of wit was almost extinguished but this was the dawn of a new age tending to take itself seriously with no time for banter. Following his retirement from the School for the Deaf Ince-Jones lived in Harpole, a village about five miles west of Northampton with his wife and two daughters. He continued to act as Tyrannus, possibly until his death in February 1954 at the age of 70. There are no minutes extant after the Summer Meeting of 1949, held at Watford Court, the *beautiful early-Elizabethan home of Lord and Lady Henley,* when *Shapland delivered a sparkling address full of quips and epigrams on "Personality and Possessions".*

NOTES

1. Obituary *Northampton Mercury* January 1925.
2. *The Spectator*. No. 560. Monday June 28th. 1714.

'Mr Spectator' writes:

'I have received the following letter, or rather billet-doux, *from a pert young baggage, who congratulates with me upon the same occasion.*

Dear Mr. Prat-apace,

June 23. 1714

'I am a member of a Female Society who call ourselves the Chit-Chat club, and am ordered by the whole sisterhood, to congratulate you upon the use of your tongue. We have all of us a mighty mind to hear you talk, and if you will take your place among us for an evening, we have unanimously agreed to allow you one minute in ten, without interruption.

I am, SIR,

Your Humble Servant, S. T.

P.S. *'You may find us at my Lady Betty Clack's, who will leave orders with her porter, that if an elderly Gentleman, with a short face, enquires for her, he shall be admitted and no question asked.'*

Few 'letters' in *The Spectator* are genuine in the sense of being from real correspondents. It says a great deal for both Addison and Steele that they were able to confuse their readers sufficiently not to be able to tell genuine from hoax. Posterity elevated the two authors and their publication to a level neither would have expected, although they would have undoubtedly have appreciated the honour - and the humour.

3. Northampton Record Office. 72.7061

7
Darker Days – and Renaissance
Summer 1949 - 2011

Between the Summer of 1949 and 1964 there is a hiatus of fifteen years. This was the Dark Age of the Club, all records lost.

The next volume of what may be called minutes starts in October 1964 and is a simple black notebook with no inscription on the cover. It only contains accounts of a few meetings and ends with the Summer Meeting of 1969 when the Club had as its guest Sir Joseph Hutchinson FRS, Draper Professor of Agriculture at Cambridge, who spoke on the *World Agricultural Policy*.

There may have been others who took on the role of Tyrannus in the ten years between Ince-Jones death and 1964 but when records resume it is Anthony Jackson who is in the chair. From attendance statistics there were six Chatterers who had survived from 1949, Hayes Dockrell, Stuart Humfrey, Ralph Lee, Anthony Jackson, Geoffrey Lowick, Eric Shaw and Alan Turner, over a third of Club membership.

New blood had been transfused into the Chit Chat. Notable were two future Tyranni, Stanley Hill, administrator at Northampton General Hospital and reader of at least twelve papers and John (Tony) Tasker, Consultant Physician at Northampton and reader of more than eighteen papers. Also from the world of medicine were Richard (Dick) Coles, consultant dermatologist and musician and Anthony (Tony) Alment, consultant gynaecologist. Robert Heygate had joined in about 1955 and was destined to be a great talker on economics.

After 1969 there is another gap lasting until October 1979. In 1971 Roy (Roley) Lee had become Tyrannus after the resignation of Anthony Jackson who had been somewhat ill in the previous few years and on occasions unable to finish meetings. During this time Peter Dalgleish, Northampton General Practitioner is said to have run day to day affairs even though not officially being Tyrannus.

The next set of documents is a series of incomplete draft minutes between 1979 and 1982 by Lee, variable in content.

After Lee the mantle of Tyrannus fell upon Stanley Hill when the post became a rotation every three years, normally the next senior member taking on the task. Club legend has it there was a somewhat acrimonious meeting, *The Night of the Long Scalpels* which heralded the death knell of Tyrannus' reign being endless but it is unclear to which end of Lee's tenure this refers.

The old arrangement had the advantage of continuity but meant no Secretary could be voted out if unpopular or incompetent without a great deal of bad feeling. Under the new system the opportunity arose for all members to take on responsibilities of chairman, secretary and treasurer all rolled into one and with few exceptions it has worked well. It has resulted however in records being transferred from Tyrannus to Tyrannus in cardboard boxes, resulting in loss of many papers and minute books. It is of interest to compare and contrast styles of minute keeping ranging from the concise and matter of fact approach to that of the more verbose and conversational.

There is a gap of three years from 1982 until a complete notebook series covers Hill's last five meetings, the complete J R Tasker years and the beginning of Fincham's reign until March 1989.

From April 1989 minutes are hand or typewritten in loose leaf and complete except for an inexplicable hiatus from the summer of 1996 to October 2001.

The missing records, minutes and papers, are a sad loss, not only for paper titles but also for interaction between members that provides the colourful unfurling saga of the Club. The post of Tyrannus evolved, adapting to changing needs over the years. Whether a Club should have a Chairman, Secretary and Treasurer combined in one person as general factotum and dogsbody is debatable but in answer to any criticism, it worked and still does, at least for Northampton's Chit Chatterers.

Since the days of Ince-Jones perhaps the most striking change seen in Club affairs is a general lack of discussion about rules and procedure. There was one exception, the rule regarding of blackballing has already been mentioned and it arose again in recent years as recounted previously. There were those who objected on principle, even to the point of resignation and those who considered there should never be a member elected if even one Chatterer would not have the candidate in his house as a guest. Regrettably these two views have been irreconcilable but did result in rule changes of 2004 creating a more informal compromise.

Chatterers appear to have come to meetings with no intention of indulging in banter so typical of pre-WW2 years. There is a more serious approach to the main business, that of presenting a paper and taking part in Chat. For the chronicler this has been unfortunate. Whereas in the past personalities had shone through, illuminating pages of minutes with their own special qualities, post Ince-Jones there is a tendency to omit any hint of disagreement between members or disapproval by or of Tyrannus. Reminiscences by past or present members would suggest there have been times when such feelings surfaced but these cannot be included in this review. Should there ever be a second edition of these wanderings through Northampton's Club no doubt the writer will expound at length upon Tyranni of the late twentieth and early twenty first centuries, the excellence or otherwise of papers and idiosyncrasies of members. The standard of papers has continued to be high as will be seen in succeeding chapters.

In spite of deficiencies in record keeping it is possible to give some idea of the Club's progress after the Dark Age.

By the 1960s Chatterers had developed a fairly strict format for their meetings. Hosts welcomed members and their guests with a cup of coffee and sandwiches, prepared by a long suffering wife, prohibited from participation in the Club's affairs but always expected to be there in the background to provide support when needed. Guests would remain in one room finishing their refreshments whilst members conducted their business in private. The host left the other members to collect guests and escort them to the Club who had risen to their feet in welcome. An introduction would be made by Tyrannus and rules governing form of address and general proceedings were explained. A paper followed, after which Chat ensued until brought to an end by Tyrannus. At this point the serious business of the evening started with liberal consumption of the host's whisky and port. These were the only two alcoholic drinks provided but within these were a multitude of variations. It was customary for the port to be vintage and the Scottish water single malt. There would appear to have been no limit to either the amount consumed or the hour when members were expected to depart.

Hospitality started to became more sophisticated towards the end of the decade. One of the wives, legend has it spouse of a Tyrannus, had recently acquired an electric toasted sandwich maker and experimented upon the Club. This was received with much approbation and presumably members returned home with tales of fantastic fillings between crisped white or brown slices. It was not long before a number of wives got together and decided their menfolk should indeed have something hot inside them before embarking on an evening of serious thought and talk. At first this was a one pot dish, a casserole, a fork and plate affair.

Time passed and with it inevitable evolution. By the mid-1970s members were greeted with a glass of sherry and wine appeared at the table. There were two members whose interest in the grape is remembered with affection, Alan Jennings and Tony Alment. Dr Alan introduced sherry and Sir Anthony added greatly to members' knowledge of wine.

Reasons for further changes in refreshments at Club meetings depend upon which version of events is believed. Some maintain the gradual emergence of three, or even four, course meals was due to the desire of wives not to be outdone by other spouses. On the other hand there may have been members who felt their social position required them to provide lavish feasts. Less judgementally and probably more true is the wish to entertain what was after all a society of friends in the most congenial atmosphere possible.

Nowadays a host welcomes members and guests with a glass of wine, red or white, soft drinks, mineral water or various other concoctions appropriate to the time of year. The assembly is then summoned to the dining table at 8 o'clock to be waited upon by host, spouse and any friends who have been inveigled into taking part in the ritual. Occasionally a hostess manages to persuade a member's wife to help with the promise of reciprocal assistance in the future. The move to a more school-like meal has appeared when members either help themselves in the kitchen or are doled out their portions by an aproned hostess. A typical first course consists of 'meat and two veg' in various guises. This is followed by a dessert dictated by the taste and skill of the hostess. Cheeses round off the meal, along with coffee. It was inevitable this explosion on the culinary front would bring forth criticism that the Chit Chat had become no more than a Dining Club with paper and discussion of secondary importance, a view strenuously denied by those who enjoy a leisurely meal with the opportunity for informal chatting. In the past twenty years there have been various moves towards the old *coffee and sandwiches* regime but this would seem unlikely although *moderation in entertainment* is always encouraged. Another tendency has been that of not entertaining at home but at some outside venue, a hostelry or more notably the Northampton Town and County Club in George Row. This move has been welcomed by some spouses but frowned upon by more dyed in the wool members.

The business part of each meeting officially starts at nine precisely. This is where problems have occurred, giving grist to the mill of those who wish a reversion to sparser fare. Assuming *the modest refreshments*, as the Rules delicately put it, start on time there is only an hour to get through a full meal. To give members their due the move to a two course repast is proving a satisfactory compromise between sandwiches and lavish feast. By definition the Club likes to chat and it is usually slower eaters who converse the most. The majority of hostesses are overly generous and second helpings of each course are not necessarily given to the faster eaters, resulting in Tyrannus glancing significantly at his watch while the host wonders if he has been too lavish with his hospitality when members linger over coffee or even dare to ask for a second cup.

Tyrannus eventually hammers on the table, reminding members of the time and suggesting they should take their coffee cups or glasses into the next room whilst leaving guests to finish their coffee or wine. This move can be unpopular with the hostess whose visions of spilt liquid are vividly underlined by stories her husband has recounted about meetings elsewhere involving ruined carpets. Eventually when the last member has returned from the comfort break seating is sorted and business begins. Only Tyrannus is aware of the time, fifteen to twenty minutes late and his agenda is longer than usual. Minutes having been circulated by e-mail are now taken as read, a welcome move if Tyrannus is a lengthy scribe and any business is transacted. It is typical that the later the start the longer the discussion on a minor point of order. The host disappears to round up guests who by this time have gravitated into the kitchen and are either helping with the washing up or otherwise deeply engrossed in conversation with the hostess. All rise to greet guests who take their seats. Tyrannus welcomes them in time honoured way:

'Good evening, gentlemen and welcome to this meeting of the Chit Chat Club. I will introduce you to the members. As a guest of X there is Mr A B (there follows a short description) and as a guest of Y, Mr C D (etc). A word by way of introduction. It is traditional that members address each other by surnames only. Except for myself, I am addressed as Tyrannus. Guests are given their correct titles. After the paper members and guests may speak continuously for no more than five minutes on the paper, only limited by party politics and sectarian religion being strictly forbidden. The penalty for any infringement is the fine of sixpence, six old pence that is. If this is not paid immediately it is up to Tyrannus to decide the perpetrator's fate.

Tyrannus then calls upon the speaker to read his paper which may last anything from twenty to fifty minutes. A round of applause will wake any member who has nodded off and it has been known for gentle elbowing in the ribs to rouse a snorer during the paper. The meeting is returned to the host's care for ten minutes or so during which time whisky or port is offered in keeping with ancient Club tradition. With the encroachment of drink driving laws it must be noted fewer members take up the host's offer these days. The Chat then takes place. During the paper Tyrannus will have made notes not only for the minutes but also to put the first comment or question to the reader, not the easiest duty he has to perform if he is either confused by details of the paper or has found the subject boring. Chatting continues until either there are no more points raised or time runs out. 10.30 is the appointed time but in practice this can be extended, especially if a reader has engendered passion and wit among his audience. It is regrettable however that more often than not a late ending is due to a late start.

*

Summer Meetings have also evolved, roughly in line with ordinary occasions. Readers may remember balmy afternoons on the lawns of Berry Wood Hospital around the end of the nineteenth century when tea was served prior to a stroll through the grounds and a paper given by one of the Club. Evolution has meant the reception of guests in early evening, standing around holding glasses filled with sparkling wine or Pimms, a move into the host's house for a paper read by the evening's guest and a discussion in which all might join and then a sit down meal or buffet with wine. Unlike monthly meetings there is no time limit for Summer Meetings. Fortunately for hosts this is rarely abused.

After more than a century and a quarter there have been surprisingly few changes in the Club.

The question of admitting ladies to normal meetings either as members or guests was raised in 2009. Discrimination laws allow institutions of less than twenty five members to remain of one sex but several members felt the matter should be aired. A confidential, anonymous questionnaire was sent out and the result was a resounding defeat for any change by a margin of two to one. One member considered it a resignation issue remarking …. *It would destroy the whole tradition and ethos of the Club.* It is interesting to note that in 1894 a similar motion was defeated by the same margin, six votes to three. There is little rancour among the fairer sex at the outcome of these ballots. I have been reliably informed that one member's wife was heard to remark she had no objection to her husband going out to play.

Another change has been in dress code. Lounge suit and tie was de rigueur until the late twentieth century when it was noted members attended in suits of light flannel or even blazer and trousers. Ties were still worn. It was not until recently after eyebrows had been raised when a member dared to attend minus tie that Tyrannus called the Club to order and asked for opinions. It was agreed that although suits were traditional 'smart casual' would be acceptable, with a tie of course. A demonstration by means of Bermuda shorts and shirt by one member of what truly casual wear signified was not lost on the Club.

Members now come from many more walks of life providing a broader base for papers and discussion although it is possible individual members may not have such varied interests as the giants of yesteryear, even when these latter are viewed through the wrong end of time's telescope.

Transport in the twenty first century is not problematic and members can be drawn from a wider radius than in earlier days, though sharing cars is essential for those intending to consume a host's generous supply of wine thanks to those restrictive drink-drive laws. Modern record keeping and production of minutes, along with electronic distribution of notices enables Tyrannus to conduct his business more efficiently, and it must be said, at less expense, than in days of postcards through the post. Papers can be produced more easily with research on the internet and there are no longer frustrating crossings out and lengthy, often indecipherable, insertions into readers' manuscripts.

Whether these changes have been for better or worse only history will tell. What is certain is that the Club has no intention of going the way of Cambridge Chit Chatterers through what M R James described as 'inanition'.

PART 2 – The Chatterers

So far emphasis has been on the Club, a Club meeting monthly at varying locations. Any historical account of the Chit Chat should ideally concentrate on its members, their backgrounds and their papers, no member being excluded, however little he may have contributed. To this point it has only been possible to include relatively few Chatterers, where they are relevant to Club evolution. The problem now arises of how to present the remaining, the majority, without introducing a chronological list of names, dates and other statistics which could become tedious and boring. The solution has been to divide members into their occupations. In this way members may be considered as individuals, each bringing unique qualities to meetings, qualities often quite unrelated to their callings. The presentation chosen provides a skeleton on which to build and hopefully decreases any tendency to monotony.

In order to facilitate identification of members a list of Chatterers in chronological order has been introduced between parts 1 and 2.

*

When Ince-Jones came to write his short history of the Club in 1951 he found that of the 112 members in the first 67 years 82 were clergymen, lawyers or doctors. Over the whole life of the Club there has to be an approximation regarding numbers with some members being untraceable as well as years missing from minute books. Of recorded members at the beginning of 2013 the percentage of the three main professions has dropped from 73 to 62 although the ratio has remained the same, clergy heading the list, law coming second and medicine trailing behind. These three will be taken in order followed by the teaching fraternity as a minority fourth.

Northampton CCC members 1885-2013

KEY

C. Moved from the area. * Papers held in archive.
D. Died.
H. Elected Honorary Member.
L. Allowed membership to lapse.
R. Resigned.

NAME	DATES	BIOGRAPHY	PAPERS READ
AUTHOR UNKNOWN			Crime and Punishment.* 1962. Ombudsman.* Morality and Foreign Policy.* Gold.* Some Aspects of National Insurance.* Longevity.* Urban Traffic.*
GEORGE Thomas John	1885-1907 R	b. 1854. FGS.Curator N'pton Mus. 1884 - whilst keeping duties as Librarian Guildhall Rd. Library. Ret. 1912. d. 1920	1885 Belemnites. 1887 Prehistoric remains in Northamptonshire. 1888 On Northamptonshire Libraries. 1891 Money. 1893 The old pottery of Northants. 1899 Museums. 1901 Who are the Celts? 1903 Edward Thring and the Classics. 1904 Recent finds of Saxon remains at Kettering. 1906 The Arts in Britain 2000 years ago.
HAMMOND Charles Edward	1885-7 C	b. 1837 Balliol Coll. Oxford BA 1858, Fellow 1859-73, MA 1861, Tutor and Lecturer. Ord. Oxford 1862. Chaplain Oxf. Female Penitentiary. Rector Wootton, Northamptonshire 1882-7, Vicar Menheniot Cornwall 1887-1912. Hon. Canon St. Rumon in Truro 1894. Examining Chapl. To Bish. 1903-12. D. 1914.	1885 Some ancient Spanish Churches.
HOOPER George Brereton	1885-7 C	b. 1849. Uppingham Sch. Cambridge Emmanuel, BA 1874, MA 1877. Ord. P'boro 1878. Curate St Edmund's N 1876-9, Rect. Courteenhall 1879-87, Woolverstone, Suffolk 1887-93. Vic. St Just in Penwith 1893-1900, Rect. Cambourne 1900-34. d. 1934.	1886 Undeveloped powers of body and mind.
EUNSON, John	1885-8 R	b. 1833 Wolverhampton Grammar Sch., Queen's Coll. Cork. Manager N'pton Gas Company 1854, consulting engineer N'pton Water Works 1877. Cons. Engineer Northampton Corpn. JP 1908. d. 1911.	1886 Roads, ancient and modern.
GORDON Charles James	1885-8 C	b. 1853. Pembroke Coll. Cambridge. BA 1875, MA 1879, Ord. Peterborough 1878, Curate St John Baptist Peterborough 1877-9, Langport Somers. 1879-82, Vicar St Mary's Northampton 1882-8, Nassington with Yarwell 1888-91, Rector Rushden 1891-5, Abthorpe 1895-99, Vicar Crosby Ravensworth	1885 Socialism.

100

Name	Dates	Biography	Publications
GREEN Thomas	1885-8 R 1898-9 L	Westmorland 1901-4, Rector Great Salkeld Cumberland 1904-25. Vicar Blawith Lancs. 1925-31. Lic. Pr. Dioc. Carlisle 1931-43. d. 1944. b.1842. Oundle Sch. BA London. Admitted Solicitor 1865. Firm later Becke Green & Stops. Poet. d. 1922	1886 Ancient Copyhold Tenure.
SMITH Harrington	1885-8 C	Left N'hants 1888.	1887 Rating Areas in Northamptonshire.
GRAY Charles	1885-9 L	b. 1842. Queen's Coll. Cambridge BA 1866, MA 1879. Curate Northwood 1866, Brentwood 1867-70, Asst. Master Epsom Coll. 1870-74, Vicar St Michael and all Angels Northampton 1874-87, Belgrave with Birstall Leicestershire 1887-91, St Mary's Peterborough 1892. JP for Leicestershire. d. 1894	1887 Earthquakes.
SANDERS Samuel John Woodhouse	1885-93 H	b. 1846. Ludlow Grammar Sch. Cambridge St John's, BA 1865, MA 1868, LLM 1273, LLD 1886. Ord. Ely 1871. Vice-Master Bedford County Sch. 1868-72, Head Master Northampton Grammar Sch. 1872-93. Curate St Peter's Northampton 1874-93, Vic. St Nicholas Leicester 1893. Canon P'boro 1890-1915. d. 1915.	1886 Protective mimicry in animal nature. 1888 Cave explorations. 1891 Criminals.
SCRIVEN Richard George	1885-98 L	b. 1845. Memb. N'ptonshire Nat. Hist. Soc. Edit. Cttee. 1880-1921. Vice-pres. Soc. 1932. Contributions to publications incl. *Drayton House, Earthworks on site of Northampton Castle, Woodcraft*. d. 1938.	1886 The Age of Trees. 1889 Chaucer. 1891 Farm Colonies. 1893 Agricultural Exodus.
JONES Arthur Henry	1886-1901 D	b. 1853. MRCS England 1874, LCA and MB Bart's.London 1876, MD London 1880, MRCP London 1882. H.Surgeon Guys, H.Surgeon Northampton Gen. Infirmary 1876-81, Hon. Physician 1882. d.1901.	1887 The Human Voice. 1889 Vegetarianism. 1891 Physical Abnormalities. 1893 The Infirmary Sesqui-centenary. 1895 Atoms & the Vortex Theory of their Origin. 1897 Spectrum Analysis.
HUTTON Frederick Robert Chapman	1886-7 R	New Coll. Oxford. BA 1880, MA 1890. Ord. Durham 1881, Curate Jarrow 1880-1, Leeds 1881-2, St Peter's Bishop Auckland 1883-4, Vicar Roade, Northamptonshire 1884-7, Lecturer Bolton 1887-90, Vicar St George's Bolton 1891, Rector St Paul Corlton-on-Medlock Manchester 1901.	1887 Fiji and its Customs.
MARKHAM Henry William Kennedy	1886-8 L	b.1848. Rugby Sch. BA St John's Camb. 1870 Solicitor 1875. Joined family firm same name. 2nd Lt. Northampton Militia 1874, later Capt. 3rd Bn. Northampton Regt. 1883. Freemason, Past Master Delapre Lodge, N'pton. d. 1925.	
BAKER Robert Sibley	1886-91 L	b. 1823. Magdalen Coll. Cambridge, BA 1846. Ord. 1850. Curate Shelton Bedfordshire 1847-65, Rector Hargrave Northamptonshire 1865.Secy Northamptonshire Society of Antiquaries. d. 1897	1887 Sports and games. 1889 Place Names in Northamptonshire.
GREENE Richard	1886-98 H	LRCS Edin. 1868. LRCP Edin. 1868, MRCP 1885, FRCP 1888. LSA Edin 1876. Med. Supt. Northampton County Lunatic Asylum 1878. Med. Supt. E. Riding Asylum, Beverley, Sen. Asst. Med. Off. Sussex Co. Asylum. Author many articles and pamphlets. d. Guernsey 1927.	1887 Facts and fancies of lunacy. 1888. Races. 1889 A Vulgar Error, or Man and his Meat. 1890 Voltaire. 1891 An historical sketch of the rise and progress of the Medical Sciences. 1891 Men and Monkeys.

			1893 Ivan the Terrible. 1894 Population, Pauperism and Production. 1895 An almost forgotten man. 1896 The wandering Jew. 1897 The root of all evil. 1900 Twin Stars or One. 1904 Pre Christian Crosses. 1906 The Ancient Religion of Egypt.
BROWNE Edward Montague	1887-1925 H	b. 1847. Solicitor 1866. 1870 moved to Northampton, as from 1905 Browne and Wells. Founded Northampton Electric Light Company 1889. d. 1928.	1887 Notes on Wills, whimsical and otherwise. 1890 Death Duties. 1892 National Pensions. 1894 Chancery. 1896 The Dawn of the 20th Century. 1898 Snake Bites & Antivenine. 1900 Illusions. 1902 Some Phases of the Drink Question. 1904 L Bridgman & H Keller. 1906 Travel. 1908 Goldsmith. 1913 The purpose of Punishment. 1916 Slang. 1917 C.C.C. – 32 years and after. 1919 Spiritualism. 1922 To Uplift the People. 1931. Gambling & the Law.
WAKE Hereward	1887-8 R	b. 1852 12th Bart. Wake of Clevedon. Eton, succeeded to title on death of father 1865. d. 1916	1887 Instinct & Reason.
WILSON William	1887-8 L	b. 1829. St Catherine's Cambridge, BA 1850, MA 1853. Ord. Peterborough 1852, Curate Isham 1851-3, West Wrathling Cambridgeshire 1855-9, Rector Teversham Cambridgeshire 1859-67, Vicar Waterbeach 1867-73, Rector Narbeth-with-Robeston-Wathen (?) 1873-85, Stoke Bruerne Northamptonshire 1885-95. d. 1895.	
BURY William	1887-89 L	b. 1839. Trinity Coll. Cambridge BA 1862, MA 1893. Ord. York 1864, Cur. Tickhill Yorks. 1863-5, Rector Fifehead-Neville Dorset 1866-7, Haselbeach Northamptonshire 1867-82, Harlestone Northamptonshire 1882-1907, est. Cooperative public house there. Rur. Dean Rothwell 1874-82, Hon. Canon Peterborough 1892-1908, Rector Ickenham Middlesex 1907-19. Canon Peterborough 1908. Canon Residentiary 1908-21. d. 1927	1888 Forgotten Man.
MILLIGAN Robert Arthur	1887-91 R	b. 1858. OBE. Entered N'pton Gen. Infirmary 1875 as pupil. MRCS (Eng.) 1881, LRCP (London), Guy's 1884, MD (Durham) 1900. Ho. Surgeon 1884. Surgeon N'pton. Gen. Hosp. 1886-1926. RAMC in WWI Camb. Mil. Hosp. JP 1908. d. 1928.	1888 Modern Treatment of Wounds.
HAVILAND John	1887-92 L	b. 1849. Solicitor. Freemason. Left N'pton 1905. d. 1916.	1888 Socialism. 1890 Poor Law.
BLYTH Alexander Wynter	1887-95 L	b. 1844. King's London, MRCS Eng. 1870. LSA Eng. 1870. Medical Offr. Of Health and Public Analyst St. Marylebone, Public Analyst Devon. Barrister-at-law	1887 Poison Lore, old and new. 1888 The germ theory of disease. 1889 A Grave Affair.

Name	Dates	Biography	Publications
MARKHAM Christopher Alexander	1888-1930 H	(Lincoln's Inn). President Incorporated Society of Medical Officers of Health, Registrar Royal Sanitary Institute. d. 1921. b. 1859. Private education & studied S. Kensington. Articled to father Henry Philip Markham. DL. Clerk of Peace Co. Northampton. Adm. Solicitor 1887. Clerk of Peace to Co. Council Northampton 1899-1904. Lt.4th Bn. Northampton Regt. 1886, Capt. 1893. Resigned 1900. FSA (Fellow Soc. Antiquaries) 1890. d. 1937. Auth (Inter alia): *The Church Plate of Northamptonshire*, 1894. London, Simpkin, Marshall, Hamilton, Kent & Co., Ltd. (50 large & 200 small copies). *The Stone Crosses of The County of Northampton*, 1901. Publ. as above. Ed. *Liber Custumarum. The Book of the Ancient Usage and Customes of the Town of Northampton from the earliest record to 1448*, 1895. Taylor & Son, Dryden Press, Northampton. *History of the Markhams of Northamptonshire*. 1901. 100 copies. d 1937.	1890 Hypnotism. 1891 The Determination of Sex. 1892 Parasites. 1893 Sanitary Law. 1888 Domesday Book. 1890 The Norman Conquest. 1892 The Liber Custumarum of the Borough of Northampton. 1894 The Church Plate of Northamptonshire. 1895 Ancient Stone Crosses of Northamptonshire. 1896 King Lear. 1898 Anachronisms. 1901 Some early text books. 1903 Iron Roads of Northamptonshire. 1905 Unparliamentary Language - Slang. 1906 Infirmary. 1909 Benvenuto Cellini. 1911 Hatchments. 1912 Northants "Ways and Means". 1914 Northants Militia. 1917 Shakespeare's Knowledge of Law. 1918 Common. 1921 Wills. 1923 The Short Cut. 1925 Franks. 1927 The Valley of the Nene. 1929 Peers taking Titles from Northamptonshire.
LAWSON Frederick Pyke	1888-91 L	b. 1834. King's Coll. Sch. London. Trinity Coll. Camb. BA 1856, MA 1859. Ord. 1858, Peterborough. Cur. St Peter's N'pton. 1857-70, Daventry 1871-2. Vic. Preston Deanery, N'hants. 1879-89. Rect. Sudborough 1889-1919. Hon. Canon Peterborough 1897-1920. d. 1920.	1890 The Channel Islands.
FAULKER John Joseph	1888-99 L	b. 1848. LLB Lon. 1872, LLD 1875. Regist. of Co. Ct. & Dist. Regist. High Ct. of Justice N'pton. 1882. Solic. N'pton. Gas Light Co. Ltd. d. 1910.	1889 County Courts. 1891 Ancient Law. 1893 Marriage Laws. 1897 Criticism of the book entitled "Merrie England".
ADKINS William Ryland Dent	1889-1903 H	b. 1862. Mill Hill Sch. BA (London) 1882. Bar, Inner Temple, 1890. MP Middleton Div. Lancs. 1906 Recorder Nottingham 1911, Birmingham 1920. Chairman Npton. CC. 1920. Knighted 1911, KC 1920. d. 1925	1889 Purple Patches. 1893 Justice & its Methods. 1893 The New Unionism & the Old. 1895 Modern Slavery. *(Reader unspecified but presumed to be WRDA by Ince-Jones 1935).* 1897 Whyte Melville, the Northamptonshire novelist. 1900 When should we tell lies. 1901 An Autumnal Civilisation. 1915 Gardens, Groves & Parks. 1917 The Problem of Poland. 1923 Scenery & the Soul.
TOM Edward Nicholls	1889-1910	b. 1830 Cornwall. St John's Cambridge, BA 1858, MA 1863. Ord. 1859. Curate Marham Norfolk 1858-60,	1890 Reign of Edward III. 1892 The Reign of Elizabeth.

		H	Kingsthorpe Northampton 1860-73, Rector St Peter's Northampton 1873, resigned 1903 on pension £60. m. Ida Smith, d of Rector of Kislingbury. S. died in infancy, 2 d. d. 1913	1894 In Memoriam. 1896 War of American Independence. 1898 Words. 1900 The Second Punic War. 1902 Proverbs. 1904 Minor Poems of Milton.
	EUNSON George	1889-90 L	b. 1866. Asst. Manager Northampton Gas Co. Rising to Chairman & Man. Dir. 1942. N'pton. Volunteers 1879. CO 3/4 Bn. Northants Regt. 1915. (Major). Capt. & Hon. Maj. N'pton Territorials. d. 1948.	
	ROBERTS, J L	1889-91 L	Canon	1889 Some tendencies of Modern Thought.
	JESSON Thomas	1890-1 C	b. 1848. Trinity Coll Camb. BA 1873. FGS. Collector fossils and bryazoa, collections to N'pton and Brit. Museums. D. 1928.	
	BEASLEY Thomas Calvert	1890-1909 D	b. 1835, Chapel Brampton, Northampton. Rugby School. Trinity Coll. Cambridge, BA 1859, MA 1862. Ord. Peterborough 1860, Curate Wellingborough 1859-63, Saffron Walden 1863, Vicar Dallington Northampton 1874-. d. 1909.	1892 Protection from lightning. 1894 Village Life. 1897 The Sense of Touch. 1898 Conversation. 1901 External Appearance as an Indication of Character. 1903 Moral Characteristics of the Sexes. 1905 Character from Hand-writing. 1907 The Martians.
	HARDING William	1891-1903 H	b. 1851. MB, CM (Scotland) 1881, MD (Univ. Edinburgh) 1893, MRCP (London) 1892. 2nd Asst. MO. N'pton. Co. Lunatic Asylum Berry Wood 1889, Med. Supt. and Asst. MO Female Dept. 1898. Administrator Northants. War Hosp. Duston. Lt. Col. RAMC. Ret. 1925.	1892 Insect and the Flower. 1894 Novels, New & Old. 1896 Gleanings, or the Humours of a Mad House, by an inmate. 1898 Predetermination of Sex. 1899 A Paradox. 1901 Second Sight. 1907 Apparitions.
	CUNNINGHAM John	1891-1917 H	b. 1842. Hatfield Hall, Durham. Ord. Ripon 1872, Curate Stanley Yorkshire 1871-3, Holy Trinity Bingley 1873-6, Gen. Lic. Dioc. Peterborough 1877. Chaplain St Andrew's Hospital Northampton 1876-1911. d. 1923.	1894 Backsheesh. 1896 Success in Life. 1898 History of Pickwick's production. 1900 Historical Names of London Streets. 1901 English Surnames. 1903 Nick Names. 1906 Some Changes during the Nineteenth Century. 1908 Curiosities in connection with Marriage. 1910 Strange Bequests. 1913 Old London Taverns. 1915 Life in London 150 years ago. 1917 Tailed Men.
	SLEIGHT William Blomefield	1891-1917 H	b. 1850. Sch. Brighton Coll. Clare Coll. Cambridge, BA 1872. MA 1875. Ord. 1877 Peterborough. Vicar Swadlingcote Derbyshire 1880-9, Curate St Katherine's Northampton 1874-80, Vicar 1889-1911, Vicar Towcester 1911-22, Vicar Easton Neston Towcester 1916-22. Member Roy. Commission Blind deaf and dumb 1886. Pres. British Deaf and Dumb Assn. 1890-1920. d. 1927.	1892 The Education of the Deaf and Dumb. 1894 Fuisorge System. 1896 Types for the Blind. 1899 Travels in Egypt. 1900 Egypt 1903 Assonan Dam. 1908 Forestry. 1909 Deaf & Dumb in Congress.

Name	Years	Biography	Papers
HARDY J	1891-2 L		1912 The tramp. 1914 Deaf Mutes.
BUTTERFIELD Henry	1892-4 R	b. 1844. Uni. Coll. Sch. London. Owner N'pton Herald, later N'pton Chronicle. JP 1896. Mayor N'pton 1909-10. d. 1929.	1892 The forward movement in Social Reform.
PERCIVAL George Henry	1892-6 L	b. 1848. Educated privately then Guy's Hosp. MRCS England 1871, LSA London 1871, MB Uni. London 1874. Med. Officer Homerton Hosp. Asst. MO Shrewsbury County Asylum. Hon. Surgeon N'pton Gen. Hosp. 1878-1919. MOH Northampton Rural District Council & Hardingstone RD. OBE. d. 1939.	1893 Sewage matters. 1895 Chinese Medicine & Sanitation.
MANFIELD Harry	1892-9 L	b. 1855. Dir. Manfield Shoes. MP Mid-Northants. 1906-19. d. 1923. Brother of J	1895 The various forms of Gambling. 1898 Mars & its marvels.
TUSON Edward Luxmoore	1893-4 R	b. 1848. Pembroke Coll. Oxf. BA 1870, MA 1881. Ord. 1872 (Salisbury). Cur. Sturminster-Newton, Dorset 1871-3, Old Windsor 1873-5. Chaplain Windsor Gt. Park 1876-84. Vicar Kingsthorpe N'ptonshire 1885-1917. d. 1917.	
WOOD Francis Henry	1894-1900 H	b. 1846. St John's Cambridge, BA 1871, MA 1874. Ord. Peterborough 1872, Curate All Saints' Northampton 1871-4, St Anne Holloway 1874-5, Rector St Kenelm-in-Rowsley Worcestershire 1875-82, Vicar St Paul's Northampton 1881-7 (resigned). d. 1906. Wife died 3 days after.	1895 Taylor's "Dunstan" and Tennyson's "Beckett". 1897 Paris under the Butchers. 1899 Shakespeare's "Merchant of Venice" and Marlowe's "Jew of Malta". 1902 Masques at Court of Ben Jonson. 1903 Browning's Paracelsus.
CHURCH W H C	1894-6 C	b. 1854. Left area 1896. d. 1929.	1894 Intellectual, not Moral, Agencies the dominant factors in the progress of Society.
GILL Anthony Clarke	1894-6 R	b. 1841. Baptist Minister. d 1915.	1895 Shakespeare's Queen Katherine.
JACKSON James	1895-1946 D	b. 1860. Admitted solicitor 1893. N'pton Counc. 1897-1940 (mostly). Alderman. d. 1946.	1896 Historical development of the House of Lords. 1898 The Czar's Message. 1900 Titles. 1901 Wordsworth. 1903 Poetry in relation to Life. 1904 What do we mean by "Gambling". 1907 What we Read, and Why. 1909 The Art of Public Speaking. 1911 What is a gold sovereign. 1914 Fear. 1916 The foreign exchanges. 1918 The only possible settlement of the War. 1921 Unemployment. 1924 What makes for Happiness? 1929 The Substance of Poetry. 1931 The Dole. 1933 The Setback to Liberty. 1936 Public & Private Employment. 1938 More about Freedom. 1941 Trade and Liberty. 1943 Post-War Reconstruction.
MANFIELD James	1896-	b. 1885. Part Owner Shoe Manufg. Co. JP 1900.	1897 Italy.

	1900 L	Mayor N'pton 1905-6. Sheriff 1916. d. 1925. Brother of H.	1899 Our Umbrellas.
TERRY George Russell	1896-1901 C	b. 1868. Solicitor, lay reader, Vic. St. Michael's N'pton. d. 1943.	1897 Thomas A Beckett. 1899 White Slaves
CROPLEY Henry	1896-8 L	b. 1860. MRCS Eng. 1884, FRCS 1887. LSA 1884. DPH Eng. Conj. 1891. MOH Kingsthorpe UDC, Med. Off. N'pton Workhouse. Priv. Pract. N'pton. Ret. 1930. d. 1940.	
HARPER Alfred Mussendine	1897-1903 R	Queen's Coll. Cambridge, BA 1883, MA 1889. Ord. Peterborough 1885, Curate St Mark's Leicester 1883-8, Vicar St Paul's Northampton 1888-1903, St Matthew's Leicester 1903, Rural Dean Gartree 111 and Vicar Bringhurst-w-Easton Magna and Drayton, Uppingham 1913. R. Dean 1913-28. Priest-Canon St Martin's Collegiate Ch. Leicester 1922-26. d. 1928.	1897 Some Social Axioms. 1899 Points of view. 1901 Suicide.
CROOKSHANK Francis Graham	1898-9 C	b. 1873. MRCS LRCP 1894, MB 1895, MD 1896 Univ. London. Junior MO. N'pton Co. Lunatic Asylum, Berry Wood 1898. Med. Offr. Health UDC Barnes & Med. Supt. Isolation Hosp. Mortlake. d 1933.	1898 Onomatopoeia.
COX John Charles	1899-1900 C	b. 1840-2. LL.D Lam . Queen's Coll. Oxford. Ord. 1881 Lichfield. Cur. Christ's Ch. Lichfield 1880-3, Cur.-in-Charge Fenville Staffs 1883-6, Rect. Barton le Street Yorks 1886-94, Holdenby Northants 1894-1900. Author numerous works on churches. d. 1917.	1899 The Black Death
PAGE, Percy Hawkins	1899-1901 R	b. 1867. N'pton. Gramm. Sch. Sec. to manager N'hants. Union Bank 1883. Manager. Borough Treas. N'pton. Treas. N'pton Gen. Hosp. 1922, Trustee local institutions. Ret. 1927. d. 1963.	1899 Alfred the Great.
THOMSON, Basil Home	1899-1901 C	b. 1861. Eton. New Coll. Oxford. Bar, Inner Temple. Dep. Govnr. HM Prison Liverpool. Govnr. N'pton, Cardiff, Dartmoor, Wormwood Scrubs. Secy. Prison Commission 1908-13. Asst. Comm. Met. Police1913 (CID). CB 1916, KCB 1919. Ret. 1921. d. 1939.	1900 Decay of Native Races.
HICKSON William	1899-1913 C	b. 1845. Head Hickson & Son, Shoe Manf. Pres. Boot & Shoe Manf Assn. Alderman N'pton 1901. JP 1908. d. 1927.	1900 Socialism in business. 1903 The Cat. 1905 How we make paupers. 1909 Poor Law Report.
PHIPPS Albert Edward	1901-10 R	b. 1863. N'pton Gr. Sch. King's Coll. Sch. Lond. Direct. N'pton Gaslight Co. 1909-35. d. 1938.	
EWEN Alfred	1901-14 H	b. 1853. Chester Gr. Sch. Solicitor Luton, Off. Receiver in Bankruptcy N'pton, Bedford & Luton Courts. Freemason. Curacy Kenwynnr. Truro 1917. Ordained Truro 1918. Vicar Laneast N Cornwall 1921-8. d. 1928.. Author vol. On Shakespeare in Bell's Miniature Biography series.	1902 Practical Use of Shakespeare. 1903 An Elizabethan Playhouse. 1905 Pre-historic Continents. 1906 Robert Louis Stevenson. 1907 Arthurian Legends 1908 Charles Lamb. 1910 Prehistoric Races. 1911 Dickens. 1913 Literature. 1915 Comparative Religion. 1916 Death and After.
TURNER Charles Simkin	1901-20 R	b. 1859. Solicitor. d 1939	1902 L'Ancien Regime. 1904 Conscription. 1906 The French Revolution.

Name	Years	Biography	Papers
STUART Frederick Joshua	1901-35 H	b. 1866. MB, BCh 1895, MD 1903 Uni. Oxford, MRCS England 1896, LRCP London 1896. Junior MO. N'pton. Co. Lunatic Asylum, Berry Wood 1898, Sen. MO. 1902. Maj. 14-18 War, Berry Wood Hosp. d. 1948.	1908 Napoleon. 1910 St. Simon. 1913 Old London. 1914 A centenary: Wellington and his tools. 1916 Spies. 1918 The Man in the Iron Mask. 1902 Odds in Gambling. 1905 Virtues, so called. 1907 Lunacy. 1909 Mendelism. 1912 Instinct. 1914 Music; by an unappreciative ignoramus. 1920 Sir Oliver Lodge's Spiritualism. 1922 Criminal Responsibility. 1924 The Bolshevik Revolution. 1928 Belief. 1930 Vice, Insanity and Crime. 1932 Convention. 1934 The Causes of the War. 1939. Freudism. 1940 Shakespeare and Medicine. 1943 Character. 1945 In Defence of Lying. 1946 Calculating Easter.
DIXON Hugh Neville	1901-44 D	b. 1861. BA London 1880, MA 1882, BA Cambridge (Christ's) 1883, MA 1886. Principal N'pton. Sch. for deaf 1883-1910. Fell. Roy. Linnean Soc. 1885, d.1944.	1902 Alternating Personalities. 1904 A medical practitioner of the 18th & 19th centuries. 1906 Education of the Deaf. 1908 Thought Transference. 1910 Some points of contact between Bryology and Humanity. 1912 Portugal. 1915 How Trees Grow. 1916 The Arthurian Legend. 1918 Class Distributions: good or evil. 1919 Some Old Letters. 1922 The Influence of Mind on Landscape. 1924 The Poet Cowper and Northampton. 1926 How Flowers came to be. 1928 A Summer Holiday within the Arctic Circle. 1930. Sicily. 1932 Personality & Personalities. 1935 Plants as the Enemies of Man. 1937 Mosses & Man. 1940 Reminiscences of a Would-be Octogenarian. 1942 Which is I?
HICHENS Peverell Smythe	1902-20 R	b. 1870. MA, MB BCh 1895, MD 1903 Univ. Oxford. MRCS England 1896, LRCP London 1896, MRCP London 1899. FRCP 1911. Lt. Col. RAMC. Hon. Physician N'pton. Gen. Hosp., spec. TB 1924-30. Retired to Guernsey. d. 1930	1904 Death. 1905 Open-air Treatment for Tuberculosis. 1907 Men & Women. 1910 Pain.

Name	Years	Biography	Papers
HANKINSON Herbert	1903-46 D	b. 1860. Tettenhall Sch. & Cambridge (privately). Solicitor. Sen. Asst. Solicitor Co. Council W. Riding Yorks., Deputy Town Clerk Bradford. Town Clerk Northampton 1909-28. d. 1946.	1904 Physical Deterioration. 1907 Legends relating to the Holy Grail and Wagner's Opera "Parsifal". 1910 The Free Student: a modern philosophy of Life. *(Paper by a Mr Hughes)*. 1912 Syndicalism. 1915 Some XIXth century memoirs. 1920 Problems of Population & Progress. 1923 British Highways, ancient & modern. 1926 The Midlands in Poetry, Ballad and Prose. 1928 Some Characteristics of the Music of the Great Composers. 1931 The Historical, Literary and Artistic Associations of the Dove Valley and its Tributaries. 1934 George Borrow. 1939 Georgian & Early Victorian Diaries and Correspondence. 1942 Problems.
ABBOTT George Edward	1904-13 R	b. 1866. JP. d. 1932.	1908 Old Age Pensions. 1910 Edmund Spenser.
STURDEE Robert James	1904-7 L	b. 1879. Jesus Coll. Cambridge BA 1902, MA 1906. Ord. 1904 Peterborough. Cur. St James' Dallington, Northampton 1903-5, Hinkley, Leics. 1905 8, St Mary's Kettering 1908-10, Vicar St Peter's, Loughborough 1912-20, Thorpe Acre w. Dishley 1917-20. Rect. Ayleston Leics. 1920-32. Principal Canon & Lecturer St Martin's Leicester 1922-6. d. 1932.	1905 Ethical Equation in Society.
WAGSTAFF Frank Alexander	1907-18 R	b. 1866. MRCS England 1890, LRCP London 1890. Registrar Anaesthetics Gt. Ormond St. Hon. Anaesthetist N'pton. Gen. Hosp. d. 1956.	1909 Precocity. 1911 A pathological view of Lying and inebriety. 1913 Self-tillage. 1914 The Crowner's Quest. 1917 R.A.M.C.
MUSCOTT Bruce Beckwith	1907-33 D	b. 1867. Will. Silvester & Son (Boot & Shoe, Leather) Man. Dir. 1905-33. V. Chair. Of Council C of E Men's Socy. d. 1933. Father of G.	1908 The marriage of Philip of Spain with our Queen Mary. 1909 A trip to Brittany and Normandy. 1910 Is the national character deteriorating? 1912 Dissolution of the Monasteries. 1917 Questions to be faced after the War. 1923 The King's Business. 1926 Problems of Population. 1929 Downland Man. 1931 Jottings from Spain.
REYNOLDS Edward	1909-21 R	b. 1874. Oakham Sch. BA Queen's Camb., MA. Asst. Maths master Cathedral Sch. Ely 1897-8, Sen. Maths & 2nd master Royal Grammar Sch. Worcester 1899-1907. Headmaster Northampton & County Sch. 1907-21. HM Insp Schools 1921-2. Headmaster Watford Gram. Sch. 1922-38. d. 1944.	1912 Some problems on Education. 1914 Greece. 1917 Classical & Modern Education.

Name	Dates	Biography	Publications
DAVIES Basil Henry	1910-13 R	b. 1879. Lincoln Coll. Oxford. BA. Ord. 1904 Rochester. Cur. Newington 1903-6, Esh, Co. Durham 1906-7, St Sepulchre Northampton 1907-10, Vicar 1910. d. 1961.	1911 A fourth dimension.
SHOOSMITH William Buxton	1910-53 D	b. 1862. Admitted Solicitor 1898. Shoosmith & Harrison, N'pton. Clerk of Peace Co. Borough N'pton. Freemason. d. 1953.	1911 Death Ships. 1913 The Tyranny of Man. 1915 Queer Law Cases. 1918 German Psychology. 1921 Laying Cable. 1925 A Voyage to New Zealand. 1928 Further recollections of New Zealand. 1930 At Sea on the Maire Leah. 1933 Things we put up with. 1938 Postage & Stamp Collecting. 1947 Looking Backward.
STREATFEILD Leonard Champion	1913-31 C	b. 1871. Oxford BA 1899, MA 1902. Ord. 1901 Gloucester. Cur. St Lawrence Stroud 1900-3, N. Creake, Fakenham, Norfolk and Private Chaplain to Bishop of Thetford 1903-4. Rural Dean N. Brisley and Tofttrees 1907-9. Vicar Weasenham, Norfolk 1904-9, Commissary Bishop of Algoma from 1912. Vicar Dallington Northampton 1909. d. 1933 Eastbourne.	1913 The Yosemite Valley. 1916 Sense of humour in animals. 1922 The Settler in Canada. 1924 Bruges and Britain. 1927 Work. 1930 Mont St. Michael.
INCE-JONES Frederick	1913-46 H	b. 1884. BSc. Lond. Bar, Inner Temple. Headmaster Cliftonville, N'pton, Sch. for Deaf. Freemason. Dir. Abbey Nat. Building Soc. d. 1954.	1914 Convention*. 1916 The Law of Psychic Phenomena. 1918 The Superman*. 1920 Some Possibilities of Northampton*. 1922 Impressions of Central & Southern Europe*. 1924 Whom ought we to kill? 1926 Luxury and Life*. 1928 Provincialism*. 1930 Standards in Art and other matters*. 1933 Gronks*. 1936 A Dull Virtue*. 1938 Progress*. 1940 The Weaker Sex*. 1942 The Unpopularity of the Jews*. 1944 The Victorians*. 1948 Where are the Outstanding Personalities?* 1951 Awakened.
WALKER William Arthur	1914-18 R	b. 1865. Solicitor, Beck Green. District Commissioner for Boy Scouts, retired 1918. d. 1958	1916 Transfigurations. 1918 Pre-War news cuttings.
FULLERTON Moore Betty	1915-21 R	b. 1873. d. 1959.	1915 Environment as a factor in Evolution. 1917 Personality.
HALL W C	1918-21 R	Rev	1919 The Mind of the Crowd.
ALDRED Cyril Clowes	1918-23 R	b. 1882. Keble Coll. Oxford BA 1903, MA 1907. Ord. 1906 Peterborough. Cur. St James' Dallington Northampton 1905-12. Vicar Raunds, Northants 1912-18. Temp. Chapl. To Forces 1915-18. d. 1971.	1919 Competition.

Name	Dates	Notes	Publications
HADLEY William Waite	1919-24 H	b. 1867. Parl. Correspondent Daily Chronicle 1925. Ed. Sunday Times 1932-51. d. 1960.	1920 What is wrong with the Middle Classes? 1922 Northampton's Great days. 1923 How can we improve Town Government? 1924 parliament & Empire. 1932 Life in Northampton and life in London. 1938 A Rural Revolution Fifty Years ago. 1943 No' 10 Downing Street. 1950 Recollections of Ten Prime Ministers. 1951 The Crown and the Cabinet.
HEANLEY Marshall	1919-27 R	b. 1866. d. 1938.	1921 Gibraltar.
SHEPHERD Arthur Pearce	1920-23 H	b. 1886. Univ. Wales BA 1907. Jesus Coll. Oxford BA 1910, MA 1913. Ord. 1911 Peterborough. Cur. All Saints' Northampton 1910-15. Asst. Secy. Ch. Miss.Soc. for young peoples' work 1915-17. Vic. St. James' Npton 1917- . Archdeacon of Dudley. d. 1968.	1920 Poetry of the Georgian Period. 1922 Punishment. 1925 The Poets and animals. 1931 Causes of Social Unrest in India. 1937 Joseph Conrad. 1948 Time & the Soul.
COOKE William Charles Cyril	1921-38 R	b. 1881. K. Edward Sch. B'ham. Queen's Coll. Cambridge. BA 1903, MA 1907. Asst. Master King's Sch. Peterborough 1903-7, Caldey Grange Gram. Sch. 1908-9, Braeside W. Kirby 1909-10, Northampton Sch. 1910, Headmaster 1921-44. Chairman N'pton Co. Cricket Club. d. 1963	1923 Choice of a Career. 1925 Humorous Verse. 1927 What is an Educated Man? 1929 The Birds & the Poets. 1932 Tea and Tattle. 1934 Some Aspects of Education. 1937 Humour.
COLLIER Thomas L	1922-3 R		
MUSCOTT Guy Bruce	1923-?1965	b. 1891. d. 1965. Son of B B.	1924 English Monumental Brasses. 1927 History of Russian Literature. 1929 The Balearic Islands. 1932 A Good Tune. 1934 The Fens. 1937 Spain. 1939 More about Spain. 1942 The Staple Trade. 1945 Wine. 1946 The Continent Revisited. 1949 More Notes on Spain.
JONES Henry Travers	1923-26 R	b. 1881. MRCS England 1906, LRCP London 1906. MB BS Lond. 1907. Sen. Asst. Med. Off. N'hants Co. Mental Hosp. Berry Wood. Sen. Asst. MO Worcester Co. Asylum. DPM RCPS 1925 Univ. Coll. Lond. Med. Supt County Mental Hosp. Camb. 1930.	1924 The Descent of some words & Customs. 1925 Labels.
KEYSELL Folliott Sandford	1923-4 C	b. 1870. Clare Coll. Cambridge BA 1893, MA 1897. Ord. 1896 London. Cur. St Paul's Finchley 1895-7, Holy Trinity Marylebone 1897, St Martin's Birmingham 1897-1900, St Paul's Haggerston 1900-4, Harpenden 1904. Vicar Weedon, Northants 1904-16. Rural Dean Weedon 1913-16. Vicar St Sepulchre's Northampton 1916-28. Rural Dean Northampton 1922-6. Hon. Canon Peterborough 1924-37, Canon from 1937. Rector Benefield Northants 1928-32.	1925 Napoleon III. 1928 Anglo-Israelism.

Name	Dates	Biography	Publications
PAGE E Murray	1923-4 R	Vicar pottersbury with Furtho and Yardley Gobion 1932-6. Vicar East Haddon 1936-45. d. 1945 Rev	1923 Kidd's "Power of Science".
LUNT Geoffrey Charles Lester	1924-6 C	b. 1885. BA Exeter Coll Oxford 1908, MA 1912.Ord. 1910 Bristol. Cur Christ's Ch. Clifton 1909-10. CMS Secy. for work among young 1911-14. Vic. St Paul Bedminster 1914-19, Chaplain Brstol Gen Hosp 1914-19. TCF 1917-19, Mil. Cross 1917. Vic. All Saints' Northampton 1919-26. Commissioner Victoria 1920-6, Timevelly & Madura 1924-6. Archdeacon CE Egypt. Subdean All Saints Pro-Cathedral Cairo & officiating clergyman RAF 1926-8, Vic. St Matthews Portsmouth from 1928, Chaplain HM Prison Portsmouth from 1928. Bishop of Ripon 1935-46, Salisbury 46-8. d. 1948.	1925 Epigrams.
De PUTRON John Percy	1925-35 D	b. 1866. BA Univ. Coll. Durham 1890, MA 1894. Ord. 1892. St Albans. Cur. Elstree 1891-3, Sandringham w. W. Newton 1893-1902, Vic. Stow Baedolph w. Wimbotsham 1902-13, Rector St Peters Port Guernsey 1913-18, Vic Kingsthorpe Northampton from 1918. d. 1935	1926 England's Economic Downfall. 1929 The Channel Islands. 1931 The influence of Canals on History. 1934 The downfall of Modern Civilisation.
CHAMBERLAIN James Thomas	1925-41 R	b. 1892. Solicitor, Hensman. Jackson & Chamberlain, N'pton. D.	1930 Charles Lamb. 1932 The king can do no Wrong.
BROWNE Harold St John	1925-46 D	b. 1882. Solicitor. Ptnr. Browne & Wells, N'pton. Maj. 4th Bn. N'hants. Regt. 1914-18 war. Mil. Cross and Order of Nile. Maj. 12th Bn. N'hants. Home Guard 1939-45. d. 1946.	1927 Joint Stock Enterprise. 1929 The Irish Free State Revisited. 1931 Gambling and the Law. 1936 Blood Sports. 1939 England in A.D. 2000. 1941 Tontines. 1943 Is the Law an Ass?
DOLLAR Joseph Bartholomew	1926-29 C	b. ?1890. BA Trinity Coll. Dublin 1911, MA 1919. Ord. 1919. Dublin for Killaloe. Cur. Creagh 1911-12, Dioc. Cur. Killaloe & Inspector of Schools for Dioc of Killaloe 1912-15, Irish Guards 1915-19, Rect. Stanwick Northamptonshire 1919-24, Vic. St James Northampton 1924-9. Rect. Ewhurst Guildford from 1929. d. c.1961.	1927 The Philosophy of Golf
HAYES Edmund Duncan Tranchell	1927-40 D	BA Dublin 1910. MB, BCh Dublin 1915, MD 1921. DPM RCPS Eng. 1921. Sen. Asst. MO. N'pton. Co. Mental Hosp. Berry Wood 1921, Med. Supt. 1940. Physician(Mental Diseases) N'pton. Gen Hosp. Capt. RAMC 1915-19.	1928 Rejuvenation. 1931 Dictatorship versus Democracy. 1933 The Psychology of Clothes. 1935 Points of View. 1937 Witchcraft.
CARTWRIGHT James Lawrence	1928-32 C	b. 1889. King's Coll. Camb. BA 1917, MA 1921. Ord. 1920 Peterborough. Cur. St Peter's Loughborough & Thorpe Acre 1919-22, St John Baptist Knighton 1922-5, Vic. Christ's Ch. Northampton 1925-	1929 George Eliot. 1930 The Testament of Beauty.
DAVIES E Meredith	1929-29 C	MD. Resigned Dec. 1929 on moving to Devon.	
HICKS Gilbert	1930-35 C	N'pton. Borough Treasurer, Treasurer Npton. Gen. Hosp. Retired 1927	1932 Changes in the Law. 1934 County Courts.
LAVER Basil	1930-4 D	b. 1894. Hon. Asst. Surgeon N'pton Gen. Hosp 1927-31, Ho. Surg. 1931. d. 1934.	1930 Devils, Drugs and Doctors. 1933 Waves.

Name	Dates	Biography	Publications
SHAW Eric Hemingway	1931-67 C	b. 1886. MB BS 1910 Univ. Durham, MD. DPH Camb. 1914. Hon. Phys. & Pathologist Northampton Gen Hosp., Hon. Path. Kettering Hosp. Examiner Gen. Nursing Council, Specialist cerebro-spinal fever RAMC.	1932 Eugenic Sterilisation. 1934 Glands and Personality. 1936. Old Age. 1939 Is Man a Machine? 1941 Time the Tyrant. 1944 Possibilities.
FIELD Ernest E	1932-39 R	b. 1890. BSc Lond. Served WWI. RE then Intelligence Corps. OBE. 2nd Master N'pton. Grammar Sch. 1927-51. Ph D. FRGS. Cambridge (Chief) Examiner Geography. Freemason. d. 1961.	1933 Problems of Progress. 1935 Trackway & Turnpike. 1937 The Struggle for Population.
CARTER Thomas G F	1933-R	b. 1887. d. 1962.	
LEWIS John Trevor	1933-	b. 1885. BA Trinity Coll. Dublin 1906, MA 1910. Ord. 1909 Richmond for Ripon. Cur. Otley Yorks. 1908-11, St Peter's Bradford 1911-12, Sheffield 1912-13. Vic. St George's Sheffield 1913-22. Rural Sub-dean & Canon St Mary's Cathedral Truro 1922-6. Vic. All Saints' Northampton 1926- , R.Dean N'pton 1926- . d. 1955.	1935 The Inter-relationship of Body, Mind and Spirit. 1937 The Contribution of Monks to English Life. 1939 On Being Original. 1942 Stoics and Epicureans. 1944 Religion & Politics. 1947 Survivals. 1949 Sursum Corda. 1950 Black Sheep.
SHAPLAND Henry Percival	1935-?	b. 1878. ARIBA. Editor *The Cabinet Maker*. Cantor Lecturer 1926. Member of Council of THe Design and Industries Assn. Author The Practical Decoration of Furniture Vols. 1,2 and 3. Payson and Clark Ltd. 1926. d. 1968.	1936 Fleet Street. 1937 Architecture. 1940 Food & Drink. 1941 Colour. 1943 Summum Bonum. 1945 Conversation Piece. 1948 Revolt. 1949 Personality & Possessions. 1951 The Press 1900-1951. 1956 Conversational Opening.
MACKINTOSH John M	1935-7 C	b. 1881. Co. Med. Off. Health N'hants. 1930-7. Chief Medical Off. Dept. Health Edinburgh. Emer. Prof. Public Health Univ. London 1944. d. 1966	1935 Housing.
ELLISON Geoffrey Walker	1936-43 C	b. 1898. County Librarian Northants. d. 1978.	1936 Atmosphere in Fiction. 1938 Should I rather have lived in the 18th Century? 1940 Some Lessons from Ancient Greece. 1942 The Village Community.
BROWNE Laurence Edward	1936-46 C	BA Sussex Sidney Camb. 1909, MA 1913, BD 1920. Ord. 1912 Peterborough. Cur. St Matthew's Leicester 1911-13, Lecturer St Augustine Coll. Canterbury 1913-14, Fellow 1914-20. Lect. Bishop's Coll. Calcutta 1921-5, Examining Chaplain to Bishop Calcutta 1924-5, Furlough 1925-6, Special Missionary SPG 1926-9. Lect. Henry Martyn Sch. Lahore 1930. Vicar Gayton, N'shire. 1935-46.	1936 The Crusades as seen from the East. 1939. Accuracy. 1941 Changes in Religion. 1943 The Political Outlook of Islam. 1945 Curiosities of Etymology.
RAYNSFORD Richard Montague	1937-?	b. 1878. 2nd. Lt. Prince of Wales LeinsterRegt. (Roy. Canadians) 1897. Queen's Medal, King's Medal, S. African War. Commander 5th Connaught Rangers & 10th Devons 1914-18 in alonika & France. DSO. Lt. Col. 1925-6 Comm. 1st Bn. N'hants Regt. DL N'hants, High Sheriff 1945-6. JP. d. 1965.	1938 The Territorial Army. 1941 The Future of England. 1943 Leadership or Linoleum. 1948 Greece. 1950 A Visit to USA and Canada.
PERRY Thomas Hattam	1938-44	b. 1892. BA Keble Coll. Oxf. 1912, MA 1916. Cuddlesden Coll. 1913. Ord. 1915. Cur. Rugby 1914-	1938 The Problem of Leisure. 1940 The Church Chest.

	R	19, Richmond Surrey 1919-21. Vic. Keresley w. Coundon 1921-31, Dallington Northampton 1931-1945, Blakesley, Towcester 1945-. d. 1948	1944 Chance and Purpose.
PARKER Henry Nichols	1939-40 D	b. 1882. Staff Capt. Oxfordshire & Bucks. Light Infantry 1914-18 War. St Peter's Coll. Peterborough. St. Catherine's Coll. Camb. MA. HM Inspector Schools Northamptonshire. d. 1940.	1940 The England of Defoe.
JACKSON Antony H	1940		1941 Shakespearean Metaphysics. 1944 Touchstones. 1946 Falstaff. 1949 Mountaineering. 1951 The Colour Problem*. 1954 An Old Title. 1968 Catesby.
HUMFREY Stuart Harold Guise	1940-?	b. 1894. BA Camb 1918. MRCS Eng. LRCP Lon. 1921. DOMS 1926 (Camb. & St Thomas). Hon. Ophthalmic Surg. N'pton & Kettering Gen. Hosp. Fell. Roy. Soc. Medicine. d. 1975.	1942 The Human Camera. 1945 Gypsies. 1949 Reminiscences of a Mother.
TENNENT Thomas	1942	b. 1900. MB ChB Glasgow 1923, MD 1930. MRCP Lon. 1931, FRCP 1941. DPH, RCPS Eng. 1926. DPM Glasgow 1927. Med. Supt. St Andrew's Hosp. N'pton 1938-62., Phyician in Psych. Med. Miller Hosp. Greenwich & Gen. Hosp. N'pton. Fell. Roy. Soc. Med., Posts in Psych. Med. at Maudsley, Lon., King's Hosp., Johns Hopkins Hosp. Baltimore. d. 1962.	1943 Compensation. 1946 Idle Hands.
LEE Ralph Owen	1944	b. 1906. MRCS Eng. LRCP Lon. 1930. MA MB Camb. 1933. FRCS Eng. 1931. Hon. Surg. N'pton Gen. Hosp. 1935-71. d. 1993.	1946 The Citadel. 1949 Medicine Men. 1952 Anything but Medicine. 1966 Russian Commentary. 1970 Sex Education. 1980 Jordan Revisited*. 1986 Flowers that bloomed in the Spring
TURNER John Alan	1945-66 D	b. 1903. Clerk N'hants Co. Council 1938. Clerk Ld. Lieut. & Clerk of Peace N'hants. Air Raid Precautions Controller 1939-45 War. OBE 1943.	1945 Local Government. 1948 Crime and Sentence. 1950 Martyrs. 1956 Holidays – Active or Idle?.
LOWICK Geoffrey Heygate	1947	MA, LLB. Notary Public. Solicitor Browne & Wells	1947 Tendencies in the Law. 1948 Slavery. 1950 Quacks. 1953 Rights and Rites. 1954 Other Novelists. 1955 Royal Marriage. 1969 Sherlock Holmes. 1980 Capital Punishment*.
DOCKRELL T Hayes	1948	MB. FRCS Ireland. Dir. Orthopaedic Surg. N'pton. Gen. Hosp. 1946. Mayor N'pton 1967-8 d. 1970.	1952 Nigerian Notes. 1967 Useful Journey.
EDEN Michael Francis	1948	b. 1914. Eton. BA Balliol Coll. Oxford. Capt. Life Guards 1939-45 War. Succeeded as 7th Baron Henley of Chardstock, Co. Dorset and 5th Baron Northington of Watford, Co. Northampton 1962. President Liberal Party 1966-7. Chairman CPRE 1973. d. 1977.	1950 Beards. 1952 Agriculture and Land Tenure To-day.
MORGAN Grenville	1948	b. 1915. BA Leeds 1940, Coll. Of Resurrection Mirfield 1940. Ord. 1943 Southwark. Cur. St Mary Magd. Newark 1942-5, Priest Vicar Southwark Minster 1945-6, Dioc. Director Youth Southwark 1946-7, Vic. Dallington Northampton 1947-60, Market Drayton	1949 Names. 1951 A Strange Rectory.

Name	Year	Details	Publications
		1960-72. Rect. Adderley 1960-72. R. Dean Hadnet 1960-72, Surrogate 196—72, Vic. Finchingfield w. Cornish Hall 1972-80.	
NETTLETON Martin Barnes	1949	b. 1911. BA, MA Oxf. FRGS. Master Rensall, Lancs. 1935-8, Repton 1938-40. Flt. Lt. (Intelligence) 1941-4.Headmaster N'pton Grammar School 1945-64. d. 1964 drugs overdose.	1949 An Arctic Mystery. 1952 "Education Act".
SKINNER A F	1949	OBE. BA. LLB. Depy. Clerk N'hants. Co.Council 1952	1950 Western Union. 1952 Nursery Rhymes.
GARNHAM Cecil John	1949-64 H	b. 1896. Manager N'pton. Barclay's Bank. Ret. 1954. D. 1965.	1951 Retribution. 1953 Can It Work? 1955 Fashionable Delusions.
HENLEY	1950 ?		1951 Planning.
LINEY, A A	1950 ?	Rev.	1953 Superstitions.
HILL Stanley	1952 pre	b. 1915.Dept. Supt. B'ham Infirmary 1937-40. Refugee Work 1940-45. Supt. N'pton. Gen. Hosp. 1945-80. JP 1961-85. d. 1997.	1952 Out of Bondage. 1962 Committeemanship. 1967 Criticism. 1980 Fragments of Calabria*. 1983 N. S. E and Centre*. 1985 The Strike*. 1987 Chance*. 1989 I.O.M.*. 1990 Irritations*. 1993 Humour*. 1995 In Memory of Heygate Sen*. ?1996 The Workhouse*.
HEYGATE Arthur Robert	1955 pre	b. 1914. Oakham Sch. JP. DL. Northamptonshire Rural Dist. Council. Chairman 18 yrs. to 1961. MBE 1957. d. 1994.	1956 Our Daily Bread. 1958 Country Life and Agriculture*. 1964 An Assortment of British Grain and Cereal Processing. 1966 Capital Gains. 1981 The Common Agricultural Policy and The Green Pound*. 1988 Merger and Management*. 1989 History and the Countryside*. ?
MONIE Peter Ralph	1956 ?	MA Vicar St James' N'pton 1956.	
HORSFALL-CARTER	1964	Chief Clerk N'hants. Co. Council.	
COLES Richard Bertram	1964 ?	MRCS Eng. LRCP Lon. 1943, MB Bs King's Coll. Lon. 1946. MRCP Lon. 1948, FRCP 1970. Ass. Lon. Coll. Music 1964. Cons. Dermatologist N'pton. Gen. Hosp. Fell. Roy. Soc. Med.	1967 Origins of Organised Sound. 1969 Aggression*.
DALGLEISH Peter Gordon	1964 ?	b. 1919. MRCS Eng. LRCP Lon. 1941, MRCP 1948. MB BS Lon. 1941, MD 1948. Clin. Asst. Dermatology N'pton. Gen. Hosp. Med. Offr. Brit. Timken Ltd. N'pton. Lect. Med. Univ. Bristol.	1964 Aspects of our future. 1967 Drugs & addiction. 1979 The Royal Naval Air Service. 1982 Hood Might or Myth 1986 Denis Burkitt. 1988 Scharnhorst and Gneisenhau. ? Happiness*. ? Health and Industry*.
HARRIS	1964?		1965 Caste & Class.
JONES Owen Meurig	1964?-?	N'ton. Co.Counc. Solicitor Browne & Wells.	1968 Beeching on Crime.
ALMENT Edward	1964?-	b. 1922. Marlborough Coll. MRCS Eng. LRCP Lon.	1968 Privacy.

Name	Dates	Biography	Publications
Anthony John	?	1945. MRCOG Lon. 1951, FRCOG Lon. 1967 (St. Bart's). FRCP Edin. Cons. Obst. & Gyn. Northampton Gen Hosp 1960-85. Fell. Roy. Soc. Med. Hon. Sec. RCOG 1969-78, Pres. 1978-81. Knighted 1980. d. 2002.	1979 Bottles*. 1982 The Womens Movement. ? The Unwanted Pregnancy*.
TASKER John Rendel (Tony)	1964?-2006	b. 1915. Marlborough Coll. and Clare Coll. Cambridge. Sqdn. Ldr. RAF (medical). MB BChir. Camb. 1940, MD 1951. MRCP 1940, FRCP 1963. Cons. Physician N'pton Gen. Hosp. Retired 1980. d. 2008	196? Two Forgeries*. 196? Florence Nightingale*. 196? Pestilence*. 196? Leviathan*. 196? The Future*. 196? The Beagle's Influence on Thought*. 1968 Science Pollution and Survival. 1980 Volcanoes and Geography*. 1983 The Zoo.* 1985 Cook's Tour*. 1987 Darwin Revisited. 1990 An Antique Land*. 1992 History and the Countryside*. 1995 Fossils. 1997 The Roots of Medicine*. 1999 Migrating Birds*. 2001 The Story of Seahenge*. 2004 This Restless Planet*.
JACKSON -STOPS, Anthony	1964?-85 R	b. 1912. Solicitor. Engineer in WWII serving in India and Cocos and Keeling Islands. Worked in Jackson Stops & Staff Estate Agents until 1975. d. 1985.	1969 Manners. ? The Cocos Keeling Islands.
FINCHAM Thomas George	1967?-2006 R	b. 1916. Educ. State Sch. Cpl. Milit. Police , Lt. Northamptonshire Regt. 1939-45. Qual. Solicitor & Notary Public. Ret. 1986.	1981 First Rights*. 1984 Denning M.R.*. 1986 Degrees of Deceit. 1989 Botany Bay*. 1992 OZ*. 1994 The Paston Letters*. 2003 Traitors of World War II.
RIGGALL John Robert	1970?-89 D	b. 1920. Farm Director, Heygate Grp. Companies. Board member Moulton College, N'pton. MBE. d. 1989.	1971 Wild Life and Modern Farming. 1980 Lost Villages*. 1985 The Ways of Water. 1987 Wild Life at Home.
HEYGATE Arthur Robert	1975	b. 1945. Oundle Sch. St. Edmund's Hall, Oxford 1964-7. MA. DL. High Sheriff N'tonshire 1997/8.	1977 John Maynard Keynes*. ? 1979 International Debt*. 1980 Boom or Gloom*. 1982 Chips*. 1986 Economic Waves*. 1989 Work*. 1992 Green*. 1994 Democracy and Capitalism*. 1996 The Right Market*. 1998 1-01-99 (In with the Euro and Out with the Pound)*. 2002 Doom*. 2004 Bubbles*. 2006 A Small World*. 2007 Change*. 2009 Crunch*.
JENNINGS Alan Maurice Charles	1979?-86	b. 1931. B.Chir Camb. 1956, MB 1957. DARCS Eng. 1958, FFARCS 1961. Cons. Anaesth. N'pton. Gen.	1979 An Anniversary to Remember*. 1982 Ordnance Survey Maps.

Name	Dates	Biography	Works
ATKINSON Douglas Mason (Peter)	D 1979-87 R	Hosp. d. 1986. b. 1918. Maj. RA 1939-45. Educ. Corps. Manager Lloyd's Bank N'pton. d. 1995.	1985 Animal rights. 1981 Mons Calpe*. 1986 Camellia Sinensis*. 1984? England Confides*.
FEATHERSTONE Cecil	1979-93 D	b. 1922. Architect in N'pton. from 1963. d. 1993.	1982 Upstairs Downstairs*. 1984 Sitting Pretty*. 1985 Customs*. 1988 Boats*. 1990 Nil Desperandum*.
GOMPERTZ Peter Alan Martin	1980-2002	b. 1940. Assoc. Lond. Coll. Divinity 1963. D 64 Ord. 1965. Cur. Eccleston St Luke's Liverpool 1964-9. Scripture Union 1969-73. Cur. Yeovil, Bath & Wells 1973-5. Vic. St Giles' Northampton 1975-96. MMin and Theol, Sheffield 96, Canon Peterborough Cath. From 1988. Rect. Aynho & Croughton w. Evenley 1996-2006, P in c Great c. Little Addington and Woodford 2006-10, Hon P Kettering St Andrew from 2010, Perm to Officiate from 2010. Chaplain to retired clergy, widows and widowers from 2012.	1981 A Damned Un-English Weapon*. 1986 Apostles of Mobility*. 1988 A Wizard with Words*. 1990 Too little; too soon; thank heaven*. 1992 Rooms with a View*. 1995 She being dead yet speaketh*. 19?? Thinking the Unthinkable*. 19?? It's turtles all the way*.
GRAHAM Andrew Noble	1980 ?	b. 1910. Cons. Psychiatrist St. Crispin's Mental Hosp. 1953-72. Consult. Psych. St. Andrew's Hosp N'pton 1972-9. Founder Fellow Royal Coll. Psychiatrists. d. 1989.	1981 Broadmoor – Without Limit of Time*.
EAMES, Peter	1982	b. ?1941. MB BChr 1965, MA Camb. 1969, DPM 1970, MRCPsych 1972. Cons. Psychiatrist St Andrew's Hosp. Northampton.	
HADDEN, Lionel Truss (Pip)	1984-92 R	b. 1923. BA Bristol Univ. RAF 1939-45. Pilot BOAC, later Capt. Brit. Airways. Ret. 1977.	1985 1997 and After. 1987 What Price Speed. 1988 Communication. 1991 Arteries of an Empire.
ELLISON Clifford James	1985-2001 C	b. 1920. Durham Sch. Chelsea Arts Sch. 1938-40. Roy. Corps Signals 1940-5 (Middle East). Teaching Dipl. (Art) Chelsea 1947. Picture Restorer. 1970 Restorer to H.M. The Queen. Retired Devizes 2001.	1987 The Decline of the English Country House*. 1989 Play*. 1989 Nor all, that glisters, gold*. 1996 A Near Run Thing*. 2001 Then and Now*.
ROBERTSON Denis Wilson	1986-2002 R	b. 1925. St. Mary's Lond. MRCS LRCP 1950, MRCGP 1967. Certif. Aviation Medicine MOD (Air), Med. Examiner Civil Aviation Authority. Gen. Pract. N'pton., ret. 1990. Med. Officer air crews incl. Concorde. Qualified pilot. JP 1967-95. d. 2005.	1987 Engineless Flight*. 1990 Lighter than Air*. 1991 Alternatives*. 1995 Without Sensation*. 1999 Lese Majesty*. 2001 1361*. ? A Victorian Genius*..
RICKETT Anthony	1987-	b. 1938. Cardinal Vaughan Sch. Lond. 1949-57. Univ. Coll. Lond. 1958-9. RIBA 1968. Farming & Architect. Pract. Everdon, N'hants. 1972- .Daventry Dist. Counc. 1879-97, Chairman 1982. S. Devon Herd Book Socy. Chairman 1998-2002.	1989 Rates of Change*. 1991 Whisky*. 1993 BLUP*. 1995 Equity and Law*. 2003 Officious Secrets*. 2005 Negativity*. 2006 This is all Rubbish*. 2009 Trotters and Troughs*. 2011 Tunes of Glory*

Name	Years	Biography	Works
SAINT Jerome P	1987-2007 R	b. 1936.	1988 Words. 1991 Stations. 1992 Invasion*. 1994 Targetting*. 1998? IV.C*. 2002 E,H,C,R. (European Convention of Human Rights)*. 2004 We don't care*. 2007 Words. ? The Eye of the Morning*.
SOUTAR Neil	1989-?	b. 1918. Uppingham Sch. Maj. N'pton Regt. & Gen. Staff 1939-46. Ment. In Despatches. Capt. N'pton Hockey 1946-56. JP 1966-88. Man. Dir. Odell Leather Co. Beds. from 1975. d. 1998.	1991 Justice. 1994 The Last Frontier*. 1996 In a Persian Market*.
JACKSON-STOPS Timothy William Ashworth	1989-2003 R	Bilton Grange School 1950-5, Eton 1955-60, Roy. Agricultural Coll. 1960-3. FRICS. Jackson-Stops & Staff 1966-93.	1991 Preservation of Country Houses. 1994 Liverish* 2003 The Paint Box*. 2004 The Lords of The Ring. 2005 Navigation and longitude.
COOCH Peter	1990-96 R	b. 1943. Uppingham Sch. Clare Coll. Camb. BA 1964. Solicitor Phipps & Troup (later Becke Phipps) N'pton 1969	1992 A Noble Experiment*. 1994 In Search of an Identity*. 1996 Heirs of Sorrow*.
CORNELIUS Michael	1991-2011 R	b. 1936. King's Coll. Taunton 1950-4. Articled London 1954-9. Admitted Solic. 1960. Practiced London 1960-5, N'pton. 1965-2008. d. 2012.	1993 What am I?*. 1995 Unavoidable Deception*. 1997 It's a Secret. 2006 Coffee for Two, Champagne for One*. 2008 A Lazy Eight*. 2009 Celtic Sense*?
UNDERWOOD Trevor	1992-2005 R	b. 1932. N'pton. Gram. Sch. 1944-49. Founder Ptnr. Estate Agent/ Comml. Prop. Consultants 1960-97. FSVA/FRICS. Pres. Northants. Surveyors' Club. Chairman Mid-Anglia Reg. Socy. Valuers and Auctioneers. Depy. Chairman Derngate Housing Assn.	1993 Any Volunteers?*. 1995 Chaos and Cavaliers*. 1998 Watch this Space*. 1999 A Giant On Its Back*. 2003 A Novel Experience*. 2005 The Long and the Short of it*.
SITWELL Francis Trajan Sacheverell	1993-2004 D	b. 1935. Eton. Nat. Serv. As Naval Offr. With Shell (Africa) 1956-66. Own PR Company. d. 2004.	1993 A Portrait of Edith Sitwell. 1996 A Notable Disappearance*. 2002 Our National Hero and the Georgian Navy*.
HARDINGHAM Peter Alan	1995-	b. 1946. Fell. Inst. Legal Execs 1976, Coll. Law Guildford 1978/9, Admitted Solicitor 1980, Notary Public 1995. Partner Law firms at Norwich, Northampton 1983-2000. Consultant Solic. Woolley & Co. and J H Law Ltd. 2000-2006. Hon. Solic. N'shire Record Socy. 1995-2006. Hon Solic. N'shire CPRE 1998-2006.	1997 Bread and Cheese for the Medical Men*. 2002 A Tale of the Old West*. 2005 Jeremiah XXXII 9-10*. 2007 A Mystery Wrapped in an Enigma*. 2007 The toy that grows with the boy*. 2008 Club History and some early Minutes*. 2009 What the Vicar Saw*. 2011 As Monty Did. (Reading) 2012 After "What the Vicar Saw" (January 2009), What the Rector Did, or The News of the World Would Have Loved Him.*
GODFREY Simon Henry Martin	1996-	b. 1955. Homeland Sch. Torquay. Britannia Roy. Naval Coll. Commissioned Roy. Army Chaplains' Dept. 1988, Major 2000. TD. Chaplain Order of St. John 1996. King's Coll. London BD 1980, AKC 1980,	2002 Evil to him who evil thinks*. 2003 An Apostolic Blessing*. 2007 The Jaw of Gerard – or Gerard's jaw*.

	St. Stephen's Ho. Oxford 1980. Ord. 1982. Cur. Kettering SS. Peter & Paul 1981-4, Rect. Crick and Yelvertoft w. Clay Coton & Lilbourne 1984-9, Vic. All Saints' & St Katherine Northampton 1989-98, Rect. N'pton. All Saints' w. St Katherine & St Peter N'pton 1998-2009. Chancellor & Canon St Paul's Co-Cathedral Valletta, Malta 2009-. Investiture as A Cross of Merit Pro Piis Meritis of the Sovereign and Military order of Malta, 2nd Feb. 2013.	2011 A City Built By Gentlemen for Gentlemen*.
TOSELAND Michael Anthony	2000-	b. 1931. Northampton Grammar School 1939-49. MB, ChB Birmingham 1954, MRCS England 1954, LRCP London 1954. Lt. later Capt. RAMC 1956-8. Gen. Pract. Northampton 1958-2000. Med. Advisor KAB Seating (CVG) Northampton 1963-.	2001 No Orchids*. 2003 1886 And All That, by Jingo*. 2005 The Little White Wonder*. 2008 A Simple Mechanism*. 2008 Bubble Bubble*. 2011 The Full Monty?*.
VAUGHAN Christopher James	2001-	b. 1948. Spratton Hall Sch. 1956-61, Oakham Sch. 1961-66, Guildford Coll. Of Law 1970-72. Solicitor Browne and Wells, N'pton 1973. Notary Public 1978. Pres. Notaries Socy. 2001-3. Member: Scriveners Livery Co., Farmers' Club.	2001 The Dome*. 2004 1658 and Still in Print*. 2005 Pass the Matches, Matilda*. 2007 ©*. 2009 A.5*. 2010 The Last Freedom*. 2013 TBA*
GALE John	2001-4 R	b. 1932. Epsom Gr. Sch. 1940-45. Kingston Tech. Sch. 1946-48. Brit. Rail – Civil Engin. Dept. 1948-50. RAF Music Services 1950-56 (Bandmaster RAF Hereford 1953-6). Mngr. Boosey & Hawkes 1956-61. Music Consultant Mather & Crowther 1961-65. Music Publisher 1965-. BA (Hons) LRAM.	2002 007 (Life of Lorenzo Da Ponte)*. 2004 Strike up the Band*.
REED Michael	2002-	b. 1948. St John School Nairobi, Kenya. Hurstpierpoint College 1960-6. Fell. Inst. Of Chart. Accountants 1974. Worked for KPMG London, Bahamas and US. Private Accountant N. Bucks. 1981, Merged Mercer & Hole 1998, based Northampton and Milton Keynes.	2004 Five letters and it's a puzzle … perhaps an enigma?* 2006 A Good Shepherd Should Shear His Flock Not Skin It*. 2009 Kathmandu – Derring Do*. 2011 Plus ca change*. Valletta to Mogadishu via Baltimore in 400 years.
NOCK Peter John	2004-	b. 1946. King's Norton Prim. Sch. 1951-62. Greenmore Sch. 1962-68. Worked with Michael Jones, Jeweller, N'pton 1969-75, Potton London Ltd. 1975-7, MBC Ltd. 1977-91, Halford Jeweller 1991-. NAG Valuer 1969, GIV Valuer 1991-.	2005 Does Charity begin at Home?* 2006 Diamonds are Forever*. 2008 Valuation, a Question of Opinion?*
SHAEFFER Gary William	2005-	b. 1943 Minneapolis USA. Carleton Coll. BA (Eng. Lit.) 1965. Wesleyan Univ. MA (Eng. Lit) 1967. Teacher Bedford NY. Copywriter & Editor for Sports Illustrated and Newsweek Magazines, New York City.To Gt. Brington, Northants 1988. Freelance Copywriter N'hants Tourism & Conference Bureau, Rockingham Forest Trust and Outward Bound. Director Popperfoto, Commercial Photographic Library 1992- .	2006 Beautiful Tragedies*. 2008 The UH*. 2010 From the 18th to the 21st … How Do You Look When I'm Sober?* 2012 Third Time Lucky – Again?*.

GEORGE David Rodney	2007-	b. 1935. MSc Dunelm 1971, PhD Leicester 1985. Dean Faculty Science Nene Coll. 1975-88, Assoc. Direct. Nene Coll. (now Univ. of N'pton) 1988-90, Fell. Univ. Salford 1987, Founder Pres. Nat. Assn. for Able Children in Education and was member Exec. Cttee of World Council of Gifted and Talented Children. Consultant to Brit. Council and UNESCO. Hon. Commdr. RAF Croughton (USAF) 2009, Paul Harris Fellow 2011. Qualified Lay Preacher. Chair of Managers St Andrew's Health Care Northampton 2006-11. Author *The Challenge of the Able Child, Gifted Education: Identification and Provision, Young, Gifted and Bored*.	2008 Gifted is as Gifted Does*. 2010 A Merry Heart is Like a Medicine*. 2010 Isopods*.
TALBOT Peter Lindsay	2008-	b. 1954. Lawrence Sheriff G.S. Rugby 1965-71, Roy. Agric. Coll, Cirencester 1972-75 (MRAC Dipl. Rural Est. Mgt, Fellow Royal Institute Chartered Surveyors (FRICS) 1995, Fell. Cent. Assn. Agric. Valuers 1981. Dir. Virgin Group PLC, Subsid. 1988-9, Ptnr. Howkins & Harrison LLP 2004-8. Consultant Tayler & Fletcher 2009-.	2010 Lost Souls*. 2012 Ways and Means*.
TASKER Matthew Howard	2009-	b. 1952. Marlborough Coll. Articled Clerk\a 1971-6 Browne and Wells, Northampton. Qualified solicitor 1978, practiced Kettering and Banbury. 1998 Legal Management Consultancy.	2010 Beam Me Up Scotty*. 2012 Metropolitan Emmental*.
LOWERY Thomas Ian	2009–	b. 1946. N'pton Grammar Sch. 1957-62. Coll. Estate Management London 1963-7. Associate Roy. Inst. Chartered Surveyors 1967, Fellow 1981. Articled Gambell & Skinner 1962-70. R L Lowery & Ptns. N'pton. Etc. 1970-2003. Consultant to Chown Commercial.	2011 The Birthplace of Civilisation?*
BULL, Derek James	2010-	b. 1943. Apprentice Eng. 1959-63. Sales RTZ 1966-75. Beam Tubes Dir. & GM 1976-99. Chairman European standard for Aluminium 1983-90.. Memb. Northants Health Authy. 1980-90. Trustee Relate 2000-, Trustee Dyslectic Socy. 2009-11. Owner Hexpak Ltd. 2001-, Memb. Rnd. Table 1972-84, Rotary 1984-.	2012 Time*.
ORTON-JONES Michael	2012-	Coventry Preparatory School 1947-53, Cheltenham College 1953-7, Various Universities and College of Law Lancaster Gate. Joined Shoosmiths & Harrison solicitors (now Shoosmiths) 1960. Retired as a partner and Chairman 2000. Notary Public 1984-. Member Northamptonshire County Council and Northampton Borough Council in 1970s. Deputy chairman of the Education Committee and chairman of Traffic and Car Parks. Governor and manager educational bodies including University of Northampton (formerly Nene College). Chairman Compton House Limited (financial services now part of JLT Jardine Lloyd Thompson), Chairman of ASIM (Association of Solicitors & Investment Managers). Member of the Council of the Law Society representing Financial Services & Investment Business. Chairman Daventry Constituency Conservative Association. Secretary Aquitaine Society. Chairman Northamptonshire Area Conservatives. Chairman Trustees of Northampton.	

Ordinary Members

1887 Edwd. Montague Browne,
    21 The Drive
1888 Christopher Alexander (Major)
    Markham F.S.A.
    The Gables
    Dallington
1889 Revd. Edwd. Nicolls Tom M.A.   Hon. Member
    32 St Michaels Av.   June 1910
1891 Revd. John Cunningham M.A.   Hon. Member
    68 Billing Road   Sep 1917
  " Revd. Wm Blomefield
    Sleight M.A. Towcester Vicarage   Hon
    St Katharines Vicarage   Member
                                      Sep 1917
1895 James Jackson. J.P.
    19 The Drive
1899 Wm Hickson J.P.   Resigned June 1913
    Highlands, Holly Road Ashigh Avenue
1901 Hugh Neville Dixon MA F.L.S.
    17 St Matthews Parade
  " Alfred Brown, 23 The Embankment Resigned
    2 St Pauls Terrace Bedford   Oct 1914
  " Albert Edwd. Phipps.   Resigned April
    Dallington   1910

Part of members' list 1910 by Tyrannus E M Browne
With later additions

120

8
Clergy

Club founders Sanders and Hooper recruited members from among their friends, resulting in five of the original ten members being clergy. Altogether 51 ordained priests are recorded as having been Chatterers and about half of these appear in the first 20 years. During this time most only remained for a year or two, contributing few, if any, papers. Three who read only one paper each resigned in 1887, Hammond moving to Cornwall, Hutton to Lancashire and Hooper to Suffolk. These moves, often unsought, provided vacancies in Club membership and a constant source of new blood, however inconvenient it may have been to the secretary who had the task of producing a yearly calendar. Several livings contributed more than one Chatterer although this is probably coincidental rather than by design of the retiring cleric. It is however a convenient way of grouping clergy rather than by a strictly chronological list.

Northamptonshire born Thomas Calvert Beasley was educated at Rugby school and after gaining a BA at Cambridge Trinity in 1859 entered the priesthood the following year. Having spent time in Saffron Walden and Wellingborough as curate he came back in 1874 as vicar of Dallington, a sleepy picture postcard village one and a half miles northwest of Northampton, where a clear stream between church and vicarage flowed down towards the river Nene. Dallington was later absorbed into the expanding town in 1901 but retained many of its original features. Beasley became a member of the Club on May 15th 1890 having attended a Summer Meeting as a guest the year before. He contributed eight papers, the first four being mentioned by title only in Jones' minutes, *Protection from Lightning* (1892), *Village Life* (1894), *The Sense of Touch* (1897) and *Conversation* (1898). More details emerged from Browne's first minute as Tyrannus after Jones' death in 1901 when *Beasley discoursed profitably on "External appearance as an indication of character.... and many remarks of a personal character were Made, the practical result being that the ownership of grey hair and blue eyes was held to be incompatible with the pursuit of a criminal career.*

Moral Characteristics of the Sexes (1903) was *marked by an evident desire to hold the scales fairly.* In his talk on *Character from Hand Writing* (1905) *Beasley proceeded with great temerity to criticise the writing of each member of the Club, as exhibited on the backs of certain postcards....They magnanimously forgave Beasley for the liberties he had taken with their characters.*

Beasley's paper on New Year's Eve 1907 considered *The Martians*, including *the remarkable increase of our knowledge of the planet Mars in the last 20 years.....*and he*…. considered the question of animal life in Mars, the physical conditions which might be expected to influence it, and the possible relations between any intelligent beings, and the system of so-called canals and oases.* This was a decade when early science fiction, particularly that of H G Wells and Jules Verne fired the imagination.

A well-known and respected local character, Beasley was summed up by Ernest Gaskell: *With his invincible faith in human nature he believes in helping men to help themselves, in fostering the spirit of self reliance, and the children have been especially the objects of his care.*[1]

Beasley last attended the Chit Chat Club in September 1908 and in November *Beasley's state of health was referred to, and Tyrannus was asked to write him a letter of sympathy from the Club.* The following February *Reference was made to the recent departure of the Revd. T. C. Beasley, for more than 18 years a valued member of the Club. Tyrannus was directed to convey to Mrs. Beasley the assurance of the members' sympathy and sorrow.* Perhaps meant tactfully but expressed unfortunately this is immediately followed by *The question of nominating a new member was considered, and deferred for the present.*

During Beasley's incumbency at Dallington Robert Sturdee, curate from 1903-5 was brought into the Club and contributed one paper, *Ethical Equation in Society* (1905) before moving to Hinckley, Leicestershire, later that year.

Leonard Champion Streatfeild, an Oxford graduate became the next vicar of Dallington and joined the Chatterers in 1913, presenting six papers over the following seventeen years. *The Yosemite Valley* (1913), a matter of fact tourist report, was followed in 1916 by *Sense of Humour in Animals* where he *did not include.....any biped animals, men or birds, but confined himself to beasts which ...... especially lent themselves to caricature. He alluded to the comical situations occupied by animals in nursery rhymes and fairy tales &c. – Aesop, Alice in Wonderland, - Brer Rabbit &c.*

Reference was also made to dogs (domestic and circus performers) which evidently enjoyed life, and (as the reader thought) exhibited a sense of humour.

Cats, lambs (not sheep) goats, pigs, cattle, horses, asses, mules sealions bears, and porcupines came in for a share of notice – and two porcupine were represented as having been on one occasion very humorous individuals .... it was clearly recognised that if (as many supposed) the quadrupeds were destitute of humour, their champion and delineator was not in like case.

In 1922 *Streatfeild gave a talk on the "Settler" in Canada, a land in which he had spent 12 of the earlier years of his life. He gave much information as to acquiring land, by free grant or purchase, development of the same, farming processes, felling timber, "Bees" for labour of all kinds, fishing, shooting. &c.*
The Club & visitors had a very good time   (24 min.)
Streatfeild's paper on the Yosemite Valley lasted 26 minutes and also contained a mine of information. It must have been difficult to include so many facts in such short times without merely producing a boring list, perhaps Browne in considering the Canada paper was being ironic with *a very good time*. Streatfeild's 1924 tract on *Bruges and Britain* in 1924 was recorded as being *interesting and informative* but his penultimate reading, *Work* in 1927 throws a different light on the reader's character….. *He asked whether one was an ass to work, and wound up the paper by quotations from the sermon of a 13th century Friar Nicholson, on the relative merits of the ass and the pig. It appeared that members of the C. C. C. who worked partook of the qualities of the ~~pig~~ ass, while those who did not partook of those of the pig; and the Club was left on the horns of a somewhat painful dilemma.* Members thought they all knew something about work but could not decide *upon a definition of what work actually was.*
Streatfeild was quite a traveller and for his last paper in 1930 extolled the virtues of Mont St Michel. Foregoing former tendencies to produce a travelogue…..*Skilfully he blended legend with fact and in a masterly way described the motives and genius that led to the building of the 'Merveille'. It was interesting to note that his taste was Catholic enough to appreciate not only the Gothic beauty of the architecture but also the gastronomic beauty of the omelettes of Mme. Poulard de Putron, whose exceptional knowledge of Mont St*

Michel & the neighbourhood, [De Putron was present at this meeting] *enabled him to speak with unusual authority...... Later ..... thoughts of members turned to the advantages & disadvantages of Monasticism. Some, wearied perchance of the world, the flesh & the devil, cast wistful eyes towards the cloistered life; but Stuart* [one of the Mad Doctors] *who doubtless knows more about it than most, intimated sotto voce that so far as he was concerned their confinement would not be voluntary.*

Streatfeild died in 1933 at the early age of 62 in Eastbourne.

Cyril Aldred, a former Dallington curate from 1905-12, became a member in 1918, whilst vicar at Abington, Northampton. He gave one paper, *Competition,* in 1919 and hosted in 1921. A desultory attender he apparently left the Club in 1922.

The next Dallington vicar to join was Thomas Perry, like Streatfeild an Oxford man. Although having been in Northampton since 1931 Perry was not elected until 1938 which indicates, like Streatfeild before him, the line of Dallington clergy owed more to chance than direct succession. Perry gave his first paper *The Problem of Leisure* on September 30th 1938. It is difficult nearly 75 years later to imagine the thoughts of his audience that night. The annexation of Austria by Germany, the *Anschluss*, in March had been followed by increasing tension during the summer with the prospect of a second war 'to end all wars' looming on the horizon. On September 30th Adolf Hitler, Benito Mussolini, Neville Chamberlain and Edouard Deladier met in Munich and signed the agreement that would, in Chamberlain's words, secure 'peace for our time.' In all probability there were many doubters among Club members. Ince-Jones as Tyrannus:

Those assembled then settled down tranquilly to listen to a delightful and very able talk.....A day or two before they had been faced by the prospect that the only leisure likely to be theirs would be enforced inactivity in a gas-proof cellar or trench. With profound relief they found themselves able to follow the Reader as lightly, deftly but penetratingly he showed the possibilities of using what time still remained for the development of life to the full.

In 1940 the war began in earnest with nightly prospects of air raids. Perry read *The Church Chest*, an exploration of his Dallington church records, including *one where the parson got his own back on two lawyers by describing them as spiritually dead, another when the church funds benefited by 6/4* [six shillings and four pence][2] *of the horse money and when folk had their last swank by being 'buried in linen'*. The ever present threat was noted, *On a very dark night, all returned home safely, thankful there had been no 'Alert'* [air raid siren].

Perry read his last paper, *Chance and Purpose*, on June 5th 1944, another auspicious day, the eve of D Day landings in Normandy. Although the meeting remembered the recent death of Dixon, a member of 43 years and Hooper who had died at the age of 91, it proved to be an occasion where in the best traditions of the Club good natured banter followed an excellent paper, recorded by master of words Ince-Jones. It is worth reproducing, only slightly edited:

He started by examples of apparently trivial things that had profoundly affected men. A dog's bark had altered the whole course of his life. The fact that his friend had a car forced him to go to a dance and there he met his future wife. .... he passed on to history. Charles Martel defeated the Saracens on the Loire and so England never became Mohammaden.... In 1612, Prince Henry died of a chance disease and so a broad minded prince with sympathy with

Parliament and Religious Reform was lost and Charles I took his place.....
Were these the finger of fate or coincidences? Was there plot and rhythm in life? Was Tennyson right in his "one increasing purpose through the ages?" or did emergencies arise one on another by chance?
The discussion started unpromisingly with a duet between Trevor Lewis [vicar] and Shaw [physician] on an alleged vision of his own funeral accorded to a well-known town-councillor. After this 'Flowers that bloom in the spring' episode, Tennent took up the mantle of Joad [Professor C E M Joad of the radio series Brains Trust who invariably prefaced arguments with 'it depends what you mean by'] and tried to insist on getting some definition of 'chance'. A number of people talked a lot without giving any definition, until Shaw in despair tried to get one out of Tennent, himself. This gallant effort was equally fruitless.
Many members pinned their faith to the uncertainty of whether a penny would fall head or tail, until Trevor Lewis professed to show how he could make it do either by throwing it at varied heights. Though his purpose was obviously nefarious, nobody believed he ever achieved it except by chance.
Some held there was no such thing as chance because every event had its cause and others could see no evidence of any purpose. Nevertheless a great deal was said about both and when the Club broke up after a sparkling, but rather indeterminate discussion, Lee [surgeon] and Trevor Lewis were left behind having a fierce argument on the dogmatism of scientists and the sweet reasonability of theologians. For all I know, they may be at it still.
Perry was 'removed' in 1945, having moved to Blakesley near Towcester.

Grenville Morgan, a Leeds graduate, had previously been priest vicar at Southwark Minster and joined the Club in 1948, the year after he came to Dallington. His first paper, on *Names*, began seriously but later *Morgan mentioned that he had recently married a Mr Gander to a Miss Gosling and had in his parish a Gracie Fields & an Albert Hall.....In the course of a brisk discussion, those present tried to trace the origins of their own names. Jackson and Jones, Turner and Skinner and Muscott were easy, but Liney, Dockrell and Manor had to be elucidated by the owners.*

A number of curious names cropped up, but it was generally felt that Humfrey took first prize when he solemnly assured us that one of his colleagues had ushered into his consulting room a lady who announced herself as Mrs Pricklybotham. To such an extent was he overcome that he had to plead indisposition, stagger from the room with handkerchief to his mouth and summon his partner to deal with the prickly lady! Ince-Jones adds, perhaps with tongue in cheek *Apparently this name is not rare in Huntingdonshire and parts of Lincolnshire.*

Grenville Morgan is recorded as giving another paper, *A Strange Rectory* in 1951, but this and any others he might have read must remain in the Dark Ages of Chit Chat when minutes were lost. Morgan left Northampton in 1960.

In the centre of Northampton is the church of All Saints, rebuilt in the manner of Sir Christopher Wren after the town's Great Fire of 1675 with 1000 tons of wood from Salcey Forest donated by Charles II. Three vicars became Chatterers.

Geoffrey Lunt, an Oxford Exeter College graduate, arrived in Northampton in 1919 on leaving the army having been awarded a Military Cross in 1917 whilst Chaplain to the Forces in France.

Elected to the Club in 1923 he gave one paper, *Epigrams*, at 1925's Summer Meeting held at Markham's house in Dallington.

He defined an epigram as 'an inscription generally in verse, engraved on a tombstone, temple, public building or votive offering'. Such was the immortal couplet praising the heroes of Thermopylae:
> "Go tell the Spartans, thou that passest by
> That here obedient to their country's laws we lie".....

.... *Quoting a XVII century writer he said*
> "The qualities rare in a bee that we meet
> In an epigram never should fail;
> Its body should always be little and sweet
> And the sting should be found in its tail."

It was an altogether delightful paper and Coleridge's verse –
> 'O that some bright inventive man
> Would patent make and sell
> An onion with an onion's taste
> But with a violet's smell'.

- brought tears to the eyes of the members.

..... *One honoured member by his grave statement 'I have seen some very funny things in the pulpit' caused the laity to gasp for a moment, until they realised by smiles on the faces of the clergy that all was well.*

The record of this meeting concluded with *A lady, having heard the minutes read, said in all wisdom and sincerity that she thought if future generations could read the minutes of the club, they would be surprised at the things which had amused their forebears.* Time alone will tell.

Geoffrey Lunt passed through Northampton on his way to higher things. He left to undertake various posts in the Empire before becoming chaplain to HM Prison Portsmouth from 1928 whilst vicar of St Matthew's Portsmouth. In 1935 he became Bishop of Ripon where he remained until 1946 when he was translated to Salisbury.

The National Archives at Kew have an interesting comment on the 1925 Summer Meeting's speaker Anthony Bevir, Sir Winston Churchill's Private Secretary, who comments when considering who to appoint as the next Archbishop of Canterbury

I believe the Bishop of Ripon to be a man of average ability who has not done badly where he is. On the other hand he has not done conspicuously well. He is a sentimentalist and rather gushing. He is quite a good judge, as far as I know, of men. He is not particularly good at handling men of character or those who do not feel his particular enthusiasm.[3]

Faint praise indeed. Geoffrey Lunt died in 1948.

Canon John Trevor Lewis obtained his degree of BA at Trinity College Dublin in 1906 and after living in Yorkshire and Cornwall arrived at All Saints' in 1926 following Lunt's departure. It was seven years before he joined the Club to become one of its more colourful characters.

On January 25th 1935 Lewis gave his first paper and *incurred a fine of 6d for not answering the intimation card. He paid with violent protests, saying that of course he must be present because he had to read the paper. Tyrannus was obdurate.* Lewis's *The Inter-Relation of Body, Mind and Spirit* was *short but learned*, the minute containing the reader's assertion that *A rabbit was soulish because it possessed a Psyche but was not Spiritua*l. Later in *....An excellent discussion.... "The Mad Doctors" took a prominent part, not always in agreement with the Reader. Shaw sat on the fence with brilliant interests. Some doubt was expressed as to whether the Reader had not given the subliminal self too low a place. Genesis was quoted but did not lead to Revelation.*

Lewis made several memorable comments on papers by others. When *Jackson read a carefully-thought-out and impressive paper on*

'Public and Private Employment' in February 1936, the *lively and appreciative discussion....reached its brilliant moment when Trevor Lewis stated that Public Officials did no creative work, they were only administrators. This was hotly contested. Mackintosh* [Medical Officer of Health Northamptonshire] *nearly broke the ten minute rule, but was so interesting that nobody minded.*

This denigration of a public body mirrored remarks on social class Lewis had made three years earlier, a month after Lewis had been elected to the Club and unfortunately bracketed with another cleric's far more serious and today unprintable accusations in the local press ... *Two vicars have been in the limelight this week – Canon J Trevor Lewis, of All Saints', Northampton, for his declaration about the upper and middle classes, and the Rev L A Ewart, of Earls Barton, who said that the Jews were mostly to blame for the existing antagonism toward them in the German Parliament.*

Canon Lewis expressed the opinion that about 80 per cent of the upper and middle classes do nothing to justify their existence. "They have every comfort and luxury," he said, "but contribute nothing in return for what they get.

"About 20 per cent, or a little more, perhaps, are doing really noble work, but the remainder do nothing. They are not interested in their homes...All they do is play bridge and breed horses and dogs".

The Rev Ewart stated: "The Jews' heartless usurious arrogance to Christian debtors before the war, their callous disregard of national interests and shameless profiteering at the public's expense throughout Germany's long-drawn-out economic agony following the war, aroused widespread indignation."

The Jews, he added, had every reason to be devoutly grateful to Hitler for protecting their lives.[4]

The Rev Ewart was never recorded as being a member or even guest of the Chit Chat.

Trevor Lewis was in a minority of one on February 29th 1936 when Thomas Carter had submitted his resignation. No reason for withdrawing from the Club is recorded but it may well have been this was on the grounds of non-attendance as Carter, initially a good attender and having hosted once, had not been to any meeting since the Jubilee Dinner twelve months before. *After some discussion it was agreed (Trevor Lewis dissenting) that the resignation be accepted but no steps be taken at present to fill the vacancy.* Reasons for resignation, apart from moving away from the Club's catchment area, are rarely given in minutes and it may well be there had been a clash of personalities or other private matters.

Lewis's train of thought could be difficult to follow at times. After Jackson had presented *More About Freedom*, discussing the state's restrictions on individuals *Trevor Lewis was understood to complain of the restrictions imposed upon his keeping cows and sheep and growing potatoes in the vicarage garden.* Tyrannus somewhat plaintively adds *Indeed everybody said a great deal and finally* "came out by the same door wherein he went".

Still with Trevor Lewis, he was always known as this, never simply 'Lewis'. In 1939 Lawrence Browne, Vicar of Gayton, gave one of his erudite talks on *Accuracy* and after Tyrannus *showed himself peculiarly inaccurate by confusing the books of Daniel and Nehemiah* it is recorded *Trevor Lewis had Zero on the brain to such an extent that some feared he had been specially unlucky at Monte Carlo. He maintained persistently that Mathematics was founded on Zero, "which there aint no such thing".* Browne equally persistently kept on asking him how many figs he had in his garden, but he never found out for the learned Canon would not reply.

Zero hour arrived at 11.0. P.M.

Later that year, on October 27th Trevor Lewis presented his paper *On Being Original*. Ince-Jones was absent – the first time for over ten years – and Dixon, in loco Tyrannus recorded the proceedings with *a good paper, rather profound and rather perplexing; a good discussion also. I cannot attempt a resume. I think my general impression was that it divided itself into three stages (1) violent disagreement with the reader leading up to (2) an understanding of what he meant, and (3) a more general agreement with his position. A good part of the time was taken up by the reader's having to enforce his point that by <u>being original</u> he did <u>not</u> mean doing original things.*

When he came to enter Dixon's notes in the minute book Ince-Jones added *From others I gathered that much of the time was spent pleasurably in baiting Trevor Lewis to his* [sic] *great joy. A general discussion before the paper led to an expression of opinion that it might be well to understand that the discussion of the paper ends at 9.00.* An excellent example of

It would seem that having managed to confuse an issue Trevor Lewis continued to sink even further into his own quagmire. The next paper, *Stoics and Epicureans* in February 1942, was no exception:

Professing to be chastened by previous receptions of his papers, he announced his intention of being quite uncontroversial. In this he succeeded about as well as usual.

Tyrannus summed up the discussion *...Though there seemed no violent desire for anarchy, it could not be said that there was any passionate support for any form of philosophy whatever. Everyone was Epicurean in his enjoyment of the cigars and liquid refreshment* *and Stoical about the prospect that they would be less good next year.*

Comment has already been made on the occasion in 1944 when Trevor Lewis asserted how he could affect the chances of a penny falling heads or tails after Perry's paper on *Chance and Purpose*. Also in 1944 Lewis presented *Religion and Politics* which *was very high-minded and much less provocative than was hoped and expected.* Having said *Perhaps it was time that servants of religion should not interfere with party politics* the reader had defused what could have been a confrontational discussion but in the best traditions of the Club *there was a wide difference of opinion as to the extent to which the church should enter public affairs.* They agreed however that *even the Archbishop of Canterbury was not well-equipped for a decision on Banking and that the average parson should not pose as a teacher of economics.* Needless to say *Trevor Lewis on the other hand maintained that the average parson was much better qualified than the average layman.*

In *Survivals* (1947) Trevor Lewis *contended ... that the highest values – kindness of heart, justice, compassion and love in its best sense – in a word – the Christian virtues showed a definite tendency to survive while cruelty and other vice springing from the baser side of man's nature were surely if slowly being eradicated.* In spite of the reader verging on sectarian religion, banned in the Club, Tyrannus did not intervene and there were few dissentions in the discussion.

There may have been later papers worthy of note, *Black Sheep* (1950) is a definite possibility, but no records survive, nor of any other All Saints' vicar being a Chatterer until 1996 when Simon Godfrey joined the Club. Godfrey had already spent time in the county at Kettering where he was Curate from1981-4 and Rector of the widespread parish of Crick and Yelvertoft with Clay Coton and

Lilbourne until he moved to All Saints' in 1989, eventually becoming both Vicar of All Saints' and Rector of Northampton. He will be especially remembered by his enthusiasm for music in church to the extent of having three choirs, one each of men, boys and girls as well as a succession of expert Directors of Music. Godfrey's first two papers were *Evil to him who evil thinks* on St George's Day 2002 where the replacement of St Edward by St George was recounted and *An Apostolic Blessing* the following year which *to the relief of Tyrannus had nothing much to do with religion (sectarian or otherwise)* but detailed the history and production of sherry. *The Jaw of Gerard – or Gerard's Jaw* in 2007, dealing with the Knights of St John of Jerusalem and their eventual home in Malta, was an appropriate curtain raiser to 2011 and *A City Built by Gentlemen for Gentlemen*, the description of Valletta by Sir Walter Scott. Godfrey had moved to Malta in 2009 to become Chancellor and Canon of St Paul's Pro Cathedral. He remained a Club member and manages to fulfil his commitments, generously hosting the Club with his normal shepherd's pie at the Chancellor's Lodge in 2012 when Nicholas Marquis de Piro spoke *on Domestic Arrangements for the Grand Master's Palace* at an additional Summer Meeting. Those members and wives able to attend enjoyed a wonderful few days on the island, including a conducted tour of the cathedral and felt a tradition could well have been started.

The vicarage of Kingsthorpe, in 1885 a village to the north of Northampton, absorbed into the expanding town in 1901, provided a home for two members. Edward Luxmore Tuson was elected in September 1893 having been a guest earlier that year. In April 1894 he *appeared at 9.40 and the Secretary wants to know whether this counts as an attendance*. Apparently it did but as Tuson had only attended once in the year he resigned in anticipation of expulsion before the Summer Meeting. It would seem he bore no ill will towards the Club as his name was among those signing the consolation letter to Jones' widow in 1901.

Following Tuson's death in 1917 John Percy de Putron became the incumbent at Kingsthorpe but did not join the Club until 1925. The following year...*In an atmosphere tense with expectation and dense with tobacco smoke de Putron tried to make our flesh creep with a paper on "England's Economic Downfall."* After discussing the decline of England's economic position and deploring *the growth of habits of luxury* (he) *ended on a happier note with the belief that the England which produced heroes in Elizabethan days would once again adapt itself to new circumstances and rise Phoenix-like from the ashes* After a break in which *Muscott had plentifully refilled glasses, members and visitors, almost without exception, tackled with enthusiasm the genial task of cheering up de Putron and proving there was life in the old dog yet.*

Such was their zeal that conversation continued without a break until nearly 11 o'clock and if lavish expenditure of words can avert economic downfall, England is saved.

This meeting was a fine example of members presenting papers on subjects outside their own field with enviable expertise. After *The Channel Islands* (1929) where he had spent five years as rector of St Peter's Port, Guernsey, De Putron read *The Influence of Canals on History* (1931). This proved to be fiery. He described three as 'diabolical ditches', Kiel had caused the Great War, Suez had turned the Mediterranean into a sea of blood and Panama was destined to set the combined Atlantic and Pacific ablaze. He wished *that by proper development of the canal system of Britain, a new era of prosperity ought to be introduced to the country. Baalam having come to curse stayed to bless and though no ass spoke, members* and visitors joined freely in the discussion. Their talk followed the lines of the Brook, sparkling whither it wished, rather than the canalized bed of the subject, but nay the less was full of interest and variety..... and some, seeking to find how far he would go in rejection of what others called 'progress', extorted him from him the admission that he profoundly regretted the invention of railways and thought their influence was, on the whole, evil.

De Putron's sermons may well have been as contentious as his papers. The last reading was in 1934 when he *definitely tried to make our flesh creep in his paper on "The Downfall of Modern Civilisation".* He assumed the mantle of the prophet and assured us that as Assyria, Greece and Rome had fallen so we too should bite the dust. Though he did not think catastrophe would fall before the next meeting of the Club, he was convinced that we were no better than our fathers and so the economic and physical superiority of the black, yellow and brown races would assert itself in bloodthirsty revenge upon our decadent civilisation.......None of the prophets had been listened to from Noah onwards except Jonah and even he had been horribly upset when Nineveh repented.....It may have been because de Putron had not taken the precaution of appearing at the Chit Chat Club fresh from the belly of a great fish that his warnings though impressively delivered, seemed to lack converting power.

Members tried to comfort the prophet. Even if one race lost dominance, civilisation might survive and permeate the world. Even de Putron's eloquence could not convince the Club that all hope need be abandoned yet, but there was some credit in being jolly.

In September 1935 De Putron died, a great loss to the Club.

It is difficult to divide clergy into categories. Remaining clerical members will be dealt with in chronologic order of their joining the

Club. Sanders and Hooper having already had their biographies outlined, only their papers will be considered.

Sanders, both headmaster of the Grammar School and curate of St Peter's church, gave three papers, *Protective mimicry in animal nature* (1886), *Cave explorations* (1888) and *Criminals* (1891), none of which was minuted by Hooper in detail. It is unfortunate Hooper left in 1887, his sole paper, *Undeveloped powers of body and mind* promised interesting subjects to follow.

Between 1885 and 1889 there were nine clergymen who contributed a total of eight papers of which none are detailed in minutes. With hindsight it was probably a mistake to recruit members from outlying villages. The most surprising traveller was Robert Baker, rector of Hargrave, lying about 21 miles east of Northampton, on the county borders of Northampton, Cambridge and Bedford. Baker was secretary of the Northampton Society of Antiquaries and as such he would have made frequent visits to the town although the prospect of travelling such a distance, particularly on winter evenings must have been quite daunting. Baker was not often at meetings and only managed to keep his membership going until July 1891 when he was forcibly removed under the attendance rule. Nevertheless he gave two papers, *Sports and games* (1887) and *Place names in Northamptonshire* (1889).

Charles Edward Hammond, Rector of Wootton joined in 1885 and read one paper, *Some Ancient Spanish Churches* and Frederick R C Hutton, Vicar of Roade, a few miles south of Wootton talked in 1887 on *Fiji and its Customs*. William Wilson became a Chatterer the same year as Hutton, 1887 but never read. His parish was that of Stoke Bruerne on the Grand Union Canal a mile of two from Roade. John Charles Cox had the living at Holdenby to the north east of

Northampton and scene of Gunpowder Plot meetings. He read on *The Black Death* in 1899.

In spite of being an excellent Secretary to the Club there are one or two instances where Greene omitted to record details. Canon Bury is an example. In January 1887 the 48 year old Rev William Bury attended as a guest. There is no mention of his being elected but exactly a year later he read *Forgotten Man* to the Club as a member when the paper *bristled with salient points*. There is no record of Bury attending any more meetings and in April 1890 *The Secretary stated that it was Bury's turn to read the Paper; and that on being applied to for the title of the Paper, Bury answered that it would be impossible for him to read as he had engagements connected with his Parish work.*

'Too busy to write a paper' could well have been an excuse rather than a reason, so did he then resign or was he expelled for not having complied with the 'less than two attendances and you are out' rule? Perhaps he found the Club too easy going. As ever, the Club kept some of its opinions to itself.

Our County by Adkins may give a clue to the character of the popular Rector of Harlestone from 1882 until 1907.

Canon Bury is a public man or nothing ..... His sermons are compositions of admirable sense and lofty ethics properly tinctured with sound doctrine..... Canon Bury's manners as a public man are as remarkable as his methods. For close and persistent reasoning put in the most trenchant language he is unequalled in the county, but he does not seem to conceal his low estimate of the opinion of others, and for so clever and thoughtful a man it is wondrously unwilling to put his case in a way to disarm opposition. One who knows him well says this is due to nervousness, and there is more in the excuse than may seem likely.

The truth is, Canon Bury is a University 'Don', transplanted to a country parsonage. He has all the intellectual acuteness, and the, in many ways, openness of mind, but alas! he has too much of their intolerance of the opinions, and unconsciously of the feelings, of the uneducated.[5]

There are no such gaps in the records of the Rev Edward Nicholls Tom. Born in 1830 he went up to St John's College, Cambridge where he obtained his BA in 1858. Ordained the following year he became curate at Marham, Norfolk, in 1858, moving to Kingsthorpe, Northamptonshire in 1860 where he remained for thirteen years. In 1873 he was appointed rector of St Peter's in the town and stayed there until he resigned in 1903 on a pension of £60. He married Ida Smith, daughter of the rector of Kislingbury village, four miles to the west of the town. They had two daughters and a son who died in infancy. Tom became a Chatterer in 1889 and throughout his long membership was always willing to host or present a paper. He read on eight occasions four of which were on historical themes, *Reign of Edward III* (1890), *The Reign of Elizabeth* (1892), *The War of American Independence* (1896) and *The Second Punic War* (1900). The 1896 paper generated a caustic ...*As this occupied an hour & a quarter, there was no discussion to speak of* ... from Tyrannus Jones. When it came to *In Memoriam* (1894) the minutes are somewhat enigmatic regarding the discussion: *The Club was rather hard on Tennyson in the discussion and seemed to think any other poet's In Memoriam was better than his.*

However with *Minor Poems of Milton* (1904) the secretary recorded ... *Tom now rose to higher things. He discoursed on the "Minor Poems of Milton", - (or preferably, perhaps, as was suggested, the*

Canon Bury
Drawing by W B Shoosmith c.1892

"Shorter Poems".) – *very pleasantly, quoting at length from L'Allegro Il Penseroso, Lycidas, etc. – very melodiously and sympathetically....* Two other papers, *Words* (1898) and *Proverbs* (1902) were recorded without comment. In 1910 Tom was elected an Honorary Member. He last attended a meeting on April 29th 1913 and at the extra summer meeting in June ... *Letter from Mrs. Tom read, thanking members for a wreath sent in their names. The acting Secretary (Markham) alluded in feeling terms to our late Friend, who had been at the last meeting and since then passed away, and asked those present to rise in their places, which all did.*

Ernest Gaskell remembers ... [Tom was] *Rector of St Peter's-cum-Upton, and during his long regime watched over the spiritual and social interests of his parishes with paternal care and anxiety. Throughout the extended period in which he held office his influence in the pulpit, and in the home never waned. The relationship between Rector and parishioners was always ideal, thoroughly approachable the people learned to come to him at all times and seasons; there were few sorrows that were not shared by the Rector and Mrs Tom, and few joys in which they did not participate.* [6]

*

In 1891, the last year of Greene's reign, the Rev William Blomefield Sleight joined the Club. Born in 1850 Sleight entered Clare College Cambridge in 1869, obtaining his BA in 1872. After curacy at St Katherine's Church Northampton he became vicar of Swadlincote Derbyshire in 1880 but moved back to St Katherine's in 1889 as its vicar and remained there until 1911. When he transferred to Towcester for the next eleven years the *Northampton Independent* described him as having been *the vicar of Northampton's poorest parish.*[7] Sleight was a member of the Royal Commission for the

Blind, Deaf and Dumb in 1886 and held the post of President of the British Deaf and Dumb Association from 1890 to 1920. Half of ten papers presented to the Club were based on Sleight's interest in problems of deafness, *The Education of the Deaf and Dumb* (1892), *Fuisorge System* (1894), *Types for the Blind* (1896), *Deaf & Dumb in Congress*, (1909) and *Deaf Mutes* (1914). Other readings showed a different side, notably in 1908 with the unprepossessing title of *Forestry*. In this *Sleight spun a yarn about the visit of the Agricultural Society to Elgin, Grantown, Castle Grant, Gordon Castle &c. &c. of which Society he was an honoured and appreciative guest.*

He explained the possibilities of works of afforestation as affording employments for out-of-works, and in providing wood pulp for the manufacture of the rotten stuff on which newspapers are printed.

The speaker's account of the banquets which formed an important part of the programme and of the abundant supplies of the National Beverage which were a leading feature of the Banquets was calculated to promote intense arboricultural cravings in the hearts of all Chatters.

Assonan Dam (1903) and *The Tramp* (1912) produced no recorded lateral thoughts on the part of Club members. Sleight retired to Kenilworth in 1922 and died there in 1927.

John Cunningham, Chaplain to St Andrew's Hospital, has his contributions to the Club from 1891 described in Chapter 10.

1894 saw the election of the Rev Francis Wood, vicar of St Paul's Church. During his membership he gave five papers, the first *Taylor's "Dunstan" and Tennyson's "Beckett"* (1895) where *The discussion turned mainly on historical points in the lives of the two heroes and the ecclesiastics were somewhat roughly handled by the historical genius of the Club.* In 1897 Wood resigned from his living although he continued to live locally long enough to read *a very carefully prepared paper on Paris under the Butchers. Which was favourably received. Wood's very excellent pronunciation of the French names, to which the members of the Club were so unaccustomed, led to some difficulty on the part of some of the members in following the story.*

Wood left the Club in March 1898 to live in Bromley but was elected to honorary status in September. He returned for the Summer Meeting in July 1899 when *with cigars, and drinks the members and guests settled down to a wonderfully careful analysis of Shakespeare's play "the Merchant of Venice" and Marlowe's "Jew of Malta" with special reference to the Jewish characters in each, viz. Shylock and Barabas, respectively.....the members recognized both the excellence of the matter, and the "record" length of the performance – Wood engrossed the Club for an hour and a half.* Papers normally lasted less than an hour, even at Summer Meetings. Perhaps he felt that having come all the way from Kent to fulfil his obligation of membership he should give the Club its money's worth.

Wood's remaining papers elicited little comment from the secretary, in 1902 the Club *listened with unalloyed pleasure to an admirable paper by Wood on the "Masques at Court" of Ben Jonson* and the following year in a very matter of fact entry, *Wood read a very thoughtful and interesting paper on Browning's Paracelsus, and this was succeeded by a discussion on Browning in general and his poem of Paracelsus in particular.*

Wood died in 1906 and sadly his wife passed away three days later.

During a clerical career of 45 years Alfred Mussendine Harper spent a third as vicar of St Paul's, Northampton and six years as a Chatterer from 1897. His first paper, *Some Social Axioms* (1897) narrowly missed being dubbed as party political by asking *which thought should influence the action of individuals in relation to many of the problems dealt with by Socialists,* but with *Points of view* (1899) he became less controversial when he.....*recommended the Club to change its points of view. How and how far to adopt this advice occupied the Club the rest of the evening to discover....*The last paper was on *"Suicide" a subject somewhat gruesome, but handled with mingled delicacy and dexterity.*

Tyrannus added, regrettably with no details *The ensuing talk went right merrily.*

The Rev Frederick Pyke Lawson, for two years Vicar of Preston Deanery, five miles south of Northampton, contributed *The Channel Islands* in 1890.

In 1096 Simon de Senlis set out on the First Crusade and returned home about 1098, when he founded The Church of the Holy Sepulchre in Northampton, one of four 'round churches' still standing in Britain and based on the Jerusalem model. Locally known as St Sepulchre's or St Sep's it is near the town centre All Saints' Church, built on the site of Simon de Senlis' other thanks offering, All Hallows', destroyed during the Great Fire of Northampton in 1675. Basil Davies joined a long line of vicars at the Holy Sepulchre Church in 1910, having served there as a curate for the previous three years. He gave one paper to the Club, *A fourth dimension* (1910), that earned the comment *A paper of remarkable merit* with no further explanation other than *(39 min)*.

Folliott Sandford Keysell joined the Club in 1923 and in his five years membership read two papers. In *Napoleon III* (1925) *when he revealed himself as a strong monarchist .... he tried loyally to show what a truly admirable though misunderstood man this* (Napoleon) *was. Jackson was heard murmuring in a corner that he regarded the sainted monarch as an unprincipled scoundrel, but, as he failed to come resolutely out into the open, a pleasant evening ended more peacefully than it might otherwise have done. Members who had enjoyed momentary visions of the monarchical Rural Dean and the Red Republican Jackson settling the matter gracefully with foils, suffered some disappointment, but gave relief to their emotions by telling stories, mostly gay, but few of them having any close connection with Napoleon III.*

The minute ends characteristically with an enigmatic *A very pleasant evening was further brightened by strains of merriment from the next room.*

On St. Valentine's Day, February 14th 1925. *The Rev. Keysell, vicar of the Church of the Holy Sepulchre.......ventured forth clothed only in the armour of righteousness to climb by outside ladders to a precarious perch 145 feet from the ground to help in fixing and consecrating with water he had brought from Jordan the weather-vane on the top of the spire. It was no light feat to undertake in ordinary weather, but on this occasion there was a positive gale blowing. Fortified by his experience as an Alpine climber..... he felt no nervousness in climbing to such a great height. He was, however, somewhat disconcerted by the way the structure swayed, which the workmen say is much worse when the bells are rung.*[8]

To prevent any misunderstanding from the reporter's rhetoric, the Rural Dean was quite properly dressed on this occasion as the accompanying photograph showed, not only was he well shielded from the elements but wore what appears to be a cross between a knitted cap and a policeman's helmet on his head. Members of the Club were nothing if not intrepid.

Anglo-Israelism (1928) was a compromise: *Keysell who was down to read on "Palestine and the Jews" made the Club a sporting offer of a paper on "Anglo-Israelism" or one on "Palestine" or both. It decided in favour of "Anglo-Israelism" with the proviso that if the after discussion languished he should be called upon for the second paper. Although Keysell seemed to have little faith in the Anglo-Israelist idea, his short paper gave rise to a discussion on the Jews so prolonged that all hope of hearing the talk on Palestine had to be postponed for another occasion........A number of excellent stories were told – of Aberdeen as well as Jerusalem.*

Arthur Pearce Shepherd came to Northampton in 1910 as Curate at All Saints' Church but did not join the Club until 1920 when he had been Vicar at St James' Church for three years. He remained an ordinary member for another three years after which he attained Honorary status, becoming Archdeacon of Dudley in Worcestershire. He gave six papers. The first took place early in 1920 as a substitute for Streatfeild, when he gave *A remarkably able discourse, the subject being the "Poetry of the Georgian Period": meaning thereby, not 1714 to 1820, but 1910 to the present date.*

Among poets mentioned were: Rupert Brooke, J. A. [sic] Flecker, Davis, Sorley, Gibson, Turner, Graves, Delamere, Nichols, May Byron, Drinkwater, Sassoon, Harwood, Grenville, Masefield. Many selections were read.

In 1922 *Shepherd gave an excellent talk on the "Origin & value of Punishment" .... Divided .... into two kinds viz. disciplinary, retributive. Tracing the idea of Punishment to the earliest times, he .... showed how in the early days of Social life, restraints became necessary, and retributive justice was naturally administered; "an eye for an eye, a tooth for a tooth, a life for a life" and how this became modified under the law of Christ. Love became the chief force in regard to Sin, and should have its part in dealing with Crime.*

After *The Poets and animals* in 1925 when *Shepherd gave a delightful paper .... in the course of which he read a great many extracts from Poetry, Ancient and very Modern* it was six years until *Causes of Social Unrest in India* was given at the Summer Meeting when *Tyrannus welcomed Shepherd, one of the honorary members, and congratulated him on behalf of The Club upon having obtained the degree of Doctor of Divinity.*

…. a delightful talk *was based on a recent visit to India lasting six months. During that time he … became acquainted with a great variety of people of all classes including Europeans, Eurasians and Indians. In spite of his great admiration for the members of the Indian Civil Service, he was conscious that a number of Europeans in India seemed never really to understand the Indians & their water-tight compartments contributed towards misunderstandings.*

Following another Summer Meeting talk, this time on *Joseph Conrad* (1937) it was not until November 1948 that Shepherd gave his next and final paper on *Time and the Soul* based on his book *The Eternity of Time.* Ince-Jones summarized it as *a stimulating evening, though occasionally some of the fog outside seemed to have drifted indoors.* Though appearing somewhat out of his depth Tyrannus tried hard *…. Though it was extremely able, it was by no means easy to summarise and at times was a little abstruse in its profound philosophy…. . Most people regarded the present as real; the past gradually faded & became unreal…. Actually past, present & future constituted a simultaneous whole…. The science of psychology by its investigation into the sub-conscious showed how a past, which was believed to be forgotten, still lived in the subconscious mind.*

The discussion included *telepathy, psychoanalysis, the unforgiveable sin, possibilities of hell in perfect memory, alpha & beta rays from the brain, dreams, Eastern & Western religions, conversion, forgiveness & ways of cheating Time…. The question of re-incarnation was raised but not discussed.*

Dr Shepherd died in 1968.

The next Vicar of St James' Church Northampton from 1924-9 Joseph Bartholomew Dollar had gained his degree at Trinity College Dublin in 1911 and served in the Irish Guards during the First World War. Regrettably he was only called upon to give one presentation, *The Philosophy of Golf*, in which *To the disappointment of the members there were no illustrations of the lurid language used on the links.*

The Paper ended with a poem on "The Muscular Woman" by Owen Seaman[10].

It was at the Summer Meeting of 1929 when James Lawrence Cartwright, Vicar of Christ Church, stepped into the breech. *All lovers of George Eliot, of whom many were present, were refreshed by the skilful way in which he recalled the leading features of her novels and made the familiar characters again to live before them.*

This was the meeting when *weight of the venerated Tyrannus* caused the collapse of one of Mrs de Putron's chairs. As was mentioned in an earlier chapter *This event brightened the proceedings considerably.*

 For his second talk to the Club Cartwright chose Robert Bridges' poem *The Testament of Beauty* and *besides explaining the general theme and purpose of the poem* [he] *read a number of passages illustrative of its beauty of language and power of description.* Later, after a somewhat complicated summary, Ince-Jones continued *The appreciative discussion that followed was directed chiefly to the nature and reality of Beauty; the difficulty of arriving at any standard of Beauty and the extent to which Selfhood and Breed contributed to human personality.* He ended on a lighter note: *Tyrannus, after explaining how the Rules of the Club permitted a paper which inevitably dealt to some extent with Religion, illustrated the need for religious instruction by confusing the Parable of 'The Prodigal Son' with that of 'The Good Samaritan'.*

Laurence Edward Browne DD, the 49 year old Vicar of Gayton Northamptonshire, became a Chatterer in 1936 although he had attended meetings earlier as guest of his father, Tyrannus IV, or brother H St John. Laurence Browne was an academic. Having spent time after his ordination in 1912 lecturing at St Augustine's College Canterbury he transferred in 1921 to Bishop's College Calcutta, where he was examining chaplain to the bishop as well as a lecturer. In 1926 he became a SPG Special Missionary and later a lecturer in Lahore. Laurence made a special study of the relationship between the Christian and Muslim faiths resulting in many books, from *Early Judaism* (1920) to *The Eclipse of Christianity in Asia* (1967).

Laurence Browne gave five papers, the first being *The Crusades as seen from The East* (1936). His years in India *had impressed him more with the squalor than the romance of the East and the romantic side of the Crusades made no appeal to him. To him they were the greatest calamity in history.* Following this contentious start Browne expanded on this theme and concluded with *When the followers of Jesus tried to win a dominion for Him by the sword and supported their mission by shifty practices, the multitudes in the East, who were watching the struggle between the Cross and the Crescent, decided against the Cross.*

It is not surprising the discussion *turned upon the question of when the use of military force was morally justified. At times there was some little liveliness.*

The paper on *Accuracy*, read in 1939 where Trevor Lewis had *Zero on the brain* has already been mentioned. Before this episode Browne had compared English *inaccuracy in the exact amount of Kruschen to go on a sixpence* with that displayed by Indians being *a few hours early or late for catching a train and missing a whole day cheerfully.*

Tyrannus commented *As he represents an interesting combination of a Doctor of Divinity who took firsts in both Science and Theology, few dared to question his orthodoxy in either department, but the scorn he poured on the idea that the 3 angles of a triangle were equal to 2 right angles, caused a flutter in the dovecotes of the Fundamentalists.*

Two years later came *Changes in Religion*, a very non-sectarian paper. He *did not find any reason to accept the idea that all religions had a monotheistic basis......differences arose more from borrowing, retrogression, fusion and convention, either forcible accompanied by persecution or peaceful persuasion. He pointed out that a new religion was rarely resisted by the government unless there was some political implication. The Romans more or less let the mystery religions alone but persecuted the Christians because they taught a new way of life.*

In *The Political Outlook of Islam* Browne gave *an excellent paper packed with argument and illustrations and illuminated by wide knowledge* to the extent *It is impossible in a short summary to do justice.* Some idea of Browne's attitudes can however be judged from *at many times various bogeys had been raised to frighten the world....One that appeared almost continuously was the threat of the Jews, a peculiarly passive race; others were The Yellow Peril, The Bolshevik Menace and the Danger of a rising of the Black Peoples.......Browne doubted whether the Moslems could ever unite......Some sort of economic union was possible and need not be feared. Actually Moslems were too much divided in race and belief to be likely to constitute a menace.*

The discussion......was at times lively, especially when one cleric seemed to regard the Crusaders as devils and another as angels......on the whole the members were comforted by Browne's paper and were encouraged not to fear an attack by united Islam. The present high cost of living rather destroys the hope engendered by the broad interpretation of the Koran that a man may have 4 wives, if he treats them equally.

The last recorded paper by Laurence Browne, in 1945, is *Curiosities in Etymology*. This turned out to be *treasures of his collection* with *a catalogue of the most interesting specimens* from the schoolboy definition of theorem - *A problem may be solved by unaided human intelligence but a theorem as shown by its origin from Greek "theos" and latin rem can only be solved by Divine Assistance* to *words deliberately invented among them the ghastly triptupious* [sic].

He retired from Gayton in 1946 and if there were further papers they are lost in the Club's Dark Age. During this time there are one or two names of clerics attending meetings but no papers are recorded.

The last Chatterer in this section appears sporadically in later minutes and three of his six recorded papers are in Club archives. Peter Gompertz came to Northampton in 1975 at the age of 35 as Vicar of St Giles' Church and joined the Club in 1980. *A Damned Un-English Weapon* (1981) was revealed as a history of the submarine starting from *Cornelius Van Drabbel, a Dutch physician, who produced 3 wooden boats with pigskin chambers to be filled alternately with air and water. ..... propelled by oarsmen using collapsible blades and King James I was said to have taken a trip in the third boat in the Thames at a depth of 12-15 feet!!!* At the end of an in depth paper Gompertz concluded *The modern nuclear submarine powered submarine has become the flagship of the Navy.*

Apostles of Mobility followed in 1986 and *To the surprise of some this proved to be a penetrating analysis of tank warfare, and nothing to do with St. Paul and his colleagues.* Given in great detail the reader ended with *Perhaps, after 70 years of dominance, the role of the tank in modern warfare is at last shrinking.* Tyrannus commented *This tightly-knit paper led to a lively discussion which made it clear that the Club, not normally a bellicose body, had its own reserves of military wisdom.*

Dylan Thomas proved to be the subject of *A Wizard with Words* (1988). *The story .... in a way sad and tragic* produced a moving and learned paper ending with Thomas's most famous line *Do not go gentle into that good night.*

Too little; too soon; thank heaven (1990), a review of naval forces on both sides in World War II and Germany's *precipitate entry into world conflict with good equipment either stored or not sufficiently tested* was followed by *Rooms with a view* (1992),a treatise on code breaking in the Royal Navy. Gompertz gave *She Being Dead Yet Speaketh* in 1995, a paper on German naval rearmament after 1919 with a detailed history of the battleship Bismark, launched on St Valentine's day 1939 and sent to the bottom about 400 miles west of Brest where *She now lies at a depth of 15,700 feet half way down the slope of an extinct underwater volcano .... upright on her keel a symbol of brooding menace still...... A ghostly presence beneath the waves.....she being dead yet speaketh.*

Gompertz had moved to Ayno in 1996 and after the turn of the century found it difficult to continue his membership and resigned from the Club.

As a footnote to the clergy, and for the sake of completeness, two untraceable clerics presented papers, Rev A J Gill on *Shakespeare's Queen Katherina* (1885) and A A Liney on *Superstitions* (1953).

NOTES

1. Gaskell E. *Northamptonshire Leaders: Social and Political.* 1908. A description of 113 lives privately printed and circulated for the sum of three guineas (£3.15p).
2. About £10 today.
3. *Church Times.* PREM 5/287.
4. *The Northamptonshire Independent.* 13 December 1933.
5. Adkins R. *Our County.*
6. Gaskell E. *Northamptonshire Leaders.*
7. *The Northamptonshire Independent* 1911.
8. Ib. 14 February 1925. *Vicar's Daring Deed.*
9. Seaman Sir Owen. Editor *Punch* magazine.

9
The Law

Only one of the ten founder Club members practised law. Thomas Green entered the profession in 1865 and by the time he joined the Club had established himself as a local poet and novelist as well as a solicitor. Having given his sole paper, *Ancient Copyhold Tenure* in 1886 he attended the next meeting, in May, but does not appear in subsequent minutes as present or as having resigned until Greene, as Secretary in early 1888, notes that *he had carried out the instructions given to him at the February meeting as to the non-compliance of certain members with Rule 8. Letters were received from T Green and Wake, both of which letters were considered satisfactory.* In October however *The Secretary announced that he had had a letter from Green T. asking to have his name removed from the list of members as he has found it impossible to attend the meetings.* Greene adds somewhat tetchily
This request came at a rather awkward time as Green ought to have read the paper at the November meeting.
Green, without the 'e' (secretary Hooper's persistent spelling of Dr Richard Greene without the 'e' made trawls through early Club archives slightly complicated) is not mentioned again until the Summer Meeting of 1897 when the axe fell on two members for non-attendance ....*Cropley only attended 1 and Scriven none. The last two have accordingly resigned and Harper and Green T have been elected in their place.* Thomas Green had been a guest earlier in the year and presumably convinced the Club he would be a better attender than in years gone by, but the following July *Green T was*

conspicuous by his absence and accordingly once more passed into the nebulous.

The next solicitor was Henry William Kennedy Markham who obtained his BA at Cambridge in 1870 and entered the family firm in 1875. Giving no papers and a poor attender it is strange he should have joined the Club in the first place. He certainly had no intention of abiding by the rules. Frederick Ince-Jones, to whom all aspiring chroniclers are indebted, records

.... a striking personality, who combined great kindness of heart with ability to call a spade by any other name, achieved the unique distinction of retaining his membership for four years without writing any paper. He said picturesquely that he would dine the Club or wine the Club, as often as they liked, but he would be condemned if he would write a paper! [1]

The same could not be said of his cousin Christopher who joined the Club in 1888. The Markhams were a family proud of their heritage, tracing ancestors in Northamptonshire back to the 17th century. During his life Christopher wrote extensively about the county and included in his publications a *History of the Markhams of Northamptonshire,* privately printing 100 copies in 1890. Having joined his father, Clerk of the Peace Henry Philip Markham DL, young Christopher was admitted as solicitor in 1887, aged 28. He soon became Clerk of the Peace for the County Council in 1899 where he remained for five years. He was commissioned in the 4th Battalion Northampton Regiment in 1886 as a lieutenant, rising to Captain of F Company in 1893 but resigned in 1900 with the rank of major. In 1890 Markham became a Fellow of the Society of Antiquaries.

During his forty two year membership of the Club Markham presented twenty two papers, the first of which, *The Domesday*

Book (1888).....*was read by the Secretary as Markham was ill and unable to attend. Owing to this the discussion was somewhat languid.* When it came to *The Norman Conquest* (1890) the discussion was anything but languid, it was *so animated indeed that at one time it seemed as if the peace loving Reader had thrown a veritable apple of discord among the astute historical critics of the Club; but the spars bent gracefully to the breeze and the good ship righted herself amid clouds of smoke and the fragrant odour of the Wine imported from the Sister Isle* - Greene at his most lyrical.

The Liber Custumarum of the Borough of Northampton (1892), dealt with the *Book of the Ancient Usage and Customs of the town of Northampton from the earliest record to 1448.* In 1894 Markham read *The Church Plate of Northamptonshire* and *Ancient Stone Crosses of Northamptonshire* the following year. Both papers were expanded subsequently and published as books, models of patient research with detailed illustrations.[2]

Six other papers were concerned with local history. *Iron Roads of Northamptonshire* in 1903 described *the wonderful system of steam locomotive railways – inaugurated in the early part of last century,......but,* Browne, as Secretary, adding.....*(almost as the ink dries on this page) becoming a thing of the past, supplanted by express automobile cars and an international service of 500 miles an hour airships.*

Infirmary (1906) was a history of Northampton's General Infirmary (now Hospital). *Ways and Means* (1912) proved to be a dissertation on *ancient roads, classed as Pre-Roman, Roman, and Post Roman......including a good account of several of the most ancient and interesting Bridges in the County.* At 58½ minutes long it might be thought Markham was testing members' attention span. If so he was apparently encouraged, *Northants Militia,* appropriately read on June 3rd 1914, just three weeks before the assassination of Archduke Ferdinand of Austria and consisting *of portions of a paper written for the press,* lasted an hour and four minutes. A long history going *back as far as 872-901*, and including *its methods, long marches, pains and pleasures, and referring to the brutal and savage punishments awarded to transgressors* it was later developed into an authoritative publication.[3]

In 1927 Markham deputised St John Browne to read his *The Valley of the Nene*, a history of the river from ancient times and referring *to the use of the river for traffic, and the opening of the line of Railway along the valley, which in time absorbed most of the trade and led to the practical disuse of the waterway.* The line to Bedford, one of two available for Chatterers to attend the 1913 Summer meeting, opened in 1872 and became disused in 1962 when intermediate stations closed to passengers thanks to Dr Beeching, leaving a small section between Northampton and Piddington station open until 1981 for purposes of the Ministry of Defence. The reopening of the line to Bedford has been proposed recently by the Bedfordshire Railway and Transport Association and is supported by local authorities.

The last paper in this local group and also the last of Markham's twenty two readings is *Peers taking Titles from Northamptonshire* (1929), another widely researched subject *from Althorpe to Wellingborough. I* [Ince-Jones] *do not remember any beginning with X, Y or Z, but most of the other letters were well represented and many titles now extinct came from modest spots little known.*

Back in November 1896 Markham moved from local affairs to Shakespeare's *King Lear......A large number of the members* [six present] *and visitors* [two] *had been festive during the afternoon in attendance on the new mayor, H. E. Randall Esq but notwithstanding a profitable evening was spent.* The Mad Doctors were missed......*A close discussion followed on the mental aberration of the King, which needed the special guidance of Greene and Harding, wanting alas! when most required. The description of psycological* [sic] *defects in fiction was also freely criticized.*

A later paper in 1917 dealt with *"Shakespeare's Knowledge of Law"* where the secretary records *He did not maintain that the poet was ever a lawyer, nor commit himself to Lord Chancellor Campbell's opinion that he had been a lawyer's clerk, but, (having been just raised to the County Bench; on which the members of the Club offered their congratulations), the reader held the scales judicially and impartially. He did however declare that, lawyer or not, the Bard of Avon was a miracle.* There are no comments on the discussion.

Anachronisms (1898), also with no comments, was followed in 1901 by Markham *discoursing on "Some early text books", otherwise "Hornbooks", and, as usual, knew what he was talking about.* It appeared Markham also knew his subject in 1905 when he presented *Unparly. Language* masquerading as *"Slang", with numerous examples of the slang of high life, low life, army, navy, stock exchange thieves, &c....*

Returning to the Arts in 1909 with *Benvenuto Cellini*, Markham.....gave *a graphic account of the life and lifework of that accomplished artist; moral and amiable man; deft and dexterous assassin.* Historical but not local was *Hatchments* (1911). These are, or were, funeral demonstrations of the lifetime "achievement" of the arms, i.e. shield, helmet, crest, supporters and any other honours displayed on a black lozenge shaped frame which used to be suspended against the wall of a deceased person's house and after six or twelve months removed to the parish church. ...*The first* he could find in the County was of the date 1656 at Stoke Bruerne and.....The most recent hatchment the reader knew of in England was that of the late Revd. J. J. Hornby D.D., Provost of Eton (1826-1909).

A common word producing an uncommon paper was *Common* in 1918. Examples were *the natural desire of many men and women to become to some extent "uncommon", different from the general....a "common" cause......the Book of "Common" Prayer......"Commons" at School and College* and ending with *the use of the word was most abundant in connection with the administration of the Law....*

An equally complicated subject was *Wills* in 1921, *the history of testamentary dispositions from Old Testament times to the present date......concluding with some examples of rhyming, quaint or comical Wills.*

A short paper, only 13 minutes, described *the Short Cut in various department of activity. There was, to most men and women, something attractive in the Short Cut, whether across fields or through woods – in making money – (sometimes by cards, racing or robbery).......In most cases...... the longer way round was best.*

It is a constant feature of the Club that the most unlikely papers produce the best Chat. *Franks*, read by Markham in 1925 and minuted by the indefatigable Ince-Jones *dealt with the ancient rights, formerly possessed by Members of Parliament, to frank letters and even large parcels through the post. Some of the members and visitors seemed to feel some regret that such opportunities of reducing expenses no longer existed, but one member rose to the occasion in the true old Chit Chat spirit, by asserting the satisfaction and even the enthusiasm with which he paid his Income Tax and, one may infer, those higher demands of which one speaks only with bated breath. Less high-minded and possibly poorer members were quite willing that he should pay theirs too; but from the highest motives he was not prepared to go quite so far and it is feared the subsequent 6d off the Income Tax has caused him no little pain.* This last is reference to the 1925 controversial budget by Winston Churchill that returned Britain to the gold standard and knocked 6d (2½ p) off Income Tax.

Among other posts Markham was Corresponding Secretary of the *Northampton and Oakham Architectural Society*, affiliated to the Association of Architectural Societies. Many Chit Chatterers appear as members of this body. The Rev T C Beasley held the post of Secretary, R G Scriven was an officer and E Montague Browne the Auditor of Accounts. Members included W B Shoosmith, B Muscott, Rev. Bury and a new member that year, W D R Adkins.[4]

Markham died in 1937. Northampton *Independent's* obituary columnist quotes Adkins as having said earlier of the Markham family *A fine carelessness of convention, a good-natured downrightness of statement, and a comic indifference to the general opinion do not hide successfully the good breeding and kindheartedness of them all.* The writer continues *The late Mr Markham possessed in excelsis the best characteristics of his forebears without that vein of eccentricity that marked and marred some of his relatives in the estimation of orthodox mortals.* Strong words, said with feeling and later *His patriotic instincts led him to join the Northamptonshire Militia, and what he lacked in inches he made up in zeal and efficiency ......*[5]

Various of Markham's writings and memorabilia found their way into the Northamptonshire Record Office. They consist of thousands of items and have not yet been fully documented in detail, although most titles of his original writings have been listed. Among these no papers presented to the Club can be found, nor does the Club get a mention although various talks to such institutions as Women's Institutes are catalogued. As elsewhere it is as if the Club is considered an intimate society of friends, not to be referred to even in private documents.

*

Edward Montague Browne was born in 1847. Following early education in Norfolk he became a solicitor in 1866 and after four years in London moved to Northampton. When the senior member of his firm died in 1872 he practised alone until being joined by John Haviland, a future Chatterer, in 1893. In that year Browne founded the Northampton Electric Light Company with which he was associated until 1926. He was closely associated with professional centres in Northampton and was a life-long churchman.

Browne joined the Club in 1887 and his first four papers were on legal matters, *Notes on Wills, whimsical and otherwise* (1887), *Death Duties* (1890), *National Pensions* (1892) and *Chancery* (1894). Browne then *held forth on the dawn of the 20th Century* in 1896. *He abused the 19th a good deal, especially in domestic architecture, sanitation, and medicine as contrasted with surgery. His hopes for the coming century included one that justice might be more prompt and less expensive.*

He could not be induced to express any opinion on the New Woman in the next century.

Among his remaining papers was *C.C.C. 32 years and after* (1917) when, being Tyrannus as well as reader and recording his own paper, *Browne reeled off a meandering sort of medley, concerning the formation of the C. C. Club and its early history, doings and adventures. He became "reminiscential" on the subject of ancient members, in, or out of, the flesh. Pursuing this theme usque ad taedium, the instinct of self preservation suddenly asserted itself,* and he pulled up just in time to avoid any serious consequence. Browne's last reading was on *Gambling and the Law* (1931) when *In view of the instability of hitherto stable securities and in the absence of all the clergy, members and visitors sat up in the hope of hearing how purchase by a modest flutter within the law they might re-establish their fortunes. No tips however were given.

Browne died in 1928. His partner, John Haviland, joined the same year as Browne and gave two papers, on *Socialism* (1888) and *Poor Law* (1890). He left Northampton in 1905.

John Joseph Faulkner gained his LLB London in 1872 and LLD three years later. He moved to Northampton and became the Registrar of the County Court and District Registrar of the High Court in Northampton in 1882. Faulkner joined in 1888 and read four papers, *County Courts* (1889), *Ancient Law* (1891), *Marriage Laws* (1893) and *Criticism of the book entitled "Merrie England"* (1897), all of which were well received but not detailed.

*

Elected to the Club in 1889 William Dent Ryland Adkins was born in 1862, the son of local JP William Adkins and his wife Harriet. His early schooling took place at Mill Hill and later he attended University College London where he attained his BA in 1882. Called to the Bar from the Inner Temple in 1890 Adkins went on the Midland Circuit and was made Junior Counsel to the Post Office in 1908. In 1911, having taken silk, he became Recorder of Nottingham and nine years later Recorder of Birmingham. He won the Middleton Division of Lancashire seat in Parliament for the Liberals in 1908, continuing to represent this area until 1923. Knighted in 1911 Sir Ryland sat on many committees both in Parliament and locally, becoming Chairman of the Northamptonshire County

Council in 1920, having first joined when the Council was formed in 1899 as member for Duston.

Adkins was not only an accomplished speaker with a ready wit but also a prodigious writer, particularly in regard to local history. His *Our County* of 1893, with pen and ink sketches by fellow Chatterer W B Shoosmith contained among others cameos of Chatterers Canon Bury and Dr Greene. The subtitle quote, *It takes all sorts to make a world* is quite typical of Adkins, to be taken in whatever way one chooses. During the First World War Adkins produced a stimulating, if rather long, *Ballad for the time*, entitled *Awake Northamptonshire!*, exhorting *You men of strength and sinew ... keep Northamptonshire Unblasted by the Hun.* Loyalty to his county had produced an outpouring of Jingoism, understandable in the context of his time. (Appendix 4)

Adkins presented ten papers in 34 years. The first, *Purple Patches,* given a month after he joined the Club in March 1889 has no comments by Greene apart from *An animated discussion followed.*

Justice and its Methods (1893), *The New Unionism and the Old* (1893) and *Modern Slavery* (1895) came in quick succession. In 1897 he read ....*Whyte Melville, the Northamptonshire Novelist* .... *Adkins then proceeded to interest the Club for ¾ of an hour with comments, extracts etc. on our local writer, not the least interesting parts being the touches of incident which gave life to the memory of the man. The discussion took chiefly the form of further enquiry, and was specially livened by the presence and remarks of one who had known the hero.*

Scottish born in 1821 George John Whyte-Melville became a captain in the Coldstream Guards and retired in 1849. Having married Charlotte Hanbury the following year the couple settled in Boughton, a village close to Northampton. 1853 saw the young man in the Crimea, a volunteer major of the Turkish irregular cavalry. On his safe return to England Whyte Melville embarked on a successful career as a novelist, producing 21 volumes in the next 25 years, starting with *Captain Digby* in 1853 and including *Kate Coventry* (1856), which appeared in Sir S J Maxwell's 1886 list of best novels at a Cambridge Chit Chat meeting. The marriage was unhappy, possibly owing to the major's life style as a country gentleman and ended in 1878 when he fell from his horse whilst crossing a ploughed field during a hunt in the Vale of the White Horse. Whyte Melville is chiefly remembered today for writing the rather melancholy words to Paolo Tosti's song *Good-Bye!* and locally as founding *The Whyte Melville Club* in Northampton, later a Working Men's Club. Two public houses are named after him, one being his old home in Boughton. The most intriguing question to the Chit Chat chronicler is the identity of *one who had known the hero*. Could this have been Adkins, only 16 years old at the author's death?

The appeal of Whyte Melville's fiction was partly due to his fox hunting 'yarns', including *Digby Grand* echoing the works of R S Surtees and historical stories such as *The Gladiators*, mirroring Sir Walter Scott.

*

Adkins had the ability to provoke discussion. *When should we tell lies?* in 1900 produced the admonition .... *Lest some high moralist among succeeding generations of Chatterers should think Adkins was anxious to lie and prevaricate, let it be here set down that only altruistic and fiduciary considerations exposed him to any temptation to depart from the truth. Prolonged and ardent discussion of the subject by the Club, which was leavened by a morality of the highest tone, left the matter at this stage "Let him that is without sin among you cast the first stone".*

165

After *An Autumnal Civilisation* (1901), dealing with the Byzantine Empire, there was a break until 1915 when he returned to talk on *Gardens, Groves and Parks*, a detailed discourse on their history with examples, most of which were in his home county. *The Problem of Poland*, in 1917 included "*How the middle cut of Central Europe ought to be disposed of*". In the middle of the First World War Sir Ryland suggested *It may be that actual formal independence will not be necessary, if there is practical autonomy* and concluded with. *Armageddon will go on until certain problems are effectually solved, Belgium, Alscace-Loraine, but chiefly and predominantly, Poland.*

For his last talk, *Scenery and the Soul* in 1923, Adkins *….Rejoicing at regaining contact with society of high intelligence, desired to consult the combined intellect of the Club upon a pet theory of his own.*

He found that the scenes in which his early life had been passed always formed the back ground for his imaginative efforts to visualise scenes in the books he had read in youth; so that even today certain classic events in such books as 'Ivanhoe' always took place for him somewhere between Hardingstone and Houghton.

If this experience was universal or common, it made the early environment of children a vital actor in the development of their souls.

The combined intellect of the Club, though scintillating with its usual brilliance and aided by coruscations from a number of visitors, welcomed unreservedly the charm with which the theory was elaborated, appreciated the local patriotism engendered in the speaker and agreed with his conclusions, but could find little corroboration in their individual experiences.

Sir Ryland Adkins never married. He died at the early age of 62 in January 1925 from *gastric influenza* [6].

*

Entering the legal profession in 1893 James Jackson was one of the most prolific Chatterers, presenting 21 papers in his 48 years from 1895 as a Club member. He wrote on various subjects including poetry, public speaking freedom and liberty.

Jackson started well in 1896 when he *apologized to the Club for his absence* [and] *sent his paper to be read by the Secretary. It was entitled the Historical development of the House of Lords.*

The Club tried its hand at reforming the House, but relinquished the task at a quarter to nine when conversational groups took the place of the Session of the Club. A hundred and sixteen years later reformation is still on the agenda.

The Czar's Message (1898) and *Titles* (1900) were read without comment from the Secretary. In 1901.... *Jackson then read & delivered a paper & address mingled with readings & recitations on & from the poet Wordsworth. What he said was very interesting & entertaining, & must have put him to some trouble to prepare. The time for discussion was short & was occupied by Adkins & Wood, to good advantage.* No doubt members hid their smiles when this was read out for approval at the next meeting. Two years later Jackson spoke *on Poetry in relation to Life* being *erudite and eloquent, shewing a deep and wide acquaintance with both Poetry and Life.* Adkins was reported as saying enigmatically *it reminded him of his own experience in often spending a whole afternoon and a small fortune in shedding cards at the doors of his friends.* The relevance of this was not explained, no doubt being clear to members.

After Jackson's talk *What do we mean by Gambling* (1904) Browne records.... *The value and interest of his paper were measured by the fury of an onslaught led chiefly by Stuart. Various other members – notably Ewen Hichens and Hickson spoke with an air of authority suggestive of a close acquaintance with the subject of the discourse. Ultimately Jackson emerged from the fray, alive, and fairly well.*

1907 produced *What we read, and Why* during which *He referred to the great advantage of cultivating habit and method in reading, and pointed out that literature was not something outside one's life, but became, as it were, part of the life itself.*

A dissertation on *The Art of Public Speaking* in 1909 was followed by *What is a gold sovereign?* two years later. He became quite philosophical …. *what do we mean by the <u>value</u> of the gold;- or of anything?………Gold soon came to be recognised as having a special value. It has characteristics of beauty and utility: it is in itself a commodity.* In 1916 Jackson delved into mysteries of *the Foreign Exchanges, which he defined to be the method by which people in one country paid their debts to people in another country with a different currency.* He continued by stating *The standard measure of value in this country is the amount of gold in a sovereign, and the currency of all great commercial countries have their basis in gold …… The cheque is now the great instrument of payment…..* and remained so for less than a century.

Between these last two papers came *Fear* in January 1914. Had this paper been written later that year the summary might have been different …. *He could only define "Fear" in a negative way – the opposite of "Courage"….. Of courage there are many kinds and shades. The highest form of courage will meet and overcome the strongest fear……. The greatest power in dispersing Fear is Love.*

April 1918, seven months before the cessation of hostilities in the First World War, Jackson gave what might in retrospect be considered a follow up to his 1914 musings in *The only possible settlement of the War.* Having given his thoughts on the current international situation ….. *He submitted, as the only Settlement really possible:- that there must be an end of the whole military system in every country, and any departure from that attitude would be an international crime. .. In conclusion we have to face a situation in which the attainment of the highest Christian ideal is the only true solution.*

Soon after the war ended disillusionment set in with rising unemployment. Jackson used *Unemployment* as the title of his paper in 1921. With insight he said *At the present time the working classes were suffering from the delusion that there is, - Somewhere – an unlimited mine of wealth. After alluding to the unprecedented taxation which attended, and followed on, the War: the speaker concluded by inviting practical suggestions.* There the minute ends, perhaps not even *the combined intellect of the Club* could make helpful suggestions.

Although the subject sounds more cheerful *What makes for Happiness?* in 1924 untypically elicited no comments from Ince-Jones as Tyrannus. This lapse was entirely compensated for by entries regarding Jackson's 1929 paper on *The Substance of Poetry*. Cooke as host was indisposed and sent a verse as apology:

The Chit Chats once met with a host,
Of whom they could venture to boast
That he no one did flurry,
Or bother or worry,
But effaced himself far more than most.

It would be difficult and negligent for any chronicler to abbreviate Ince-Jones' minute….. *Jackson, obviously stimulated by this sublime verse, delivered a talk on "The Substance of Poetry" but prefaced it by a statement that a truer title would be "Art & Life with some reference to Poetry". He omitted to say that the supreme Art of Life was to avoid flurry, or bother ~~and~~ or worry and to efface oneself except for self expression in the loftiest poetry. He set the brains of the members working by such conundrums as "What is Poetry?" "What is Art?", "Who reads Poetry?" "Why do Poets stand so high in our esteem?" He felt that behind & beyond all material things existed an ultimate reality of beauty; that at rare moments the true artist, panting to escape from routine, caught glimpses of this mystic harmony and, gifted with exceptional powers of expression, crystallised his vision for all time to share.*

The Artist felt more deeply, saw more clearly than ordinary men and so in Poetry and other Arts were recorded the best & happiest moments of the greatest minds.

Jackson was quite unnecessarily apologetic for a very suggestive paper which gave rise to a well-sustained, interesting discussion.

The depression of the 1920s stimulated Jackson to talk on *The Dole* (1931).....

which was, by universal consent, a masterly effort, and, to the relief of Tyrannus, did not transgress the rule of the Club against party politics.

The paper dealt ...... with the necessity for fair & generous public assistance in times of unusual depression & bad trade ......He feared that if the Communistic experiment in Russia was successful in providing an improved standard of life under a system of equal division, there might be a demand for similar economic arrangements in this country & therefore he pleaded for no reduction in the Social Services & no lowering of the standard of living.

Jackson's papers provide a valuable insight into the changing scene of the first half of the 20th century. By November 1933 it was realised there could be problems ahead for democracy and in *The Setback to Liberty ... He cunningly avoided any definition of Liberty,*

NORTHAMPTON GRAMMAR SCHOOL

Grammar School Headmaster's House, 81 Abington Street today

W C C Cooke (front row centre), Headmaster 1921-45
at Northampton Grammar School front entrance, early 1930s.
Two other Chatterers: front row second from right J Trevor Lewis.
Back row, third from right E E Field.

NORTHAMPTON GRAMMAR SCHOOL HEADMASTERS

Canon S J W Sanders 1872-92

E Reynolds 1907-21

M B Nettleton 1945-64

NOTABLE CHATTERERS

Thomas Green

Sir Hereward Wake

Sir Ryland Adkins

W B Shoosmith

NOTABLE CHATTERERS

Dr Percival

Dr Cropley

Alfred Ewen

Herbert Hankinson

CHRISTOPHER A MARKHAM, NORTHAMPTON CHRONICLER

Young newly commissioned C A Markham

Major Markham

Clerk of Peace Markham

NOTABLE CHATTERERS

Rev Tom   Rev Beasley

Ince-Jones and School for Deaf, Cliftonville c.1927

TWO CHATTERERS AT WORK

Ince-Jones and School for Deaf 1929-30

Stanley Hill (third from right) receiving a cheque for £40 from the East Midlands Ladies' Football Alliance to buy equipment for Creaton Hospital
October 1972

A DISTINGUISHED CHATTERER

Sir Basil Thomson KCB 1925

A THANK YOU FROM THE CLUB

Rose-bowl presented to E Browne, Tyrannus IV
July 1923

but stated that everybody knew what it was ….. *The question was whether democracy could be purged from its drawbacks or whether such atrocities as now were established in Russia, Italy & Germany were likely to afflict us.* The next comment is a reminder of how members of the International Brigade would have felt a few years later …… *If he were a young man he would regard it as his mission in life to defend the sacred principles of Freedom of Speech.* In the discussion …. (members) *tried to discover a way by which the welfare of the whole world could be secured, while preserving the reasonable freedom of the units.* Jackson repeated that it was impossible without some form of Democracy. His radical treatment of Conservative Liberalism was much enjoyed.

By 1936 there was increasing concern about *Public and Private Employment* and in his paper *Jackson ….. drew attention to the increase in the number of people wholly employed by the State & Local Bodies. Probably there were about 2000 in Northampton & 2 million in the whole country. In all probability this would reach three million ere long.*

It was difficult to get rid of officials who were mildly incompetent but in spite of this he paid a high tribute to the British Civil Service, the finest in the world. Already Public Officials had great voting power & as they increased in number it might become a question whether it was not dangerous for men to have such a large say in the choice of their employers & the policy to be pursued. It was at this meeting …. when Trevor Lewis stated that *Public Officials did no creative work, they were only administrators. This was hotly contested. Mackintosh nearly broke the ten minute rule, but was so interesting that nobody minded.*

State interference surfaced two years later with *More about Freedom.* Two issues arose ….. *the freedom to select the people to govern us & make the laws* [and] *the extent to which the State should interfere with individual liberty and private enterprise ….. He speculated as to how far a government ought to legislate to affect taste; to enforce such things as vaccination or prohibition, & to interfere with trade & employment …. a very long discussion …. continued without a break until 11.30.*

Everybody took part & Tyrannus was threatened with censure for breaking the 10 minute rule! Ellison complained bitterly that he was not allowed to career over the county in a car with a trailer at 40 miles an hour. Shapland wished the govt. would concern itself chiefly with the putting down of wrong-doers. Mr Russell Chamberlain [visitor] *in a thoughtful contribution suggested that the State must act as an umpire between the haves & the have-nots. Trevor Lewis was understood to complain of the restrictions imposed upon his keeping cows & sheep & growing potatoes in the vicarage garden.*

Indeed everybody said a great deal & finally "came out by the same door wherein he went".

Jackson's first wartime paper in 1941 …. *was entitled "Trade and Liberty" and it revealed all the wisdom of a veteran but no sign of advancing years …. he made three assumptions (1) That we are fighting for Liberty (2) That we shall win (3) There will be an attempt after victory to build a better system.* So far as trade was concerned he was worried about …. *Tariffs and Socialism. He thought it inconceivable for a more united world to bear a continuance of prohibitive tariffs and advocated subsidy for agriculture as the best form of protection.*

The question of Socialism would have to be settled in the light of new facts and a different political situation.

Jackson's last reading, in 1946, was predictably *Post-War Reconstruction*. It was a thoughtful paper reflecting the optimism of many but containing reservations held by those with insight. *In considering lines of future progress, he recalled the achievements of man in government and social arrangements during the long period he had been upon earth. He asked himself what hope there was of cleansing and equalisation and he answered that in spite of the present outbreak of savagery there was a lively hope because men had increasingly a bent towards freedom and justice ….. resistance to change did not always spring from selfish motives. ……. In the future he hoped for ….more sensible international trade, planned before the end of the war; more cooperation with China and definite plans for feeding starving people; more employment based on well-developed export trade; the end of the Poor Law with the establishment of universal subsistence and medical treatment; more equal distribution of incomes and a better relationship between employer and employed.*

If this was to be accomplished he could give us no hope of reduction of taxation. …. he expressed the conviction, based on over 84 years of life, that mankind had been, was and would continue to be beneficently guided and so all would be well.

James Jackson took a great interest in local affairs, serving with only a short break as a town councilor, latterly as Alderman. He died in 1946. Jackson's partner James Thomas Chamberlain became a member in 1925 and read two papers, *Charles Lamb* (1930) and *The King can do no wrong* (1932).

The year after Jackson joined the Club George Russell Terry became a member in 1896. A solicitor at that time Terry, a keen lay reader, later took orders and became vicar of St Michael's Church in Northampton. He read two papers, *Thomas A Beckett* (1897) and *White Slaves* (1899) which was read by Secretary Jones, *Terry having sent an apology for his absence on important business.*

Fortunately he arrived in time to conclude the paper which was of a thrilling character, and the sympathy of the members was elicited and warning expressed in the discussion which ensued.

Alfred Ewen, who joined the Club in 1901 at the age of 48, held the post of Official Receiver in Bankruptcy for the Northampton, Bedford and Luton Courts but from eleven papers he read his heart was more in literature and the higher things of life. His first reading in 1902 on *the Practical Use of Shakespeare* included the *opinion (inter alia) that numbers of people throughout the world, who had read Shakespeare in their own tongues, were craving to understand him in the original, and that this would greatly tend to make English the language of the world, a consummation devoutly to be wished.* He followed this with *the many sided message which the great Poet and Philosopher delivered, was as applicable, now as then, to the needs of mankind.* Regrettably the Secretary, Browne did not enlarge upon what Ewen considered this message to be.

On June 15th the following year *In obedience to the rules this was called a "Summer Meeting", but the temperature was that of November and the rain descended in torrents.*

Ewen endeavoured, and with much success, to disperse the prevailing gloom. His yarn was entitled "An Elizabethan Play House" and produced a lifelike impression of the theatre in the days of Shakespeare, both as regards the structure and the stage arrangements – the nature and behaviour of the audience being also clearly portrayed.

With *Pre-historic Continents* in 1905 Ewen discussed the *famous Island of Atlanta* [sic] *described by Plato, lying between Europe and America, and by charming sketches of various islands. Ewen supposed that Atlanta formed the connecting link almost joining the* two continents, and accounting for the similarity between the civilization and worship of the mighty Egypt and the tiny Easter Isle.

Ewen's next three papers were largely factual, *Robert Louis Stevenson* (1906), *Arthurian Legends* at the Summer Meeting of 1907 and *Charles Lamb* (1908) that included comments *on the distinction between wit and Humour and on the quality of those gifts as exhibited by Lamb.*

This literary trend became interrupted in 1910 with *Prehistoric Races ….. illustrated by numerous coloured sketches of prehistoric monuments &c. drawn and coloured by himself.*

Ewen's last two papers might have been written by a member of the clergy. In *Comparative Religion* (1915) he professed *that Christianity was one of the great religions of the world – that we looked forward to the day when it would be <u>the</u> Religion of the world, but as that day had not yet dawned, he proposed…..to treat Christianity in relation to other religions, and then he considered that no controversial question would arise.* A detailed analysis followed of Body, Soul and Spirit. This paper could well have been described as flouting the rule against sectarian religion but perhaps due to it being given at a Summer Meeting no comment was made apart from its being *an excellent and uncommon talk illustrated by a Chart or Diagram.* Ewen's theme was extended the following year, again at a Summer Meeting, by *Death and After* when *Ewen pointed out that: "all must die, passing through nature to eternity", and if death was inevitable as birth surely we have been in the habit of regarding it quite wrongly.* Ewen wrote his own summary of the paper which concluded that ……… [at death] *all that is lost is the physical body, and that, in his view the evidence pointed to the conclusion that at death we enter into a higher vitality because not hemmed in and limited by the physical body.* He had been a mild critic of the established church for some time and two years after this paper Ewen resigned his post as Official Receiver to take up a curacy near Truro. As he said at the time …… *Criticism of any institution is no good unless you can be prepared to provide a substitute. My principle is, don't condemn unless you can help to construct something better….*[7]. Alfred Ewen died in 1928.

*

Charles Simkin Turner, a Northampton solicitor, joined the Club in 1901 at the age of 42. The following year he spoke with authority on *l'Ancien Regime in which he showed clearly the respective positions occupied by the nobility and the peasantry under the French Monarchy anterior to the Revolution, & the miserable state of poverty and slavery to which the poor were reduced by taxation & oppression.* In …. *A lively discussion …. a Town Councillor suggested that there were lower depths than Northampton: The Club wisely abstained from entering into controversy upon so debatable a point.*

Turner continued to show Francophilia with four papers. *The French Revolution* (1906), *Napoleon* (1908), a survey of the early 18th century memoirs of the (Duc de) *St Simon* (1910) were followed by The *Man in the Iron Mask* (1918). After *quotations from Voltaire's record of the noted but mysterious prisoner* Turner revealed …. *The victim of the 24 years imprisonment is supposed by the best authorities to be Count Matthioli, a Mantuan diplomatist who had offended Louis XIV, was kidnapped in May 1679, carried by Pignerol, and many years after removed to the Bastille in Paris, where he died on the 19th Nov. 1703.*

Another paper by Turner was *Conscription* (1904) where he reviewed current practices in France and Germany and *strongly advocated a modified form of conscription, or at least a military training for all the youth of England, so that the work of the schoolmaster might be supplemented by drill and training. A good talk followed a good paper, there being a general consensus in favour of military training – but Jackson stood out and spoke with his usual ability against the inculcation of the military spirit.* The Club would appear to have been as divided as the nation at that time regarding views of Baden Powell and Kipling.

In *Old London* (1913) ….. *Turner took for his paper "Besant's London"* [8]*, which he boiled down for the benefit of the Club …….The subject was too vast and the time at his disposal too limited to go much into detail, or to dwell upon any special phase of London life, but he succeeded well in sustaining the interest of his hearers …..*

When it came to *A centenary: Wellington and his tools* (1914). *Turner …. lightly sketched the career of the "Iron Duke", bringing into prominence his great qualities, while not ignoring the failings in mind and manner which at times detracted from his popularity and even from his usefulness.*

When Turner gave his paper on Italian Spies in 1916 *The reader gave an inventory of some noted spies, beginning with Joshua the Son of Nun and Caleb the Son of Jephunneh, and going down through the ages to present times.* Browne added his comment in the minutes, pertinent to the mid-war date ….. *Frederick II of Prussia, sometimes called the Great, and unquestionably great if you supply three or four appropriate nouns to follow the adjective, - was said to be the founder of modern spying, - a pleasant thought for the modern spy!*

Turner died in 1939.

Town Clerk of Northampton from 1909 to 1928 Herbert Hankinson had varying interests judging by his talks to the Club. In 1904, the year after joining …. *He read a long but interesting paper on Physical Deterioration …… the general opinion seemed to be that things* might be worse, but ought to be much better. – Various remedies were proposed but the Club, not being fortified with Parliamentary powers could not carry matters any further.

Hankinson's diversity may be judged by his next seven papers, *Legends relating to the Holy Grail and Wagner's Opera "Parsifal"* (1907), *Syndicalism* (1912), *Some XIXth century memoirs* (1915), *Problems of Population and Progress* (1920), *British Highways, ancient and modern* (1923), *The Midlands in Poetry, Ballad and Prose* (1926) and *Some Characteristics of the Music of the Great Composers* (1928).

In 1931 Herbert Hankinson read the somewhat unusually long titled treatise, the longest until 2012, *The Historical Literary and Artistic associations of the Dove Valley and its Tributaries.* Ince-Jones records:

He discussed the correct pronunciation of the name of the Valley arising out of a verse sent by Streatfeild which, though almost illegible appeared to run as follows.

"I should like to have heard
How Hankinson rove,
By the banks of the Dove
Or from heights far above
Watched the swift current move
As mimsy as a Borogrove
As burnished as a dove."
and finally came down definitely in favour of 'duv'.

Tyrannus then waxes lyrical with ….*In this he spoke with real authority, for the district is memorable and dear to all Chit Chatterers as his birthplace and furthermore he delighted them with tales of tickling trout near Leek and quaffing beer at Buxton in carefree days ere responsibility had covered, as with a veil, his joyous spirit.*

After *George Borrow* (1934) and *Georgian and Early Victorian Diaries and Correspondence* (1939) Hankinson gave his last paper in 1942 having been a member for nearly forty years. It was a cold January night when there were …. *15* [members and guests] *in all, in spite of weather that would have been difficult to beat for unpleasantness.* The title was *Problems* which *proved to be problems of Population, Race and Colour, and Labour. They were set out with admirable clearness, facing the Club in their alarming, stark nakedness, but the reader refrained from suggesting any solution......Naturally such a provocative paper led to a sustained discussion, ranging over fertility; progress; the inevitability of civilised people being overwhelmed by barbarians; the causes of war and agricultural policy.*

Hardly anybody agreed with anybody else, though everybody was very polite. The result was that we came out by much the same door wherein we went, but when we came out of Dixon's door we found our cars covered with snow, though it had been raining cats and dogs, when we came in.

Herbert Hankinson died in 1946.

William Buxton Shoosmith entered the legal profession in 1898 and became a Chatterer in 1910. The following year *Shoosmith gave his paper (a maiden effort) on Death Ships and a précis appended will speak for itself.* Unfortunately for such an intriguing title there is no trace of this despite the previous two months' papers having résumés pasted in the minute book. Shoosmith could be controversial as in his 1913 *The Tyranny of Man*. He used recent events to show *that an attempt to anticipate the natural growth of public opinion by violence and clamour would prove a failure, but that all things (within reasonable limits) would come to her who knows how to wait.*

As the paper was read in April this could not have been a reference to the death of suffragette Emily Wilding Davison who threw herself under the King's horse at the June Derby but rather the rising tide of violence, an example of which would have been the partial blowing up of David Lloyd George's house in February.

After *Queer Law Cases* (1915) came *German Psychology* (1918) in which Shoosmith included propaganda ….*In recent years the mind of the people was filled with a Great Delusion, artfully and deliberately contrived, they were surrounded by jealous enemies, chiefly England and France waiting their opportunity of falling upon the peace-loving Teuton.* His papers then became more anecdotal. *Laying Cable* (1921) was taken *chiefly from the journal of his uncle Capt. Henry Shoosmith, on the laying of the first Atlantic cable from Valencia to Hearts Content N.F.L. and produced specimens of the cable a map and a representation of the Great Eastern Steamship.* Two accounts of Shoosmith's 'voyage' to New Zealand were followed by tales of his yacht *At Sea on the Maire Leah* (1930), when *the members felt they had enjoyed many of the pleasures of a voyage with Admiral Shoosmith (as he is sometimes affectionately known to his friends) without any of the inconveniences inevitable on such a trip.*

At the end of the paper, he answered innumerable questions on subjects as varied as "Cooking" and "Quelling a Mutiny at Sea."

In *Things we put up with* (1933) ….. *he was eloquent in protest against the restrictions imposed upon his liberty to purchase pork pies and alcoholic refreshment at all hours of the day and night and, lawyer though he be, quoted Queen Elizabeth in support of the statement that we suffer from too much law.*

A paper on his hobby *Postage and Stamp Collecting* (1938) was followed in 1947 by *Looking Backward* being more extracts from his

Uncle Henry's cable laying voyage. Owing to the absence of minutes after 1949 it is impossible to say whether Shoosmith read to the Club again.

Shoosmith is chiefly remembered by the Club for his artistry, not his papers extensive though they were. His younger siblings, Thurston Laidlaw (1865-1933) and Fanny Violet (1870-1924) were noted local water-colourists but W B entered his father's firm and only occasionally showed his artistic capabilities. In 1935, for the Jubilee Dinner he produced a pen and ink drawing of Tyrannus guarding the Club's Tree of Knowledge and its record book. This symbol has been used on many occasions since, gracing notices to Chatterers to the present day. WBS died in 1953.

In 1913 guest speaker William Arthur Walker, solicitor with Becke Green in Northampton had talked about *The Scout Movement* of which he was County District Commissioner until 1918. After his somewhat contentious election the following year Walker read two papers as a member. *Transfigurations* (1916) dealt with *a pine tree in Switzerland which became as incandescent with white light by the rising of the snow edge behind it* and among other stories *the burning bush in the wilderness, the descent of Moses from the Mount, and lastly the Transfiguration of our Lord on the Mount.....* Not all members were entirely happy. C A Markham added an initialled note in the minutes *The paper was very nearly transgressing the rule that no religious subject should be discussed.* It did, the amendment to *sectarian religion* was not passed until the next year. Even so Walker would have sailed close to the wind after 1917.

Walker's other paper, *Pre-War Press Cuttings* (1918) gave a serious look at articles in the European press prior to 1914 that boded ill for

England and were largely ignored. Walker resigned from the Club in 1918 but lived for another 40 years, dying at the age of 93.

Harold St John Browne, the elder son of Montague E Browne became a Chatterer in 1925 after serving in the 1914-18 war as Major in the 4th Battalion of the Northamptonshire Regiment and being awarded the Military Cross and Order of the Nile. He practiced as solicitor in the Northampton firm of Browne and Wells.

The first paper, *Joint Stock Enterprise* (1927) is described by Ince-Jones as *comprehensive and very interesting*. The general tone of the meeting however may be summed up by the discussion:

The whole subject was treated in a masterly way and those present, in order to show their deep appreciation, proceeded to discuss at great length the important question as to whether Shoosmith ought to have caught a certain train at Paddington.

Opinion was very equally divided. About half the Club was in passionate sympathy with Shoosmith and the other half indignant that he should even expect to catch any train whatever.

The members, having thoroughly enjoyed this vital controversy, suddenly turned and rent Tyrannus for allowing them to enjoy themselves at all ..... This was a classic Chat.

Two years later St John Browne had been travelling. In *The Irish Free State Revisited* he noted *the elaborate and expensive preliminaries necessary to get a car into the Free State made one wonder if the game was worth the candle but....the freedom of action was very welcome*, a somewhat cryptic phrase partially explained later in referring to *a run of five miles at top speed, 52 miles an hour.* He praised *the efficiency of local government in Dublin, the good roads, and the absolute tranquillity of the country.....but not.....the poverty of western districts.* He also referred to *the high value attaching to the Irish language, though no one understood it.*

Browne gave a history of gambling and its inevitable debts, once enforceable, in *Gambling and the Law*, (1931) when......*in the absence of all the clergy, members and visitors sat up in the hope of hearing how purchase by a modest flutter within the law they might re-establish their fortunes. No tips however were given. Cooke,* [Grammar School headmaster] *the Classic, announced some remarkable successes he had gained in operations at Newmarket in supporting horses with alleged Latin names, but few of those present seemed to be either, desperate or confirmed gamblers, unless indeed they were very reticent. In this respect the absence of the clergy was regretted.*

In 1936, after a gap of five years, St John Browne ventured into the realms of controversy with *Blood Sports* which he claimed *was not to be taken too seriously.* He included *chivalrous championing of the shark's point of view when fished and caught* [and] *most of the forms of sport, when animals are killed, not for food or safety but for fun* [which] *made him feel uncomfortable. Cruelty was a matter of conscience and conscience varied in different ages.* Later....*At least one hardened pikesman seemed so moved by the paper that one imagined him about to lay aside the rod and take up growing cabbages. Others, perhaps more hardened, put up spirited defences for their favourite blood sports and even the cry that 'the fox enjoyed it' was raised.*

As Tyrannus recorded in January 1939 *Browne indulged in his first attempt at prophesy with a paper on "England A.D. 2000".* Although with hindsight it is easy to look upon his conclusions as being unbelievably naive and optimistic much of his forecast was logical – at the time. *He believed there would be no new European War because the nations would be too much afraid of one another. The British Empire would continue to hold together, though the outlying* parts would be more independent and industrialised. There would be no increase of population at home, but probably a decrease.

The money centre of the world would be New York not London. We should return to a 2 Party System. The rights of the individual would become more subordinated to the State and Local Authority. Existence would be more complex and materialised. There would be more wage earners with high wages and no small shop-keepers. Class distinction would disappear, but prisons would remain. Voluntary hospitals and blood sports would go. Less land would be under cultivation. It would be possible to travel to the ends of the earth in 2 days.

Tontines was the subject in 1941. This *system of long-term annuities upon nominated lives* (where) *holders of the bonds upon the last remaining lives received much larger annuities and in many cases the whole of the capital value* was not entirely popular with the Chatterers as...*It was a form of long-distance gambling in which the final benefits accrued after eighty or more years* and *everybody felt the rewards would be too remote.*

St John Browne's last paper was read in 1943 was *Is the Law an Ass?* where *Against this foul aspersion Browne drew his sword.* In the discussion *thanks to the undue preponderance of legal luminaries the Law was dealt with tenderly.* In conclusion *on the whole the opinion seemed to be that at any rate The Law was a clever ass* and *After the meeting somebody said the Law was more of a mule than an ass.*

Harold St John Browne died 1947.

*

Gilbert Hicks gave the Club the benefit of his legal mind with *Changes in the Law* in 1932, two years after he joined and *County Courts* in 1934. He moved to London in 1935.

Anthony Jackson was the son of Chatterer James Jackson. A solicitor like his father he joined the Club in 1940 and read at least seven papers, the first of which was *Shakespearean Metaphysics.* Jackson *.... Without giving any definition of metaphysics, announced his intention of trying to find out what the man Shakespeare was really like......*[and] *arrived at some of the underlying ideas, which included;- hatred of flattery and tyranny, individualism, love of order but the belief that love was greater than order and was the only quality to survive.* The discussion started off at a tangent *with a devastating attack by Dr Tennant on the accepted idea that the Shakespeare, who was supposed to have written the plays, was really the man who went from Warwickshire to London and ran the Globe Theatre.*

Though he said he was no Baconian and did not know who wrote the plays, he was convinced such an uneducated man, as was Shakespeare, could not have done so. After some time......Some attempt was made to synthesize the philosophy of Shakespeare but the final result was a little nebulous.

Shakespeare was prominent in the next two papers, *Touchstones* (1944) in which *he meant standards that could be applied as criteria of values in Art and Literature* and *Falstaff* (1946) but Jackson came down to earth with *Mountaineering* in 1949. Minutes are not extant for Jackson's archived paper *The Colour Problem* (1951), it will never be known how the Club reacted to the speaker professing the most beautiful person he had ever met *was a Cingalese man who was up at Cambridge with me....his skin was as dark as a ripened chestnut.* After advancing the opinion it was never possible to disregard colour in others there follows an admirable account of the history and contemporary situation regarding colour throughout the world.

A 1954 paper by Anthony Jackson is *An Old Title*, listed but not detailed. During his tenure as Tyrannus there is only one reading minuted, *Catesby* in 1968 when with classic Tyrannus self-effacement ....*Jackson wanted to show the Club Some old deeds relating to land near West Haddon which had been in the occupation of a Heygate & his own grandfather (both of West Haddon) and which had been exacted inter alia by Robt. Catesby of Gunpowder Plot fame. He tried to make up a story – not very clever – but produced the deeds.*

Geoffery Heygate Lowick, notary public and member of the legal firm Browne and Wells, became a Chatterer in 1947 and straddled the Club's Dark Age. *Tendencies in the Law* (1947) *was mercifully lacking in that legal phraseology which bewilders the layman.* Lowick considered that regarding *Recent legislation....Much of it is hasty and ill digested....laws should be based on popular assent.*

In *Slavery* (1948) Lowick dealt with the *history* and status of these *rightless* people ending with *Archbishop Temple's statement that, if material standards are the sole criterion, as they should not be, slavery might be justified for producing the greatest good of the greatest number.* The Club, as ever, drifted towards a less serious view of the subject, including domestic service, washing up and hankering *after the introduction of some forced female labour to lessen them in domestic servitude.* On this occasion one of the guests, *Judge Forbes almost exceeded the ten minute rule* [9] *by his able summing up, but it was so interesting and to the point that nobody would have minded had he completely over-shot the mark.*

Listed papers on *Quacks* (1950), *Rights and Rites* (1953), *Other Novelists* (1954) and *Royal Marriage* (1955) with no doubt others in the fourteen year gap were followed by *Sherlock Holmes* (1969) where Lowick was amazed *why so much was centred.....on Holmes and Dr Watson as* [if] *they had been real people.* Another gap until an archived typewritten paper emerges, *Capital Punishment* (1980), a consideration of whether the death penalty abolished in November 1965 in England should be reintroduced. The conclusion was doubt as to whether restoration of the death penalty would act as a deterrent. Lowick ended with the view that normal 'life sentence' being an average of nine years *a murderer would probably come out a bigger blackguard than before rather than a reformed and useful citizen.....The question remains what we are to do with them.*

A F Skinner OBE, later deputy Clerk to the Northamptonshire County Council in 1952 joined the Club at the beginning of the Dark Age in 1949 and read two papers, *Western Union* (1950) and *Nursery Rhymes* (1952). In 1964 Horsfall-Carter, Chief Clerk to the County Council became a member, as did Owen Meurig Jones, another local authority lawyer and member of the Browne and Wells firm, but of them and any papers they may have read there are no records.

Thomas George Fincham was a member from the latter part of the 1960s and remained in the Club for forty years until retiring in 2006. Tom was a lieutenant in the Northamptonshire Regiment in the 1939-45 war and afterwards joined the Browne and Wells firm as solicitor and notary public. Five of his seven papers are held in the archives, the first of which covered *First Rights* (1981), a review of parental responsibility and child custody. *Denning M.R.* (1984) was a review of the life of Lord Denning, Master of the Rolls, still alive at the age of 85, a charismatic figure, the 'people's judge' who would override precedent and in words attributed to Mr Justice Walton:

Here come I, my name is Denning,
What I don't know is not worth kenning.
Twice a day I make new law,
If there were time I'd make much more.

In 1986 *Fincham read a paper entitled "Degrees of Deceit", and drew the attention of the Club to the word "Con" which is new to the English language. It may be used.....to describe a transaction which though not actually criminal, is nevertheless designed to defraud a fellow man by means that fall some way short of complete honesty. He distinguished a con from criminal deception, without wholly convincing Tyrannus* [Tasker] *of the distinction.* No doubt others agreed, for *In the end the club was inclined to agree, somewhat reluctantly, with the reader that life was just the big Con.*

Botany Bay (1989) and *OZ* (1992) recounted the colonisation of Australia by convicts in the 18th and 19th centuries. Back to England and *The Paston Letters* (1994), a collection of over 1000 documents covering a period from 1418-1506 giving *a fascinating insight into the thoughts and activities of an English squire's family in the 15th century.* Leaping forward some 500 years Fincham talked about *Traitors of World War II* in 2003, which *mainly related to William Joyce – otherwise known as Lord Haw-Haw, John Avery and Norman Bailey-Stuart and the respective fates which awaited them on being convicted.*

District Judge Jerome Saint became a member in 1987 and the following year spoke on *Words*, a review of the English language which *threw off its shackles of Latin, adopting and adapting words from other languages and developing a fluidity of expression which is still with us.* The second of nine recorded papers, *Stations* (1991) covered *a journey, sometimes nostalgic, often factual, mainly through Victorian England...*and the next, *Invasion* (1992) the period during the late 19th and early 20th centuries when thoughts turned to possible intrusions from Germany. *Targeting* (1994) dealt with police concentrating on a group or individual suspected of criminal activity, uncorroborated confessions and *juge d'instruction* in

France. His 1998 paper told the story of Colditz Castle, including anecdotes and pictures, under the title *IV.C*. Saint's next paper, *E.C.H.H - The European Convention of Human Rights* in 2002, covered rights and freedom. Two years later Saint presented *We don't Care,* saying *I am hoping to generate a spirited discussion about the lack of interest shown by the vast majority of people towards the government of this country.* After an admonition to remember the rule regarding party politics *the discussion was lively* with regrettably no details. At one meeting Saint read the passage from *As We Were* by E F Benson describing the Cambridge Chit Chat Club much to the interest and amusement of members. For his final paper before resigning later in 2007 Saint returned to *Words,* updating his first talk from Dr Johnson and *the Oxford English Dictionary down to our own time.*

The next 'legal' Chatterer to be considered in detail is Peter Cooch, solicitor in the Northampton firm of Hewitson Becke and Shaw, formerly Becke Phipps. His first paper *A Noble Experiment* (1992) dealt with the history of prohibition in America and the second *In Search of an Identity* (1994) was a study of the Armenian people in the early 20th century and in particular the genocide they suffered at the hands of the Turks, abetted by the Kurds, in 1915 and the events leading up to that. In 1996 Cooch expanded on his theme with *Heirs of Sorrow.* Tyrannus Ellison waxed lyrical …. In *a long and complex paper dealing with a forgotten part of the Middle East …. it was an account of the tragic history of the Armenian people …. The earliest Christian nation, great architects, builders and explorers ….*[and] *suffered many centuries of persecution and oppression …. Indeed none of us seemed to know much of these terrible events.* There followed *a lively discussion on the iniquity of man and his ability to destroy.*

During his twenty years membership of the Club from 1991 Michael Cornelius, practicing Northampton solicitor from 1965 to 2008, read six recorded papers, starting in 1993 with an enigmatic *What am I?* This turned out to be a dissertation in cosmology in the broadest sense *full of what I* [Clifford Ellison as Tyrannus] *suppose are unanswerable questions, the number of stars, the limits of space, the age of the universe* ....and...*summed up by a member saying he had enjoyed it very much, particularly the bits he had understood.* For his next paper, *Unavoidable Deceptions* (1995), Cornelius quoted Massimo Piattelli-Palmarini, at that time founder and director of the Department of Cognitive Science (DIPSCO), of the Scientific Institute San Raffaele, in Milan as saying in his book *L'illusione di sapere (Inevitable Illusions)* ...*humans are illogical in trying to impose logic on purely random events*...such as choosing numbers for the National Lottery or a roulette wheel. This was a complicated subject, explained in detail. At its close *A little goggle eyed, the club (certainly Tyrannus* [Ellison again]) *reached for the port and whisky.* A lengthy discussion ended with the well-known saying *There are lies, damn lies and statistics.*

Following *It's a Secret* in 1997, of which there are no details, there is a gap until 2006 when *Coffee for two, Champagne for One* explored the history of duelling along with stories of particular duels, including ones between ladies. Coffee was drunk before a duel and champagne after, hence the enigmatic title. *A Lazy Eight* two years later *harked back to the deep waters of time, space and infinity,* of which an eight on its side is the symbol, ∞. Cornelius ended with a quotation from *Rosencrantz and Guildenstern are dead,* [the play by Tom Stoppard], *Eternity's a terrible thought. I mean, where's it all going to end?*

For his last treatise, *Celtic Sense* (2009), Cornelius presented the Club with the question *King Arthur, fact or fiction?* He came down firmly on the side of fiction based on *The Raven* or *Bran, Protector of Celtic Lands*. The Club was deeply divided into *passionate believers..... and those to whom it was a tale told by fools and signifying nothing but a good yarn*. Cornelius left the Club in 2011 and died the following year.

Peter Hardingham, solicitor and Notary Public, joined in 1995 and presented *Bread and Cheese for the Medical Men* in 1997. This was a history of Doctors' Commons, both an area of London where Doctors of Law held sway and a Society of those worthies going back to 1494 and lasting until the last elected member, Dr Henry Tristram, died in 1912. As previously noted the tradition of disguising a paper's subject had gradually advanced since the closing years of the 20th century until it was a brave Chatterer who would profess to know what the evening's talk would be about. Certainly *A Tale of the Old West* that Hardingham related in 2002 hid its subject well, being the story of the West Northamptonshire Culworth gang who had terrified surrounding villages for many years before six of them were hanged in 1787. *Jeremiah XXXII 9-10* was a text that gave no additional clue to the uninitiated but proved to be a history of Notaries Public from the 2nd century AD to the present day (the text of the title recounting the recording of a conveyancing transaction) when the Club was surprised to hear there are still about 1100 of these worthies in England. When Hardingham announced in 2007 the title of his next paper was *A Mystery Wrapped in an Enigma* a more erudite member might have assumed it was about Russia, the quotation being a description of that country ascribed to Sir Winston Churchill. It was however the sausage, its history from Sumeria five thousand years ago and its contents, a mystery if ever there was one. Later the same calendar year but at the start of the Club's year Hardingham gave *"The toy that grows with the boy"*, a quotation all members should, but not all did, recognise. The speaker *unfolded the Meccano tale from first marketing in 1901....through the glory days between the wars* and *the end of Meccano production in the United Kingdom in 1981.* Interest in the construction toy is still widespread and many imitators around the world produce their own versions. Hardingham read both these last two papers whilst occupying the post of Tyrannus, breaking a tradition where Club Secretary, Treasurer and Chairman is excused reading a paper or hosting. With low numbers at that time he felt it only right to be included in the calendar. In 2008 the Club was let down by the Summer Meeting speaker being unable to attend with the result Hardingham gave a brief history of the Club's founding with readings from some of the minutes. This *tour de force* gave additional encouragement to the present Tyrannus in his quest of delving deeply into Club records.

Hardingham continued with *What the Vicar Saw* (2009), the Reverend Benjamin Armstrong's chronicles about the market town of Dereham in Norfolk, where he was vicar from 1850, *giving a fascinating insight into early Victorian life.* This had its sequel in 2012 with *After "What the Vicar Saw" (January 2009), What the Rector Did, or The News of the World Would Have Loved Him!* a title exceeding in length the previous record by Hankinson in 1931. In it Hardingham recounted the scandalous affair of Edward Drax Free whose frolics in the early 19th century both horrified and entertained the Club. *As Monty Did* (2011)was a presentation of M R James' ghost story *Canon Alberic's Scrapbook,* read to the Cambridge Chit Chat in 1893 by the author and referred to in Toseland's paper about Monty James three months before. After an introduction by Hardingham and with electric lights turned off and room in soft candle glow the Club listened to a recording of the story read by character actor David Collings. In 2012 Hardingham relocated to Rugby and resigned from the Club the following year. It was appropriate he was elected the first Honorary Chatterer of modern times having drawn up the rules for this office.

Over the years the Club has enjoyed the company of many Notaries Public, one being Christopher Vaughan, Secretary of the Notaries Society of England and Wales. Vaughan joined in 2001 and presented his first paper, *1658 and Still in Print* in January 2004, being an account of *The Compleat Angler* and its author Izaac Walton who lived through the reigns of four monarchs and the Commonwealth until his death in 1683. *Pass the Matches, Matilda* (2005) mystified members but all was revealed on the night, a gripping story of cricket's Ashes from a spoof report in the Sporting Times to their being given substance at the home of Sir William Clarke, whose wife was not named Matilda. The latter was a reference to Belloc, not Dahl, a young lady whose adventures with matches ended in tragedy. 2007 saw a more mundane but nevertheless fascinating account of copyright, the title being ©. Continuing with brevity Vaughan read *A.5* two years later, taking his audience on a journey through space and time *along the Watling Street from Marble Arch in London until the highway is submerged under the M54.* Perhaps one of the most contentious matters ever to have been the subject of a paper *The Last Freedom* (2010) dealt with suicide, or more specifically assisted suicide. After an analysis of the legal position Vaughan concluded *My Last Freedom, I can take my own life but probably you cannot help me.*

Matthew Tasker of Tasker's Management Consultancy for legal practices and son of Tony Tasker, had been a guest on many occasions and was welcomed as a member in 2009. Like his father Matthew attended Marlborough College and having been articled at Browne and Wells in Northampton qualified as a solicitor in 1978. In 2010 under the title *Beam me up Scotty* he *traced the evolution of communication from prehistoric times to the present day, leaving the Club to meditate upon future developments*. The title *Metropolitan Emmental* neatly introduced Matthew's paper of 2012 on the many tunnels under London, carrying rivers, railways and sewers. A bewildered but impressed Club *wandered off* (into the night) *contemplating their capital city being riddled with holes, the Big Cheese rather than the Great Wen*[10].

The latest member of the Club is another Notary Public, Michael Orton-Jones, yet to provide a paper but taking on the onerous duty of hosting a Summer Meeting as his first contribution.

There is no doubt the legal profession will continue to be represented in the Club in the future. With their wide interests and knowledge spreading far beyond the law they have always provided food for thought – and Chat.

NOTES

1. Ince-Jones F. *A Short History of the Chit Chat Club*. 1951.
2. Markham C A. *The Church Plate of Northamptonshire*, 1894. London, Simpkin, Marshall, Hamilton, Kent & Co., Ltd. (50 large & 200 small copies).
   The Stone Crosses of The County of Northampton, 1901. Publ. as above.
3. Markham C A. *The History of the Northamptonshire Militia 1756-1919 by Major C A Markham FSA, the last Captain of F Company, 4th Battalion*. By subscription 1924. London, Reeve and Turner.
4. Northampton and Oakham Architectural Society *Reports and Papers MDCCCXCV, Vol. XX111 Part 1*. Northampton Central Library archives.
5. *The Northampton Independent*. Obituary 1937.
6. *Northampton Daily Echo*, front page Friday January 30th 1925.
7. *Northampton Independent* November 10th 1917. *This Week's Gossip*.
8. *The History of London* (1892) by Sir Walter Besant (1836-1901), prolific writer and champion of the poor. Author of *The Golden Butterfly* (1876)
9. There is no mention until rule 7 of 1950 regarding the length of chat. It may well be an unofficial understanding between members at this date.

10. The Great Wen – A derogatory term for London, originally by William Cobbett, champion of rural England in 1820s. Quoted in Cobbett's Rural Rides (1830) *But, what is to be the fate of the great wen of all? The monster, called, by the silly coxcombs of the press, "the metropolis of the empire".* A wen is a sebaceous cyst, a non-malignant swelling.

10
Doctors, Mad and Otherwise

During the first year of the Club's existence Sanders and Hooper had looked to their colleagues for additional members. There could well have developed an almost exclusively clerical society but fortunately other professions and callings were recruited, notably law and medicine.

It was Dr Richard Greene, joining as a Chatterer in 1886 who started a long tradition of psychiatrists being Club members. He had been appointed to the position of Medical Superintendent at the Berry Wood Asylum in 1878 and in those days would have been responsible for both day to day running of the hospital as well as practising his chosen speciality. The system worked well and lasted until after the establishment of the National Health Service in 1948 when hospital administrators were invented.

During his twenty years in the post he was responsible for overseeing modernisation and development, the management boasting they had never had to pay out on architects' fees whilst Greene was around. It is reported the average cost per patient per week fell from 10s. 6d. (52½p) in 1878 to 7s. 6d. (37½p)[1] when Richard Greene retired in 1897, a model of efficiency in administration. There is no mention of decline in patient care with this 30% cut but in the latter part of the nineteenth century inmates would have had little say in the matter and their relatives could well have been either uncaring or unaware of conditions. It can only be hoped the popularity of Greene inside the institution was as great as that outside. When he retired the local press reported with some surprise that a substantial pension was granted *with practical unanimity* by the County Council. *There are, of course, a great number of people who object to a pension being granted to anyone but themselves* the column writer adds, with feeling.[2]

Ryland Adkins gives a sketch of Greene, full of insight. *Behind the gold-rimmed spectacles and easy smile of Dr Greene there lies a gifted and versatile mind* and in keeping with Club tradition and humour ...*Spite of his surroundings, there is not a trace of lunacy in his conversation. Stranger still to those who believe the current libel on doctors which accuses them of no interest outside their work, he can talk well and pleasantly on almost everything. There is said to be in Northampton and district a private club wherein professional men meet monthly at each other's homes to exchange ideas and hospitality. Unless Rumour lies beyond her wont, Dr Greene has been the life of this society, and, if any essayist should fail or a discussion flag, he can be reckoned on to 'keep the ball rolling' with effect.*[3]

It is possible this last comment refers to the occasion in April 1890 when Bury claimed he was too busy with parish work to write his paper.

Later Adkins opines ... *He is a devotee of that coldest and most cheerless of creeds – vegetarianism.*

The Northampton County Lunatic Asylum at Berry Wood had opened in 1876 at a cost of £162,176. 14s.6d. of which £149, 600 was borrowed. The original Medical Superintendent, Dr. Millson resigned in 1878 and was replaced by Richard Greene. Millson's assistant, Dr. Bowes continued in his post, apparently without rancour at not being promoted, until 1881.

Dr Richard Greene, Tyrannus II
Drawing by W B Shoosmith c.1892

On appointment Greene's salary came to £750 a year (as a rough guide a multiplication factor of 50 may be used in the last quarter of the 19th century to compare with 2012 values) together with a £30 coal allowance. By the time he left in 1897 the annual remuneration had increased to £1200 (£60,000 in 2012 money).[4]

Greene gave a total of fifteen papers during his twenty years' membership of the Club, the last eight as Honorary Member, latterly residing on the island of Jersey. His first talk was on *Facts and fancies of lunacy* (1887) during the last year of Hooper's secretaryship and the second in November 1888 when *The Secretary* [now Greene] *reported that since the October meeting, no one had volunteered to take Green T's place* [he had resigned the month before] *and as he failed to find anyone outside the Club willing to enlighten the members, he would read a paper to them on "Races".*

A Vulgar Error, or Man and his Meat, presented in March 1889 extolling the virtues of vegetarianism unfortunately suffered the fate of almost all readings at this stage in the Club's evolution, there are no details of papers or Chat.

Greene took secretarial responsibilities seriously. If a member was due to read and at the last moment reneged, became ill or moved away it was the Secretary's task to find a replacement. This was often not possible and Greene took it upon himself to step into the breach, as he had done when Green T resigned. Several Tyranni, following in this tradition, have found it advisable to have a paper prepared, just in case. It happened again to Greene in April 1890 when *The Secretary stated that it was Bury's turn to read the Paper; and that on being applied to for the title of the Paper, Bury answered that it would be impossible for him to read as he had engagements connected with his Parish work.*

The Secretary further reported that he had tried to find a substitute, but failed in his attempt. He therefore offered to read a paper on Voltaire at the same time hoping that the members would not think he wished to force himself on the Club. (Cries of "No" from one corner of the room, and silence elsewhere).........

The Paper on Voltaire was then read by Greene, and the discussion which followed was almost unprecedented in the annals of the Club, inasmuch as no one particularly distinguished himself.

In the time he was Secretary Greene read more frequently than was strictly required. A full complement of members meant that with eight ordinary meetings annually and an additional Summer Meeting a maximum of a paper every two years would be expected from each Chatterer. Programmes for each season were printed in advance with the host's name and date. Readers were named but not always the paper title, then as now some members had a tendency to leave writing until the last minute. In addition to occasions already mentioned, in March 1891, four months before he resigned as Secretary, Greene *explained that he had received a letter from* [Canon] *Roberts stating he was not prepared with a Paper and as it did not appear that any attempt had been made to find a substitute, the Secretary saw that there would be no meeting unless he read the Paper himself.*

A Paper "Men and Monkeys" was then read and the usual discussion followed.

It is rarely possible to assess Tyrannus, when both reader and author of minutes, as he tends to denigrate his efforts but the next entry gives some idea of how much Greene was appreciated in the Club.

It was proposed by Tom, Seconded by Sanders and carried that the Secretary be thanked for coming forward at such short notice.

It was further proposed by Adkins, seconded by Jones and carried that the above Resolution appear on the minutes.
The Secretary is well aware that he blushed deeply on receiving such unexpected and undeserved honours and doubtless he blushed equally as much when he read the minutes.
Greene read one other paper during his reign as Secretary. On the earliest programme in the archives, for 1891-2, the Secretary had announced his subject would be *By-Walks of Medicine* but when he came to write up the minutes he recorded it as the more prosaic *an historical sketch of the rise and progress of the Medical Sciences.* The discussion was dismissed as *desultory*, perhaps if he had stuck to *By-Walks* there would have been a more lively Chat.
The first time Jones, as the next Secretary, records Greene as a reader in 1893 he implies an off the cuff performance ….*Greene, with his usual ability, "spoke" his paper on Ivan the Terrible, and the subsequent discussion mainly centred round Russian Local Government, and social conditions.*
At the next three Summer Meetings, all held at Berry Wood, Greene addressed the Club. There was no June or July meeting in 1896 but during April *Greene read a well written paper on "the Wandering Jew" in which there was much new and little true.* In 1894 *Greene…..gave utterance to his views on Population, Pauperism and Production in which he in turn had a tilt at early marriage, unlimited procreation, charities, hospitals &c. but proposed no remedy.* The following year it was by default of Wynter Blyth that Greene volunteered and *read a contribution on "an almost forgotten man." Why Greene did not let the Club know beforehand that he was going to enlighten them on the History of Cavalier, did not appear……Greene proved a true prophet, for the Club had <u>almost</u> forgotten his hero. One member saved the Club, but as his name has*

appeared frequently in the annals, greatly to the wounding of his modesty, it is not set down here. Looking through a list of those present it is likely this would have been Adkins.

In 1897 *Greene ably held forth on what he termed "the root of all evil". His sketch of the origin, uses and other relations of money was characterised by that clearness and individuality which never fail him.* Jones is likely to have had doubts about a third, or fourth, annual paper being presented by the same Chatterer but his choice of reader was evidently vindicated. *The chief feature of the discussion was Green T's question "How were those present to acquire a little more of the commodity in question" and Greene's reply by Assiduous Industry.*

By 1900 Greene had become an Honorary Member and was invited back to read once again at the Summer Meeting with *Twin stars or one......which proved to be an enunciation of the Baconian theory of the authorship of the Plays usually ascribed to Shakespeare. He read it with all his old vigour and lucidity, while his paper evinced great research.* Jones, as Tyrannus, could not help adding somewhat enigmatically.... *It was listened to as all Greene's papers have been listened to, and provoked sharp retort from Adkins.*

The last time Greene addressed the Club at a Summer Meeting was in 1904 when he *discoursed in most interesting fashion, more suo, on Pre Christian Crosses and revealed the extent of his researches by mentioning that he had read or consulted 26 works bearing on the subject.* E M Browne was Tyrannus after Jones' death and made no comments on the discussion and when Greene read his last paper *The Ancient Religion of Egypt* in December 1906 the report was even more terse.*......Greene, an occasional visitor to C.C.C. of which in past days he was so strong a pillar, discoursed in quite his old form on this large and interesting subject, and a good talk ensued.*

Greene was joined at the Berry Wood asylum by Harding in 1889 whose Salary as Senior Assistant Medical Officer was £175 p.a. with beer allowance of £5 and free gas, laundry and vegetables.[5] When appointed Harding was 38 and although having no higher qualifications than his Scotland Bachelor of Medicine and Surgery was soon to obtain his Membership of the Royal College of Physicians (1892) and Doctorate in Medicine (1893).The year following Harding's arrival Greene invited his assistant to give a guest paper to the Club. *The Balance of Nature* evidently passed scrutiny by members as the reader joined in 1891. During the next 15 years he gave seven papers, starting in 1892 with *a most interesting paper on the "Insect and the Flower" and a fair discussion followed...*not the most informative of Jones' minutes as it appears at that time he was more interested in recording Club business than details of papers. Two years later Harding was no better served, he *read an interesting paper on Novels New and Old and the discussion was brisk, at times hot.* By 1896 Jones had developed a style of reporting that included comments and December saw the first reference to the word 'Mad' in the minutes: *Harding gave his paper on "Gleanings, or the humours of a Mad House by an inmate." His racy anecdotes, though sometimes necessarily clothed in unparliamentary language were very amusing and entertaining. The discussion resolved itself into story-telling by other members of the Club, but Harding's were the best.* The term Mad House was a throwback to the days of the Bethlem Royal Hospital, repository for the insane where insanitary conditions combined with the punitive treatment of inmates gave rise to the word 'bedlam'. Eighteenth century Bethlem was most notably portrayed in a scene from William Hogarth's *A Rake's Progress* (1735). Harding was using the term in an ironic manner, echoed by

Jones' minute. The term stuck and became a group name, *Mad Doctors*, for all those Chatterers employed in lunatic asylums, the phrases mental hospital and mental health were yet to be brought into common usage as more politically correct. A certain charm of style was lost when the old appellation fell out of use in the 1940s. Harding had given himself a hard act to follow but in 1898 … *Harding read his paper on the "Predetermination of Sex" or some such title. He treated the subject with his usual skill, & narrated some amusing anecdotes.*

The discussion which followed was brisk, every member having some knowledge of the subject. One member who somewhat actively propounded or upheld theories informed the Club that he had four boys and four girls to whom Harding replied that his practice was excellent whatever may be said for his theories. The member is not identified but Frederick Ince-Jones in his 1951 historical survey names Thomas Beasley, vicar of Dallington, on 'internal evidence'.

1899 produced a reading which can be described as monumental but brief, lasting a mere quarter of an hour. Harding presented *"a Paradox", which was that all apparently unselfish actions were in reality selfish. He contended that a man's conduct was entirely resolvable into the resultant of an amount of force with which he was possessed at birth, and such forces as were brought to bear upon him by his environment, so that under any fresh Circumstances he always took the line of least resistance.* A heady subject but Chatterers always rise to the occasion.

This produced one of the few discussions that Jones summarised in detail, fearing *the Club would regard the minutes as defective were the unusual discussion passed over with the usual silence.* It shows the standard of discussion to be high and gives insight into members' beliefs

... Harding's vital parallelogram of forces provoked Harper's attack. Life was more than a calculable force. Adkins as the priest of Altruism, distinguished between the pleasure derived from self indulgences, and that gratification which arises from seeking the welfare of others. Brown[e] discovered a new test of altruism, viz. whether a man would be willing to "die for his aunt" and introduced a new study in Philhippics, or the counterpart amongst horses of Philanthropy – did it exist? Beasley's deep interest in the maternal strategy of the Partridge in protecting her young rather obscured the line of his argument and took away his appetite for this kind of game till he was assured that the indulgence of the latter did not interfere with the observation of the former.

In 1901 Browne as the new Tyrannus recorded at the Summer Meeting.....Harding proceeded to discourse on Second Sight, which, as he was careful to observe, was a misnomer, not being "second" anything, nor any kind of "sight". Harding, on this occasion, evidently had a lucid interval, to the great advantage of the Club. It became apparent indeed that he didn't know everything about Second Sight (falsely so called), but that what he didn't know wasn't worth knowing.

When Greene retired in 1897 Harding became Medical Superintendent the following year, a post he retained until his retirement in 1925. Although Harding resigned from the Club in 1904 he was unanimously elected as an Honorary Member and continued to attend meetings without the obligation of having to present papers. He did read in 1907 however, with *Apparitions....which reminded one of the famous chapter on "Snakes in Iceland". - There are none....."To see a Spook, you must be built that way" – And the reader's explanation was "Illusion" or*

"Hallucination", the difference between the two being explained by him.

During the 1914-18 war Harding commanded the Military Hospital at Berry Wood with the rank of lieutenant colonel in the RAMC. He retired from Berry Wood in 1925.

Dr. Francis Crookshank arrived at the asylum in 1898 as Junior Medical Officer and was quickly absorbed into the Club but resigned the following year when he left the hospital, becoming Medical Officer of Health in Barnes. He died in 1933. He presented one paper to the Club, *Onomatopoeia*.

Dr. Frederick J Stuart, an 1895 Oxford graduate, also became a Junior MO in 1898 and was promoted to the post of Senior Medical Officer in 1902.

An advertisement of about this time reads:

Berry Wood Asylum Northampton.
Senior Assistant Medical Officer wanted. Salary £200 rising to £250 with board, lodging, washing etc.
Candidates must be under thirty-five years of age, unmarried, and be doubly qualified.[6]

There is no mention here of Harding's beer allowance.

Stuart joined the Chit Chat in 1901 and apart from a break during which he served as major in the RAMC from 1914-18 gave talks for forty four years. Although not required to talk regularly he nevertheless contributed papers after having been made an Honorary Member in 1935.

His first paper in 1902, *Odds in Gambling* centred on *horse races, when, as he ...... informed the Club, the odds were far from even, but that in any case there were always points in favour of the bookmaker. Although Stuart stated that he knew little about horse racing and nothing at all about horses, he certainly knew more about the odds than any member present.*

Three years later came *Virtues, so called* in which ... *murder, compassion; lying, truth; deceit, sincerity; cowardice, courage; were all submitted to critical inspection. Judicial executions, military murders, justifiable homicide, and the massacre at St Petersburgh were successively brought under review. The writer concluded by expressing the opinion that the acts which we characterise as virtues or vices depend for their rightness or wrongness, not so much on their intrinsic nature as on the circumstances of each particular case.*

Stuart only gave three readings that could be considered directly Asylum based. Like so many who worked among the insane Stuart displayed a sense of humour necessary to cope with his institution's conditions. In *Lunacy* (1907) *he showed how easy it was to get into Berry Wood, what a pleasant place it was when "got into" – consequently how attractive to malingerers:- what an amusing crowd was usually to be found there &c. &c. His account of the asylum life and the peculiarities of the inmates was quite entertaining – but the question of family history and heredity gave much occasion for serious reflection.*

Many papers later came *Vice, Insanity & Crime* (1930) when Ince-Jones records Stuart... *was suffering from a grievance, better-founded than the delusions of many of his patients, in as much as an oppressive Tyrannus, conscious of the reader's skill, had called upon him for a paper six months before it was strictly due. This sense of injustice kept cropping up like King Charles' head.*

However, he appeared cheered by the happy memory of an occasion when he had been given the attributes of the Supreme Deity and proceeded to give several learned definitions of insanity all of which he dismissed with a scornful gesture, if not with a divine hand. With

Chit Chat capacity for lateral thought the chronicler continued ... *One member asked ingenuously whether the appropriation of other people's matches was "Vice or Crime or a symptom of incipient Insanity". Next morning the hostess, who was quite unaware of this question, stated that she had placed ten boxes of matches in the room for the meeting, but only five remained at the end!*

November 1939 brought forth *Freudism*, a subject not normally noted for a lighter touch. Tyrannus records....*It was really a humorous but devastating attack on Psycho-Analysis, which he regarded as false and mischievous. He did not doubt that patients recovered but he did not believe the explanation of their recovery. He had never practised psycho-analysis though he had dealt with mental disturbances all his life. He gave a startling example of his power over the fair sex, no doubt specially strong in his earlier life. As a young locum, resplendent a new frock coat, he was called in to deal with a girl suffering from hysterical paralysis. With the authority of a Hitler, he instructed the mother to order the father of the girl to give her a good hiding the moment he entered the house. He then left. There was no need for him to return for the moment 'fayther's hand was on the latch', the girl recovered.*

 He ridiculed the idea of dreams being always unfulfilled wishes, especially with respect of a man who dreamed he had become bald, and he made fine play with the libido of lascivious and incestuous infants possessing the Oedipus complex ....

The discussion …. included the unconscious, dreams, shell-shock memory, Doctors and not a word about Hitler or the war.

Stuart gave several papers not directly concerned with psychiatry. *Mendelism* in 1909 centred on the edible pea *but he also pressed into the service, sheep: horned and hornless, rams and ewes:- fowls with various and comical combs:- and the family of our first parents, ascribing to Adam and Seth brown eyes, to Eve and others blue eyes: and so demonstrating quite clearly what might or might not be expected in regard to the organs of sight of Enos* [biblical son of the 105 year old Seth].

Instinct read in 1912 was apparently matter of fact, not reported in detail by a temporary Tyrannus, Markham.

In Criminal Responsibility (1922) Stuart touched *first on the purpose of punishment, which, in his opinion was manly retributive.*

He passed on to consider the circumstances under which a person committing an offence would be held irresponsible on grounds especially within the scope of the Reader's knowledge and wide experience. Examples of unsound mind included epilepsy, obsessions, delusions &c. Infancy of course was associated with criminal irresponsibility, which during the first seven years is conclusively assumed &c. &c

Belief (1928) was *a witty paper…. Though too light and airy to have much 'substance', it afforded clear 'evidence' of 'unseen' humour …. The paper in no way violated the law of the Club forbidding religious subjects, but its catholicity may be judged by the fact that it dealt faithfully with such varied subjects as spirit photographs, brown bread, the large intestine and Cooke's handwriting. I understand that the last must be seen to be believed and when seen cannot be understood. So is it with all great mysteries!*

In 1943 *Stuart read a characteristic paper on "Character"…..He regarded Action as the summing up and expression of character and discussed the influence upon a man's moral nature of heredity, glands, parental control, books, marriage after long cohabitation, games, drama, the Cinema and wireless.*

The discussion …. was occasionally even more profound than the paper …. such questions as – the Will, Justice, Truth, Beauty,

Judgement, Values, influence of early training and many others which were toyed with …. Tyrannus Ince-Jones concluded ….. *Even if some regard human characteristics as glandular, whereas others think they may be divine, they are still of importance and perennial interest.*

There remains a collection of papers on more miscellaneous subjects. In *Music; by an unappreciative ignoramus* (1914), Stuart explained *His chief inspiration was derived from a visit to the Royal Albert Hall, where he paid one shilling to get shelter from the rain, ……. Persons of weak intellect and their attendants were more addicted than other people to a taste for music: but it did not appear whether or not medical alienists were included in the category. Wagstaff and others ragged Stuart considerably, but did not lead him into the paths of repentance and conformity.*

With *Sir Oliver Lodge's Spiritualism* (1920) Stuart gave *a very critical examination of the book "Raymond" and the position taken up by the author.*[7]

Returning to the factual a paper on *The Bolshevik Revolution* (1924) was well received.

Convention in 1932 proved to be one of those papers that defines the Club and is the bugbear of the historian by its absence in the archives. Fortunately Ince-Jones was present. *Stuart …. discussed Academic Dress, the undesirability of wearing shorts & sand shoes when hunting with the Pytchley, his own equestrian performances on a long-eared quadruped, the table manners of porcupines & his unconventional ideas of music.*

He attempted to find a boundary line between convention, etiquette & morality but his line was very hazy…..

Finally he declared it to be a convention of The Club to leave plenty of time for discussion & his intention rigidly to conform to this convention …. *his conventionality in this respect produced a long and at times very animated discussion …. If at times the Canon* [Trevor Lewis as guest] *went off rather explosively, the explosions certainly contributed to the liveliness of the debate, which covered an area so wide as to include :- the proper use of spoon & fork: double-collars; ladies' underclothing; Cooke's views on widows; and the C. of E. Burial service. It continued until after 11.0 p.m.*

Stuart's *The Causes of the War* in 1934 was *a very thoughtful, well-balanced paper* apportioning blame around Europe generally. *For more remote causes he cited the system of alliances & the commercial spirit.*

In *Shakespeare and Medicine* (1940) Stuart *regarded Shakespeare as possessing the keenest intellect of his time and being very well-informed, so his writings probably gave a fair reflection of the medical science of his age. Nevertheless in spite of references to cobwebs to stop bleeding, Falstaff on the excellence of wine for the liver, Helena as a provider of patent medicine, the value of moderation in diet, the dangers of night air & repressions, it was plain that Stuart had not a high opinion of the medical lore of the Elizabethans.*

The discussion was concerned more with medicine than with Shakespeare. Most of the laymen tried to get free advice from the doctors and were learnedly repulsed without realising it. Ellison made a gallant attempt to get back to Shakespeare with argument as to Lear's madness, but Stuart insisted he was mad all the time.

There is no doubt Stuart enjoyed being contentious. With *In defence of lying* (1945), he suggested *reasons for telling the truth were 1. To satisfy the prejudice of parents. 2. To lessen the demands made on intelligence due to its simplicity. 3. To help in the acquisition and increase of knowledge 4. Etcetera (meaning e.g. propaganda, advertisement, politics and the like…..Instances were given in each of the readers four categories when in his opinion it was proper to dissemble the truth, to decieve* [sic] *one's opponent, and to make life easy and comfortable for all parties.* Inevitably *The age-old question "What is truth?" received no more definite answer than it had received in the past centuries.*

Stuart's last paper was in 1946 when he gave an erudite explanation regarding *Calculating Easter*. Dr Stuart died in 1948.

An interesting sidelight to the history of Berry Wood is that in 1913 the Clerk to the Committee of Visitors was the Chatterer C A Markham, ubiquitous chronicler of all things Northampton, who edited an extended pamphlet *Northampton County Lunatic Asylum Berry Wood and how it was established. A sketch of its history from its opening to March 1913.*

In 1923 Dr Henry Travers Jones, assistant medical officer at the asylum, joined the Club. Although only remaining for two years, after which he moved on eventually to become medical superintendent of the Cambridge County Mental Hospital in 1930, Jones found time to give two papers, on *The descent of some words and customs* (1924), when *Travers Jones read at great pace a long and very interesting paper* and *Labels* (1925), seemingly on a similar theme as *He dealt mainly with the origin and history of words and names,* with Tyrannus adding…..*the ready way in which he answered questions and threw fresh light upon the subject revealed a profound knowledge.*

1927 saw another 'Mad' medical addition to the Club, Dr Edmund D T Hayes, a Dublin graduate who had joined the Asylum staff as assistant medical officer in 1921. Hayes remained a member until he became medical superintendent of Berry Wood in 1940. Although there is no reference to his resigning that year he only attended one meeting which would have forfeited his membership. Hayes gave five papers. In *Rejuvenation* (1928) as *one of the youngest members and in no immediate need of his nostrum, he caused his more aged listeners enviably to lick the chops of anticipation, as he discoursed learnedly on what Steinach had done to rats and what Voronoff had done with wisely selected slices of apes suitably applied to parts of what once were men. He nearly convinced us that with proper management of the ductless glands; here a spot of pituitary; there a touch of thyroid; by a little titillation to the testicle and x-rays to the sex, men o'years might be prolonged in renewed health & vigour to the extent of 25 to 30%.*

In ... *a sparkling discussion ..... Jackson [J]in more pessimistic vein than usual, seemed doubtful whether he wanted his own life prolonged by 25% and sure that he did not want the lives of certain of his contemporaries prolonged by .5%. He had got 'em on a list & they'd none of 'em be missed.*

Some of the younger men were a little anxious about the prospect of old men lingering unwanted upon the scene. Mr Laver was rather sceptical about Steinach's rodents. Did he smell a rat? But, on the whole, members regarded the larger hope a little wistfully, if not furtively, and, though unwilling to make any unholy bargain with Mephistopheles, felt that a longer life in full enjoyment of mature powers would be a not unwelcome gift even from a high-frequency current or a surgeon's scalpel.

Hayes carried on the Mad Doctor tradition with a sideways glance at *Dictatorship versus Democracy* in 1931..... *In order to impress the Club with his beautiful impartiality he treated it to a history of living matter from primordial protoplasm through the amoeba to Mussolini.*

After pointing out that the Hykros Kings in Egypt, the longest continuous dynasty known to civilisation, was apparently produced by the monarchs consistently marrying their sisters, he demonstrated to his complete satisfaction that the true remedy for all social & moral evils was to seek for long-headed dictators with well developed anterior pituitary, thyroid & adrenal glands.

In discussion certain members were a little uncertain about the value & sacredness of democratic control. Jackson, scenting the wobbliness of their liberalism, abandoned a pretence of sleep …. His pleas for liberty and his fine defence of British constitutional methods almost persuaded the new fascists to abandon the hasty idea of making Mr Neville Chamberlain dictator with full power to marry his sisters.

In *The Psychology of Clothes* (1933) Hayes *gave a penetrating analysis of the motives that caused us to clothe – the desire for decoration, modesty and the need for protection …. decoration was the predominant aim in clothing throughout the ages. In modern days women …. were the peacocks, men the dowdy hens. The sober hues & conventional trousers of the members of the Club seemed to give illustration to his dictum, though the yellow waistcoat of Shaw may have exemplified that other occasional primitive function – to strike terror to the heart.*

….. Women were setting an excellent example by wearing next to nothing …. . he made it clear that clothing could be used for purposes the reverse of modest, so that both men and women could be altered so lewdly as to make the undraped human form relatively a model of decency.

….(in) a talk that was well-sustained until 11 o'clock there appeared a restless spirit in the Club, & though at the next meeting there will

probably be no cod-pieces worn, it may be anticipated that the quiet greys & blacks will give place to more brilliant spectroscopic effects.

Points of View (1935) could have been a very pedestrian paper but Hays managed to infuse it with *the attitudes of* [various] *people towards crimes such as theft, murder & cannibalism. Some African tribes regarded theft as a more serious offence against society than murder. He put up an eloquent defence of cannibalism from the cannibal's point of view & assured the members that human flesh was indistinguishable from veal.*

After discussion (of) *marriage customs & Parliament from the point of view of a Moslem, he described the various effects on personality caused by modification of the pituitary & thyroid glands, finishing with a poem on "The gland that rocks the cradle rules the world".*

A good discussion followed ….. but Jackson failed to draw the reader into a pronouncement on the extent of human responsibility.

Hayes' last paper, *Witchcraft* (1937) where *After reading a Papal Bull, extracts from the Mosaic Law and instructions to Inquisitors in the Middle Ages…. he suggested that …. The horned devil was once the god. The witches' broomstick was a vestige of the ancient swords or branches of broom, across which primitive men & women straddled in their pagan dances before their masked god.* Current affairs again were in the minds of members, notably the Second Sino-Japanese war,[8] for Tyrannus notes *The discussion on the paper was very animated. Perhaps at a late hour it strayed slightly from the subject; for Japanese air-bombing has no immediate connection with witchcraft, though it may be pagan……*

The supply of Mad Doctors coming from St Crispin's Hospital, as Berry Wood became known after 1945, dried up, although as will be seen one psychiatrist deserted to join the private St Andrew's Hospital in 1972, a few years before becoming a Chatterer.

*

The parent asylum from which Berry Wood sprang also contributed to Chit Chat membership.

Northampton General Lunatic Asylum was founded in 1838.[9] Following the Lunacy Act of 1808, largely driven by the Home Secretary, Northamptonshire's 2nd Lord Spencer, the way was opened for the establishment of asylums for the insane. With local funding from local worthies and a generous gift from the Northampton Yeomanry the appeal had raised £12,038.18s.9d. by 1833. An area once occupied by St Andrew's Priory on the west side of the town was purchased from Robert Hardy Esq. for £2,900 the following year, over £150,000 today. The first stone was laid in 1836 and the Asylum opened for business on August 8th 1838. Under the direction of Dr T O Prichard it soon expanded to become one of the most foremost, some believed *the* foremost, institution of its kind. During the early years the most famous inmate was the poet John Clare who spent the last 23 years of his life from 1841 living at the asylum, although not confined to it, writing his verse.

Clare would have known the hospital Chaplain, Chit Chat member the Rev. John Cunningham, considered here rather than among clergy. The history of this post and its duties cast an interesting light on Cunningham's character. In 1864 Samuel Charles Haines, curate of Long Sutton, Lincolnshire and one time member of *The Canadian Mission* which gave pastoral care to immigrant Irish and Scottish backwoodsmen was appointed Chaplain with a salary of £250 per annum. He worked hard, two services with sermons each Sunday as well as daily prayers and occasional extra services along with up to 25 a year on Saints' days. He had also been fairly successful in teaching patients to read and write. It is scarcely surprising that in 1868 he requested and was granted six months leave, apparently having suffered a nervous breakdown, on condition he provided a substitute. This was the Rev. R B Woodward, late of Great Houghton, Northamptonshire. Haines finally resigned in November 1886 and Woodward succeeded, still on the same salary and remained until his death in 1875. There were problems finding a successor. The Very Rev. Lord Alwyne Compton, vice-chairman of the hospital management committee supported a vote to increase a Chaplain's salary to £400 but this was overruled by Lord Charles Fitzroy in an amendment stating not only the salary should remain at £250 but the Chaplain should undertake no duties outside the Asylum nor take pupils. John Cunningham, ordained at Ripon in 1872, curate at Holy Trinity Bingley, was appointed Chaplain to the asylum in January 1876, aged 34. The following year he was granted a general diocesan licence by the Bishop of Peterborough. It says a lot for his devotion to the hospital that he remained in the post until retiring in 1911 with no salary increase although there was a 'maximum pension', amount unrecorded. In the meantime other posts such as medical superintendent and medical officers had received substantial rises. It is worth noting his successor the Rev. E J Whitall was appointed at only £310 annually, £90 less than that suggested in 1875.

Cunningham, a loyal member of the Club from 1891 presented 12 papers. The first in 1894 was entitled *Backsheesh* in which *It was a remarkable fact that all those present had experience on the subject from the givers point of view. The discussion was, however, saved from being one sided by Adkins, who accepted a brief on behalf of tipping, & drew forth high moral utterances from Beasley & Mr Church* (a visitor, W H C Church was elected to the Club later that year).

Two years later Cunningham gave …. *a short paper on "Success in Life"* after which *Much difference of opinion was expressed as to the part "opportunity" took in the attainment of success. The combined acumen of the Club & the visitors did not eventuate in a satisfactory definition as to what Success in Life was.*

1898 saw the *History of Pickwick's production & formed an admirable prelude to a Pickwickian debate. The first part of the time given to discussion was devoted to a coaching up of the Club for Calverley's examination on that Classic*[10], *& the members proved themselves well up in the subject.*

Historical Names of London Streets (1900), *English Surnames* (1901), *Old London Taverns* (1913) and *Life in London 150 years ago* (1915) were all largely documentaries.

In 1903 *Cunningham held forth, with profit to his hearers, on nicknames, but including therein many observations on surnames in general. A general conversation followed, in which it need hardly be said the name of Mr Joshua Bugg occurred.*[11]

In *Some Changes during the Nineteenth Century* (1906) it was noted *Unfortunately the lecturer would not commit himself to any statement as to the improvement or deterioration of the said manners and customs, and the club were therefore not able to criticize in the way they would have wished.* Such restrictions did not normally stop members saying what they felt.

Cunningham's next two papers reflected his calling. *Curiosities in connection with Marriage* (1908) was *chiefly concerned with the whims, and vagaries ….. of the British people. Marriages in the Fleet, runaway matches blessed by the far famed Blacksmith and numerous other matrimonial eccentricities …… while the sale of wives, for whom their owners had no further use, appealed to practical men as a cheaper & simpler mode of cutting the connubial knot than a resort to Courts of law.*

Two years later Cunningham regaled members with *Strange Bequests,* including those *of odd and quaint dispositions, especially those of a charitable nature including marriage portions awarded by ballot at St. Ives (Hunts) – casting dice for Bibles; the foundation of the famous Lion Sermon at St. Katherine Crees.*[12] *Also he quoted from wills of a spiteful character, such as one of a testator who described his wife as an "old pig" – another whose spouse was likened to a "vinegar cruet".*

Cunningham had retired from St Andrew's Hospital as it was now titled in 1911 but continued his Club membership, giving his last paper *Tailed Men* in 1917, *with which Travellers' Tales seemed to be closely associated. Not pledging himself to the historical truth of numerous narratives and incidents which found a place in his paper, he yet led the Club to exhibit a lively interest in the subject......*

John Cunningham died in 1923.

During the 1860s the mixture of pauper and private patients had caused problems and a new hospital was built in the village of Berry Wood, to the east of Northampton town. Its austere brick appearance and clock tower, a western landmark for the town, still in ruins in the midst of a housing estate, contrasted strongly with the more graceful classical stone design of the previous establishment. In 1876 the old asylum became the *St Andrew's Hospital for Mental Diseases for Middle and Upper Classes.*

Chit Chat membership at St Andrew's did not extend to medical staff until Dr Thomas Tennent, Medical Superintendent from 1938, at a salary of £2000 p.a. and generous allowances, joined the Club in 1942. He had studied at the universities of Glasgow, London and John Hopkins, Baltimore, USA. On appointment Tennent was allowed to retain his lectureship in Psychological Medicine at London University. During 28 years at the St Andrew's he oversaw treatment changes in schizophrenia including insulin and cardiazel (shock) therapy, ECT (electro-convulsive therapy) and, with reservations, prefrontal leucotomy. Tennent's first papers, Compensation (1943) *dealt with the subject, not from a legal point of view in the sense of recompense or repair for injury, but psychologically ..... as in some cases of heart lesion ... muscles of the heart became enlarged and .... hypertrophy compensated for the injury, mental compensation took place; small men tried by a loud voice and blustering manner to make up for physical inferiority. Sometimes the effort to assert superiority led to unpleasant neurotic symptoms: there was over compensation.*

The Arts gave many examples of special energy seeming to arise to compensate physical infirmity..... Sullivan, Keats, Ruskin, Michael Angelo, Byron, R. L. Stevenson, the Bronte's and Jane Austen. Sometimes genius was associated with mental disorder, as with Rousseau, Strindberg, Van Gogh, Cowper & Clare.

This suggestive paper gave rise to a good discussion, which centred on such difficult subjects as – Thought, the Mind, the pre-conscious, Genius, Insanity....it was lively, well-sustained and compensated for frequent wanderings from the subject of "Compensation".

Three years later, on March 29th 1946 when John Williamson, Chief Constable of Northampton Borough Police Force from 1923-55 was present as a guest Tennent gave his second recorded paper *Idle Hands*, examining the association of mental abnormality with crime. He focussed on recent sharp increases in crime, *caused by the unsettlement of war, the presence of many deserters from the forces and the shortage of goods.* In development of his thesis *There should be closer cooperation between the legal & medical professions with a view to discovering how far mental disturbance was co-related to crime.* Further, *Punishment had no deterrent effect on psychopathic individuals and served only to render them increasingly bitter against society .... Psychiatry should be used to help the law but not to displace it..... During the discussion lack of parental control, the weakening of moral standards owing to the decline in religious observance were mentioned as contributory causes of crimes. It was also urged that while punishment might possibly be ineffective in reforming the criminal, it served a useful purpose as a deterrent to others. No habitual criminal was present to give his point of view though many members confessed their own youthful peccadilloes.* There is also no record of the Chief Constable's thoughts.

It would appear Tennent left the Club in the first half of 1947 although his resignation is not minuted but his short period of membership had contained two stimulating papers. Thomas Tennent died suddenly whilst on holiday in Switzerland in 1962.

Andrew Graham, founder Fellow of the Royal College of Psychiatrists, became the last Mad Chatterer in the late 1970s, having left St. Crispin's Hospital, the successor to Berry Wood Asylum, in 1972 where he had been a consultant psychiatrist since 1953 and spent 16 years as Medical Superintendent. He *contributed fifty years of his life to psychiatric care* [and] *transformed St Crispin's from a lunatic asylum into a modern mental hospital*[13]. St Crispin's loss was St Andrew's gain. It is unfortunate the only paper of Graham's to survive in the Club's Dark Age is from 1981, *Broadmoor – without limit of time*. Having discussed ways in which patients might be admitted to this secure hospital, not to be regarded as a prison, by the courts Graham went on to discuss *some ten patients with whom I have had the privilege to meet* [in his capacity as an approved psychiatrist on Mental Health Tribunals] *in order to help them, however little, with their problems, if at all* [these last words in pen as an afterthought, the paper is in typescript]. The patients were lucky, Andrew had, in the words of a General Practitioner colleague *an uncommon amount of common sense* [14].

There is one other Mad Doctor documented as being at St Andrew's. Peter Eames, a Cambridge graduate held the post of Consultant Psychiatrist but his membership of the Club was probably brief, there are no papers recorded during this period of the 1980s.

Nine members of the Club associated with mental care contributed over 60 papers, mostly in the first half of the Club's history.

*

Having dealt with the Mad Doctors it is time to consider members of the profession in the free community outside Berry Wood and St Andrew's Hospital. Of these, 26 known Chatterers produced a total of nearly 100 recorded papers and no doubt there were more in the Dark Ages after 1949 when medical Club members were at their most prominent. Although scattered among the General Infirmary (General Hospital), general practitioners and local authority Medical Officers of Health it is less confusing, if possible, to deal with them in a chronological order rather than in their various callings. This is especially so as in early days a doctor might fall into more than one category. Cropley, a Fellow of the Royal College of Surgeons, enjoyed private practice in 1896. He also held a Public Health qualification as Medical Officer to the Kingsthorpe Rural District Council and found time to act as Medical Officer to the Northampton Workhouse.

*

Early doctors did not remain long as Club members. Until the end of Edward VII's reign in 1911 only two of those actively engaged in community or general hospital practice contributed more than four papers.

Arthur Jones, Honorary Physician to Northampton Infirmary and third Tyrannus, gave five papers starting with *The Human Voice* (1887) where he *illustrated in a very practical and interesting manner.*

In September 1889 a *Paper was read by Jones on "Vegetarianism", being a reply to Greene's paper on the same subject read at the Meeting in March* [A Vulgar Error, or Man and his Meat]. *A long discussion followed, but the chief opponents failed to convince each other.*

The next two readings, *Physical Abnormalities* (1891) and *The Infirmary Sequi-centenary* (1893) are merely listed as is Jones' last, *Spectrum Analysis* in 1897. In 1895 however he ventured into unknown territory with *Atoms and the vortex theory of their origin* (1895), where *Jones tried to be scientific and the Club would talk metaphysics, while everybody acknowledged to being a bit out of his depth,. The general tendency was for every member to seek to explain what he did not understand. It was a most interesting discussion.* A modern reference[15] states: [This Vortex] *theory, advanced by Thomson (Lord Kelvin) on the basis of investigation by Helmholtz, that the atoms are vertically moving ring-shaped masses (or masses of other forms having a similar internal motion) of a homogeneous, incompressible frictionless fluid*. It was the precursor of 20th century string theory. This ordinary mortal is still out of his depth.

Dr Arthur Jones died in harness as Tyrannus in 1901.

Dr Alexander Wynter Blyth is not mentioned in Ince-Jones' 1951 list of those who 'made good' but is one of the Club's unsung heroes. Wynter Blyth was born in 1844, the son of a Woolwich surgeon. Educated at King's College, London he showed interest in chemistry, obtaining his membership of the Royal College of Surgeons. He entered the field of Public Health becoming Medical Officer of Health and Public Analyst for St Marylebone, London as well as Public Analyst for the county of Devon. Later he was appointed President of the Incorporated Society of Medical Officers of Health and Registrar of the Royal Sanitary Institute. Branching out he became a barrister-at-law of Lincoln's Inn, London. One of his best known works is *Poisons: their Effect and Detection* (2 Vols. 1885), still referred to today. Wynter Blyth holds the distinction of having read all his eight papers at consecutive Summer Meetings. After his first paper on *Poison Law, old and new* in 1887, the year he joined the Club ..... *conversation, in which most members and visitors joined, took a very wide range – from Cleopatra to Pasteur and from the Rugeley murder case* [16] *to the use of hypodermic poisons in Sensation novels.*

The germ theory of disease (1888) and *A Grave Affair* (1889) were followed in 1890 when ... *the Secretary instinctively asked Blyth to forsake the pomp and vanities of a London Season and come to this Hill-top* [Berry Wood] *to enlighten the Club. Blyth consented, as he always does, and said he would turn the full blaze of his Scientific mind on the dark, mysterious subject of Hypnotism,...*

The Determination of Sex (1891) .... *provoked a long discussion.*

In May 1892 ....*when arranging for this* [Summer] *meeting the Secretary's* (Greene at this time, one of his last tasks) *thoughts fled straight away to a paradise of Health, Comfort and Learned ease in Marylebone where sits a man great in all things and especially in little things like microbes and parasites. Need the Secretary say that he alludes to Wynter Blyth, who with his usual kindness consented on a morn to lighten our darkness; but on some further Correspondence it turned out that he also insisted upon darkening our light for he, politely but very firmly refused to speak to us unless all the rays of the Sun (the glorious orb, he called it) could be excluded from the room. The members of the Club and the welcome guests will unite with the Secretary in respecting this evidence of modesty:- rare even in an eminent man of Science*

The reasons for the darkened room were explained in Browne's minutes:

After Business Blyth talked of Parasites, from the newly discovered intra-cellular protozoa, to tape worms and measly pork; illustrating his remarks by means of the Blackboard, Lantern & Microscope. The avidity with which the members attacked the subject in the after discussion, demonstrated their large experience of – flukes, et <u>*hoc genus omne*</u>.

Blyth was thanked for coming so far to introduce us to the creatures we might possibly become hosts to ….

His last lecture, no details recorded, was *Sanitary Law* (1893). In March the following year Wynter Blyth regretted he was unable to present the paper that year but continued to attend meetings until July 1895 when he regretfully gave up his membership. He died suddenly in January 1921 and as his obituary recorded.... *Outside his work Wynton Blyth took a lively interest in everyday affairs, was a genial companion, an enthusiastic motorist, and latterly a not unsuccessful farmer.*[17] He left a widow and three children.

Robert Milligan is reported as having entered Northampton General Infirmary as a pupil in 1875 at the tender age of 16. He qualified as a doctor in 1881 in London and returned to Northampton three years later as House Surgeon and was appointed Surgeon in 1884. During the 1914-18 war Milligan forsook private practice for service in the RAMC at Cambridge Military Hospital for which he was awarded the OBE. He continued to work until 1926, two years before his death, taking an active part in local affairs, including sitting as a magistrate. In 1888, the year following his election as a Chatterer, Milligan presented his only paper, *Modern Treatment of Wounds*. Two years after retirement Milligan suffered a seizure outside the George Row Club when about to start his car.[18]

Another doctor to receive an OBE was George Percival, the third of four generations of medical men, who, already mentioned, joined the Club in 1891. In 1893 Percival *enlightened the Club on Sewage matters. The discussion was for a time well maintained, but finally became desultory.* Two years later *Percival read an interesting but blood curdling paper on Chinese Medicine and Sanitation, which went far to reconcile the members to the existing state of Medical Science in the country.* Percival allowed his membership to lapse in 1896 and died in 1939.

Peverell Smythe Hichens, a Member of the Royal College of Physicians, held the post of Consultant Physician in Northampton for over 25 years. His first paper, *Death,* appeared in 1904, two years after joining the Club, dealing with 'The King of Terrors' both in Man and lower forms of life.

In 1905 he *discoursed with his usual success on the open air treatment for Tuberculosis,* (his speciality) *as applied to the poorer classes.*

His personal experiences of Nordrach and its methods were particularly interesting, but the kind and quality of the provender compulsorily consumed by the afflicted patients did not appear attractive to the frugal habits or refined palates of the ordinary

Englishman. A long and improving discussion followed upon the paper in general and upon the provision of institutions for open-air treatment. This paper was taken from an article by Hichens in the British Medical Journal of March 1903 regarding treatment for pulmonary TB started in Nordrach, Germany by Dr Otto Walther in 1888. Readers of Thomas Mann's 1924 novel *Der Zauberberg* (The Magic Mountain) will be familiar with open air treatment of TB and may agree with Hichens' view in his 1903 lecture[19] *I do not think it necessary to send out patients to sit for hours in the woods in the worst weather. It is perfectly true they never seem to get colds, even if they get thoroughly wet, but, judging from my own experience, they certainly often feel miserable, and may suffer severely from rheumatism as I did.*

In 1907 the Secretary (Browne) was guarded in his minute. *Hichen[s] read a carefully prepared paper on Men and Women, in which the several characteristics, virtues and vices of the Sexes were dealt with in a masterly manner, and the discussion which followed was instructive.* The last of Hichens' four papers, *Pain* described *an insoluble mystery, with which the world was always confronted; there was no escape from it....Keeping clear of theological controversy, the writer yet referred to varying views concerning pain in its relation to God's dealings with man. In a physiological sense "Pain is Nature's Danger Signal".... in the brisk conversation which followed, Hichens' dictum was generally accepted: that "all suffering has a redemptive power". Pain, far from being unmixed evil, was often a great blessing.* Hichens resigned from the Club in 1921 in spite of members' entreaties, no reasons were given and eventually retired to Guernsey in 1930 where he died the same year.[20]

Honorary anaesthetist at the Northampton General Infirmary Frank Wagstaff joined in 1907 and gave five papers, the first being

Precocity in 1909 when *The reader gave the views of many eminent men on this subject ranging from those who, like Crichton Browne* [21] *[already met in chapter 4], "take an extremely grave view" of Precocity, and others regarding it as "usually pathological, morbid, atavistic" – to the more optimistic members of the medical profession (including, it would seem, the learned reader himself) – whose estimate of the Infants Phenomenon was far more hopeful, in respect of that young person's prospects. The after talk, if somewhat discursive at times, shewed a keen interest in the subject. (24 minutes)*

In 1911 came *A pathological view of Lying and inebriety.* There are no manuscripts extant from this time but fortunately Browne continued his habit of summarising texts as well as noting the time taken by the speaker:

He threw much light on Liars of various grades and qualities: Liars who lie wide awake, with eyes open:- born liars who lie because they must, and perhaps unconsciously; Liars whose weakness is in combination with Hysteria, or with Alcoholism. In elucidating what he termed "pathological drunkenness" he traced a connection between the alcoholic habit and mental defects of various kinds, including those with a criminal tendency. The paper lasted 29½ minutes and gave rise to a brisk conversation.

Like many an anaesthetist Wagstaff dabbled in matters philosophical. With *Self-tillage* (1913) he …. *pointed out that great interest was shown, at the present day, in "culture", resulting in part from the introduction of free education & cheap literature, the twin keys of the Temple of Knowledge …. "culture has a high mission, which is no less than the emancipation of mind and soul, with a view to the development of all their powers and emotions". The writer lamented ….. slavish devotion to the idea of Specialisation, …. that* *one man would give his whole life to the study of the Dative Case, while another would concentrate, not on the "Order of Beetles", but on <u>one</u> of the Species [150,000 in number] of that Order.... Wagstaff insisted* (also*) that physical balance (in other words true bodily health) should also be sought for and attained.*

Although he was called away *on a professional errand* Wagstaff managed to give a factual paper with *the Coroner and his Court* in *The Crowner's Quest* in 1914.

Appropriately for the third year of war Wagstaff read another descriptive paper in 1917, *RAMC* (Royal Army Medical Corps).

Wagstaff found it difficult to undertake the duties of membership, and reluctantly resigned in October 1919. He died in 1956, aged 90.

The next doctor outside the Mad circle to join the Club was E Meredith Davies MD, in 1929. He paid his entrance fee of 2s. 6d. in March along with an annual subscription of 1s. 6d. and attended regularly until October when it was announced he was moving to Devon, which he did without hosting or reading.

Basil Laver was appointed Honorary Assistant Surgeon at Northampton General Hospital in 1927 and Honorary Surgeon (Consultant Surgeon today) in 1931. He entertained the Club in 1930, the year he joined, with *Devils, Drugs and Doctors, a most interesting summary of the progress of medical and surgical science....and dealt among other subjects, with expectation of life, dissection, haemorrhage, anaesthesia, infection, faith healing, hygienic therapy, and drugs.* [We] *ranged ourselves on the side of the angels (the doctors and drugs) and vowed to renounce the devils.*

In 1933 Laver explored *Waves*, an attempt to make *the Quantum Theory and Relativity as clear as crystal......with similes, culled possibly from the Children's Encyclopaedia, such as that the relative crowding of the electron in an atom was about the same as that of 8 wasps in Waterloo Station.* Enigmatically he concluded *with Prospero's statement "We are such stuff as dreams are made of".*

Basil Laver had the makings of a great Chatterer and *The untimely death* [at the age of 40] *of this well-loved member was universally mourned* in January 1935.

Nineteen thirty one and Eric Shaw, Consultant Physician and Pathologist at Northampton General Hospital was elected to the Club. He gave six papers over the next thirteen years, never failing to talk on subjects of interest. His first was *Eugenic Sterilisation* and it is to be regretted members' opinions were recorded under an umbrella of anonymity. Shaw postulated that due to the increased number of people with mental defects and *80% of these suffering from defect in germ cells and most of them* [having] *neuropathic antecedents .... there was grave danger of the country being swamped by undesirables.* This was due to *the fertility of these classes, who did not use birth control, and the fall in the birth rate of the higher social classes.* Having recommended sterilisation, which he admitted might be against the law in 1932, *the discussion that followed was animated and sustained. It was remarkable too because it never wandered from the point.* The idea of segregation in colonies was put forward.[22] *One highly valued member produced evidence that appeared to prove by all the laws of medical wisdom he ought never to have been born and the rest of us shuddered at the thought.* Voluntary sterilisation for those *suffering from all kinds of transmittable defects* was suggested but others feared *such action would lead to the extinction of the human race.* The minute ends with one member waxing indignant *in the name of liberty of the subject that the State should put any barrier in the way of his self-mutilation.* It was evidently a thought provoking evening.

With *Glands and Personality* Shaw dealt *more with the effects of the Endocrine Glands than with Personality* and with *the controlling influence of the anterior pituitary upon other glands provided a fascinating story for the lay members.* This was in 1934 and …. *Although Tyrannus ruthlessly prevented any further debate upon Hitler, cleverly disguised by a pretence of discussing his glands, the conversation continued in an animated manner until 11.15 p.m. & members returned home far too late to purchase flowers or chocolates as peace offerings to their wives.*

Nineteen thirty six saw Shaw in fine fettle with *Old Age* for …. *If any body expected quotations from Cicero or Browning on the delights of growing old, he was disappointed, but in nothing else. Though "Rabbi Ben Ezra" was not mentioned, there were poetical extracts, including the immortal "Father William".* He considered the …. *immortality of paramaecea, though whether there is much immortality in being bisected every few minutes remained another question….* he even *gave tips for reaching old age; some possible, others less hopeful, such as :- choose your parents well; avoid worry; take reasonable exercise; live in the open air & cultivate new interests. In an atmosphere dense with smoke, he relieved the feelings of those present by telling them that there was no evidence that tobacco shortened life appreciably. He was less re-assuring on alcohol. Less wine than usual was drunk… After such a paper …. Even Shapland's cynical remark; that all progress was an illusion, passed almost unrebutted. The company hardly seemed to care; they were getting old.*

In 1939 Shaw asked the question *Is Man a Machine?* and Tyrannus Ince-Jones found *a proper summary is impossible in the time permissible…. In the main, without answering his own question, he* [Shaw] *dealt with the workings of some of the mechanisms that seem to have play in human life. He discussed learnedly the mechanism of heredity; breeding, eugenics, Mendelism, genes, chromosomes & development, yet he would not express an opinion on the old question whether acquired characteristics are transmissible.*

Dixon substituted for Ince-Jones as Tyrannus in 1941 when *Shaw read an admirable paper on "Time, the Tyrant", thus introducing a new Tyrannus in the absence of the old….*

It was a very able and partially comprehensible paper; its purpose being to give a précis of the recent book by one of the Honorary Members of the Club, A. P. Shepherd, "Time and Eternity" with special reference to his religious point of view….. The discussion …. rather veered from the question of time and eternity to that of judgement & self judgement in eternity, with a tendency to recur to Hitler.

Time had a tendency to fade out of the discussion, until at 7. o'clock the Club was reminded of it. It will be remembered that during wartime meetings were held during the day. It was not until 1948 Dr Shepherd returned to give his paper on his book.

It was Monday 28th February 1944 when Shaw gave his last paper, *Possibilities*, asking *whether a free world was possible. Was democracy damned?* The idea of Public Schools had been *attacked because of jealousy, as perpetrating a caste system, producing the wrong types and over emphasising the body, but though possibly too exclusive, they had provided men of character. How could the best of the Public School system be spread through all classes?*

Despite an unprecedented request from Dixon for the paper to be read for a second time *the members preferred to embark upon a sea of talk. Public Schools, Democracy, Moral Ideals, Naziism, and many other topics were dealt with and practically everybody made a useful contribution.*

John Mackintosh, County Medical Officer of Health, made a brief appearance at the Club, contributing a paper on *Housing* in 1935 before moving to Edinburgh where he became Chief Medical Officer in the Department of Health. He also held the post of Emeritus Professor in Public Health at the University of London from 1944. In 1945 Mackintosh returned to address the Summer Meeting, July 5th, on *New Houses for Old.* Ince-Jones recorded:

Raynsford's garden and Mrs Raynsford's hospitality constituted a Midsummer Day dream which Dr Mackintosh endeavoured to turn into a Midsummer Night-mare by his recital of the horrors of housing in this country. The houses of the working classes were the worse heated in the modern world. The open fireplace was dirty, wasteful and expensive. The houses were also the smallest and worst insulated in the modern world. The plumbing was primitive they had the poorest kitchens and equipment In the U.S. 75% of such houses were fitted with baths, electric washing machines rustless steel sinks & capacious cupboards Here in this country much emphasis was laid on structure but little on function.

The reader's main suggestion for betterment was a modern stove in place of the open fire place. He declared that the official mind was 25 years behind the times and impervious to the infiltration of new ideas. The company broke up in an atmosphere of philanthropic energy tempered with philosophic calm in view of the inevitability of graduations in bettering existing conditions.

The vision of a future where everything would be bright and cheerful, a Brave New World, was emerging with the end of the Second World War in Europe having been declared two months earlier. Forward looking innovators had come forth to take over establishment dinosaurs and with Mackintosh being 64 at the time not all were as young as might be expected.

Stuart Humfrey became a member in 1940. As a consultant ophthalmic surgeon he was well placed to read on *The Human Camera* two years later:

He blended essential information, illustrated by diagrams and specimens, with many light touches of humour and wisdom. At various times false eyes, tests for colour blindness & a bottle, containing lenses that had been removed from human eyes because of cataract & looking like small acid drops, were passed from hand to hand...... he dealt with a number of interesting points. These included ...... mediaeval treatment for eye defects, which happily included chastity on the part of doctor as well as patient; the Cyclops, which he dismissed as fabulous; and butterflies' eyes. .....After a description of the difficulties overcome by a one-eyed pilot of an aeroplane, he told us that Joe Davis, the champion snooker player, had only one useful eye, but this probably improved his play!

A number of points came up for discussion .... the effect of tobacco smoking; vitamins; the yellowing vision of old age, as affecting the work of artists, and being well-caught in the deep field by a man with a pronounced squint.

In 1945 Humfrey gave a particularly unsympathetic talk for a Chatterer. He *read a very interesting paper on Gipsies. Although he had chosen this subject and quoted from Borrow and Lady Eleanor Smith, who certainly had partiality for the Zingare, he did not seem to be inspired by any undue admiration for them; indeed, he attacked them with unremitting scorn... Though admitting their picturesqueness and disserting learnedly on their mysterious origins, he dealt more upon their dirt, their thieving ways, poaching, pickpocketing, and cannibalism and, though he acquitted them of the charge of kidnapping, so often levelled against them, and praised their horse medicine and abortifacients, he left little doubt in the minds of his hearers that he regarded them as a bad lot…...some members tried to put up a defence for these wandering tribes. They even confessed to an occasional desire to throw their caps over the hedge and be off with "The raggle-taggle gipsies O!" Interest was shown in the extent to which gipsies were free from the ordinary burdens of rates and taxes, their good fortune in being free from the tyranny of the Church, Law, Medicine and Education, their undoubted good health.* Unfortunately who the *some members* were is not recorded.

His third paper *Reminiscences of a Mother* (1949) was an early example of obscuring the subject of a paper by its title. Ince-Jones records:

Thus, from the outset, any idea that he was going to be mildly maternal with a time when he was a "Mother" was dispelled. He was entomologically rather than gynaecologically minded....Not only did he convince us that mothing was an interesting, healthy hobby with many aesthetic attractions, but by his accounts of hunting tiger-moths in the jungle, elephant hawks in the forest, death-heads in the dark and proud purple emperors over the tree-tops he introduced romance.

His tales of capturing eggs barely visible to the naked eye; of luring emperors by rotten rabbits; the amazing life-cycle of the large blue, the wonderful way in which plagues of cabbage white butterflies were prevented by ichneumon flies; the mating which took place almost as soon as the females were hatched, before they could fly; the cause of sexual attraction, which he thought could not be smell, because the males often flew against the wind to find their mates .... were among the topics he introduced. He concludes....

A very interesting paper....only an intimation that The Club was usually closed at 11.0. p.m. caused the members to disperse with reluctance.

How long Humfrey continued as a Chatterer is not known. There are no minutes between 1949 and 1964, only some Club programmes in which Humfrey last appears, as host, in 1951.

*

Ralph Owen (Roley) Lee entered the Club in January 1944. Consultant Surgeon at Northampton General Hospital since 1935 Lee soon became a regular reader at meetings with sideways glances at medical matters, starting with *The Citadel* in 1946, *a spirited defence of the medical profession designed to dispel any lingering doubts resulting from the aspersions in Cronin's book 'The Citadel'.*

With the National Insurance Act of 1946 and creation of a Welfare State along with the possibility of a National Health Service in Britain this was a topical matter. A J Cronin in 1937 had painted a picture of dedication by a doctor in South Wales treating the tuberculous poor and his subsequent move to Harley Street, abandoning high principles in favour of money. The book had been made available to a wider audience in 1938 with King Vidor's Oscar winning film starring the four Rs, Robert Donat, Ralph Richardson, Rosalind Russell and Rex Harison. Lee considered the Wales' section to be fairly accurate *but in the final section dealing with Harley St and specialists Cronin had expressed dangerous half-truths. In medicine as in other walks of life there were rackets, ramps & charlatans. The orange cure, removal of gall stones without operating, better sight without glasses, & long series of expensive injections giving transient relief to patients were mentioned....The Paper was followed by a keen discussion. It was suggested that in medicine as in other branches of learning the heresy of yesterday had, on occasion, proved to be the orthodoxy of today ..... It was a stroke of genius on Lee's part to bring as a visitor (or Exhibit) Dr Noel Stone a prototype of one of the many characters in the Citadel & described therein (under another name) as being addicted to strong drink. He protested that this was mere literary licence and was, like the rest of the visitors, on this occasion quite sober!*

Nineteen forty nine and .... *In the printed programme his subject appeared as "Medicine Men" but it proved to be "The National Health Service".... even his sweet reasonableness and his quotations in French & Latin could not disguise the fact that he regarded the new scheme as ill-conceived to a large extent unnecessary, dangerous to the medical profession and sure to prove so appallingly expensive that it was likely to break down....* After a summary of Health Care by the state prior to 1945 *Under the new Act doctors were threatened with restrictions of personal freedom, destruction of morale, overwork, lowering of professional standards & loss of income.... If the money being spent on the new scheme had been devoted to food & housing, the health of the community would benefit more.* In the discussion .... *Except on minor points, everybody seemed roughly in agreement with Lee, though some thought the doctors would not do too badly and many wished they had taken up dentistry or making spectacles, when they were younger.*

In 1952 Lee spoke on *Anything but Medicine* and with the absence of records the content may only be guessed at......

With scanty records in the years of Jackson and Lee being Tyranni it is impossible to give accurate accounts of papers read. In Lee's 40 years with the Club there are only seven of his recorded and even fewer detailed.

In 1966 Roley recounted a *visit to Russia that he had made with the Surgical Sixty Club (1960) a group of general surgeons The Commentary was admirably illustrated by slides. They travelled by air and did not seem to be much impressed. They stayed in hotels & were profoundly impressed by the general lack of anything approaching a welcome or interest in guests The food on the whole was poor, with little indistinguishable meats & chips with everything He did not comment much on the surgical side of things – perhaps as well, as we might not have understood.*

In 1980 Lee made two visits to Jordan, giving a paper on both to the Club in October. There are no minutes but Lee's handwritten manuscript, in characteristic but rather untidy capitals, is fortunately in the archives. The first was a Swan Hellenic Tour with his wife Julia in which he gave a tourist's view of the country. The second, a month or so before the paper, was another Surgical Sixty Club outing. Coincidence being rife in these memoirs, Lee commented that the Medical Director of the Royal Jordanian Medical Services, Major General Hanania, was once a house officer and registrar to a Chit Chat member and they received VIP treatment. There was much sightseeing as well as professional engagements. One is significant.

Official visits to hospitals do not tell one much about the patients and their treatment. Amman was no exception; we saw a lot of people, of both sexes in uniform, mostly standing around doing nothing, very few patients, many empty beds and not a single operation in progress.

Between these two travel papers came *Sex Education*, chiefly notable for Lee's *personal reminiscence of a visit to a nudist colony at St. Tropez which led him to realise the fundamental truth that nudity is clean and wholesome and obscenity lies in covering up. He instanced the anticlimax of Strip Tease and pointed out that the clothing and entertainment industries were vitally concerned in suggestivity.*

After *making a plea for universal teaching of biology in schools from the age of seven* along with country visits *to see the natural processes at work* he suggested that *Biology might well replace Old Testament Scripture as a basic subject for the 'O' level examination.* Lee went further with another *plea for special classes of instruction for engaged and newly married couples to be included in the extra-mural curriculum of technical colleges.* It is scarcely surprising *the paper provoked a lively discussion.*

The last title of Lee's to be recorded is *Flowers that bloomed in the spring* in 1986. *This outlined the early development of man, and described the origin of the crops upon which he was largely to depend...... There was apprehension about CO_2 in the upper atmosphere but opinion was divided as to whether it would make the world colder or hotter. On the question of whether another ice-age impended the club was wisely non-committal.*

Ralph Lee died in 1993 and at the November meeting ... *flowers were sent to Lee's widow Julia on behalf of the Club. She sent a letter of appreciation and said the Rolly had left two bottles of port to the C.C.C. which we proposed to drink at our next Summer Meeting.* The minutes of this 1994 meeting contain no reference to the port's location.....

Another victim of Tyrannus' poor record keeping was T Hayes Dockrell, Director of Orthopaedic Surgery at Northampton General Hospital from 1946 and a Chatterer from 1948, apparently giving no papers between *Nigerian Notes* (1952) and *Useful Journey* (1967).

The latter was *compiled from the logs of a great uncle whilst serving as a midshipman in the RN.... a journey to the China station and back..... the main purpose of the cruise was showing the flag.* Hayes Dockrell, mayor of Northampton 1967-8, died in 1970.

There is a gap of about 16 years before Peter Dalgleish, Northampton general practitioner, became a member. The date is unrecorded but from internal evidence it would have been about 1964. Apart from medicine Peter's main interests included the Royal Navy which figured in three of his six recorded papers. *The Royal Naval Air Service* (1979) described its beginnings in 1914 as a response to Zeppelins and continued to what the reader saw as a loss of sea-air power potential due to development of the Royal Air Force. *Hood Might or Myth* (1982) was the story of HMS Hood, Britain's biggest battle cruiser built during the 1914-18 war and finally sunk by the German battleship Bismark in 1941. *Scharnhorst and Gneisenhau* (1988) told the history of two formidable German battleships completed in 1939 which had been twin thorns in the flesh of the Allies in World War 2. Both were put out of action in 1942 but the Scharnhorst lived to fight another day and was finally sunk by the battleship *Duke of York* on Christmas Day 1943.

Dalgleish's first paper was presented in 1964, entitled *Aspects of our future* with Jackson recording in his notes …. *He pointed out 3 problems that now face us – Destruction by nuclear war – overpopulation & the great increase in leisure Finished by postulating that "we are a communal animal & we cannot live & enjoy ourselves in either spiritual or physical isolation".*

Continuing in 1967 with another depressing theme *Drugs & Addiction* Dalgleish described *Opiates, Amphetamines Barbiturates and Hashish, together with their action and the groups of people who used them. The psychopathy and immaturity of the user was* stressed as more important in all groups. Measures for suggested improved control of the problem were discussed.

For his 1986 paper Dalgleish chose the story of *Denis Burkitt*, the scientist who discovered the connection between recurrent malaria and the lymphoma that bears his name. It is not clear when Peter Dalgleish left the Club, it was certainly after 1988.

J R (Tony) Tasker, Consultant Physician at Northampton General Hospital from 1940-1980, was a pillar of the Club from 1964 until 2006 during which time he contributed at least eighteen readings. This number exclude others missing from the records due to Tyrannus' failings. Tony's studied and meticulous preparation of papers, excellent minutes as Tyrannus and enthusiastic involvement in discussion where he raised pertinent points will be long remembered.

John Rendel Tasker was born in 1915 and following schooldays at Marlborough went up to Clare College Cambridge where he obtained his Bachelor of Medicine in 1940 as well as his Membership of the Royal Society of Physicians of London. There followed time as a medical officer in the Royal Air Force with the rank of Squadron Leader and it is assumed by the family he acquired the name of Tony at this time as alliteration was all the rage during the Second World War. Appointed Consultant Physician at Northampton General Hospital Tony soon became a popular local figure in the world of medicine. He joined the Chit Chat around 1964.

One of Tasker's first papers, possibly in 1969 or 70, was *The Beagle's Influence on Thought*, a treatise on the five year voyage starting in 1831 by a *tall young naturalist of 27*, Charles Darwin and publication of *The Origin of Species* twenty three years later. It was typical of the reader to venture into realms of philosophy …. *By what* creatures shall we be succeeded? Here indeed the gondola of conjecture is supported only by the balloon of fancy and guessing becomes ridiculous…. We must wait millions of years. By then we shall all be comfortably seated upon the cloud reserved for the meetings of the Elysian Chit Chat Club …* Nearly twenty years later Tasker presented *Darwin Revisited* in 1987, professing with reference to his earlier paper, presumed lost, *perhaps this is just as well for its chief fault …. was a serious lack of balance.* Tasker set about this unjust self-assessment with a discussion on evolution as Darwin viewed it and opposition to the theory headed by T H Huxley and the Bishop of Oxford, Samuel Wilberforce. As ever Tasker returned to the Club, regarding fossils … *Members of the Club who are ambitious for such immortality must see that their bones come to rest in some calm shallow sea. I would suggest the Persian Gulf or the Amazon delta….. Darwin is a colossus … he transformed our view of the world and of man's place in it, just as Copernicus, Galileo and Newton had done before him. Surely his name should stand as their equal.*

Continuing the theme of voyaging Tasker commenced his paper on *Cook's Tours* (1985-6) with *It is a jealously guarded principle of the Chit Chat Club that a member may, from time to time, choose a subject of which he knows next to nothing. Accordingly, Tyrannus, a practising landlubber, now begs leave to read a paper on life at sea.* A factual treatise followed with the typical sting in its tail …. *"We debauch their morals"*, he wrote (Captain Cooke of the Tahitians) *"and we introduce wants and perhaps diseases which serve only to disturb their happy tranquillity…."*

Another reading, on *Leviathan*, (early 1960s) of which he *know*[s] *little* was an academic paper ending with a heartfelt plea on behalf of whales …. *Man has eliminated species in the past. One day he

may be forgiven for this, for the sole reason he did not know what he was doing. ...with whaling it is different....If we in the 20th century exterminate the great whales, history will not be lenient.
An Antique Land (1989) derived its title from the opening lines of *Ozymandias* by Shelley and dealt with Egypt's history.
Two papers, *Volcanoes and Geography* (1980) and Tasker's last reading, *This Restless Planet* (2004) dealt with monumental subjects of continental drift, creation of land masses and the contribution of German scientist Alfred Wegener who, Tasker felt *should be invited when the Olympian Chit Chat Club meets in 200 million years …. as guest speaker … because he got it right all along.* Starting along similar geological lines *History and the Countryside* (1992) Tasker lamented man who *had behaved badly ...smothered the land with concrete ….* but ended on an optimistic note glancing at *nature reserves acting as reservoirs from which wild life may spread.*
Previously, in January 1968, Tasker had tackled problems associated with *Science, Pollution and Survival*, likening the human race to the Sorcerer's Apprentice who cannot stem the tide of his magic. After accusing detergents and pesticides he came to *the greatest single act of pollution which the human race has ever committed ….. the release of radio-active material into the atmosphere by the explosion of nuclear weapons*. Having outlined a few measures that might be taken Tasker did not end on his usual optimistic note …. *There seems an excellent chance that man, that brilliant but foolhardy animal, will in the not too far distant future, by means of his chemical excretions, render the world unfit for habitation.*
Potential doom and gloom figure again in one of Tasker's earliest, undated papers. *The Future* traces the past, *transience of the throw-away society* and the possibility (then) of cloning mammals…. *Pressures of the accelerating world* will need *control* [of] *research*

and technology and the proposition that *Education should be increasingly geared towards the future ...... If we fail to face these problems then western civilisation may well vanish*

In another early undated paper on *Pestilence* a rather more hopeful outlook for the human race is foretold, covering the progress of medical science in the control of infectious disease where .... *as in many other spheres of human activity the price of peace is eternal vigilance.*

Archaeology figured in a later paper *The Story of Seahenge* (2001), Tasker summarising his own paper as *the recent discovery of a Bronze Age Monument on the coast of Norfolk, and about the impact this discovery had upon a small neighbouring coastal village.*

Disease and its control was never far from Tasker's thoughts and with *The Roots of Medicine* (1997) he let his mind wander not only over origins of medicine but the role played by plants over the millennia.

A trip to London Zoo in about 1982 led Tasker to ponder the history of *The Zoo,* recounting captivity of wild animals from ancient times to the present day. With a sideways glance at Humphrey Davy and Stamford Raffles as well as the Zoological Society of London he progressed from horrors of early zoos to more open planned establishments of the late twentieth century. The wisdom of breeding of rare breeds was questioned .... *Animals from this cushioned background do not easily adjust to life in the wild.* Tasker ended on a typical note. *"Man"* he [Mark Twain] *wrote " is the only animal that can blush, and the only one that needs to"....During the last 40 or 50 years man has treated his fellow creatures badly. It is about time he exercised this unique capacity and started blushing about it.*

In 1999 a paper on *Migrating Birds* provided an authoritative survey of current thought on this complex subject. He summed up with clear admiration for *swallows, cuckoos and all the rest … Their migrations, undertaken annually with the least possible fuss and bother, are a chief wonder of the natural world.*

The last paper to be considered in extant writings of this widely read and thoughtful Chatterer is *Two Forgeries*, an early undated reading. This paper, *conceived by ignorance out of curiosity*, recounted the 'discovery', in the first decade of the twentieth century, of human remains in Sussex by Charles Dawson. Piltdown Man became famous but there were doubts, *the bones of Piltdown Man became to some extent bones of contention*. In the 1950s the hoax was revealed.

The second forgery was the work of Han Van Meegeren, the Dutch painter whose hatred of art critics led him to believe *these self-appointed judges were unable to distinguish between the true and the false*. His forgeries brought him a fortune and it was not until after the Second World War an *arrest on a charge of collaboration with the Fascists* resulted in exposure. Tasker considered *these forgeries have two things in common … their meticulous attention to detail* and *the choice of subject….. I commend these two points to members of the club wishing to set up in the same line of business.*

Tony resigned from the Club in 2006 having found it increasingly difficult to attend and died in 2008.

*

E A J (Tony) Alment was appointed Consultant Obstetrician and Gynaecologist at Northampton General Hospital in 1960 at the age of 38 and about four years later joined the Chit Chat. He is chiefly remembered for doing more to further women's rights than any other doctor of his generation. He realised the extreme dissatisfaction felt by many women placed in the clutches of his profession and by discussing the patient's opinions and worries with them earned their eternal gratitude whilst annoying administrators who considered his efforts merely extended clinic times. It is regrettable there are no details in Lee's scanty 1982 notes when Alment talked on *The Women's Movement* in 1982. These jottings are enigmatic but suggest an encyclopaedic grasp of the subject. With *The Unwanted Pregnancy* Alment ventured into even more contentious territory. Having explained the title really means 'The Unwanted Child' he goes on to examine in detail the sociological, human, legal and emotional problems involved and their various possible solutions and outcomes.

Tony became Secretary of the Royal College of Obstetricians and Gynaecologists in 1969 and its President from 1978 to 1981. During this time he indulged his interest in wine by becoming the College buyer. In the words of his hospital colleague Robin Sheppard[23] .... *he left a well filled cellar whose memory lives on.* This love of bottles and their contents led to *Bottles* in 1979. Lee's notes, summarising the paper, extant in the archives and fuller than usual indicate the history of these containers, of wine, milk, oil and poison was enthusiastically received. He concludes with *The reader presented a series of corks including the composite champagne cork with three sections each of different calibre and hardness. A compendious paper by which I mean Comprehensive and Stupendous, was followed by discussion until 11.30 pm.*

Between papers Tony was knighted in 1985 and retired from professional activities. Robin concluded his obituary notice ...*An expert fly fisherman, he also worked in his engineering workshop repairing farm machinery for friends. He wrote about wine and studied church architecture, making a particular study of 11thcentury* *church fonts. He took up bell ringing in his seventies.* Sir Anthony Alment died in 2002.

Richard B Coles, Consultant Dermatologist at Northampton General Hospital developed a lateral view of his speciality that included the way the psyche influenced skin conditions. His paper to the Club *Aggression* (1969) proposed that aggression is a natural characteristic of man (Coles refers to *he* throughout the paper, inferring ladies never suffered from this affliction) and continued with analyses of animal behaviour. He concluded with the remedy for aggression in all its forms being in education. It is significant that shortly before writing this thesis a brick had been thrown through his toilet window.

Dick Coles' other love was music, being an Associate of the London College of Music from 1964. His paper on *Origins of Organised Sound* (1967) produced draft minutes from Jackson:

He examined organized sound from its primordial beginnings to the present day. Primitive ideas about the production of the Universe from an acoustical substance were discussed and Man's emotional responses to music were evaluated. The pre-genital connotation of the "raspberry" and an imperfect quotation from Shakespeare were mentioned as examples of the unpleasant effect of certain noises. An effort was made to define the whys and wherefors of the modern attitude to sound from the esoteric Third Programme Cult to the blanket effect of BBC 1. Perhaps this was not what the members were expecting from an accomplished musician. Dick Coles' other contributions to the Club are lost.

Alan Jennings is reputedly responsible for welcoming sherry at Club meetings, a symbol of his warm nature. The son of two head teachers, he was a Cambridge graduate and qualified in medicine at Leeds in 1956. After training as an anaesthetist he became consultant at Northampton General Hospital where he specialised in teaching and the relief of pain. With hobbies covering railways, mathematics and music he was an ideal Chit Chat candidate. Alan gave his first paper *An Anniversary to Remember* in 1979, detailing the great Tay Bridge disaster of December one hundred years before. Tyrannus records:

The bridge, pinnacle of the career of one Thomas Bouche, completed in 1877 and crossed successfully by Queen Victoria who knighted him therefore, gave way under the stress and strain of a severe climatic storm, associated with a lunar eclipse. The cause of the collapse was neither climatic compulsion nor Act of God but faulty foundings of iron girders, the left honeycombed with holes which had been filled with Beaumont Egg, which fell out in due course – a mixture of beeswax, fiddlers' resin, iron filings or borings & lamp black for colouring. The rest of Jennings' paper dealt with safety measures subsequently brought into being.

Ordnance Survey Maps (1982) and *Animal Rights* (1985) followed, the latter being a sensitive discussion as to the moral responsibilities of Man towards other animals with the thought summarised by Tyrannus:

We help animals most by euthanasia, which allows us to end life when in our view sickness or injury have made its continuance intolerable. In this respect man treats animals better than he treats his own kind.

This was Tony Tasker's first meeting as Tyrannus and somewhat apologetically the minute concluded:

But, perhaps through the inertia of Tyrannus, the crux of the paper was missed. This was the question whether or no animals, compelled to share the globe with a highly developed and philoprogenitive ape, possessed by their very existence unassailable rights of their own. On this key point the club preserved an enigmatic silence.

It is remembered with feelings of trepidation tempered by affection by one member that Alan would *pick anything to pieces in an academic way* when any paper was presented.

Alan died suddenly the following year aged 54.

1986 saw general practitioner Denis Robertson enter the Club. A qualified pilot and medical examiner to air crews, including the ill-fated *Concorde*, Robertson was well qualified to talk on flying, his first two papers being *Engineless Flight* (1987) and *Lighter Than Air* (1990). In the first he *sketched the history of gliding from Leonardo to hang-gliders and from Icarus to Arnhem*, and in the second the evolution of balloons from Montgolfier to Graf Ferdinand Von Zeppelin and concluded with asking *the Club to pray with him for a calm day on his 65th birthday as his wife was giving him as a birthday present a flight in a Hot Air Balloon!* In his 29 year membership of the Club Robertson read seven or eight times including *Alternatives*, a comprehensive review of both orthodox medicine and the alternatives, homeopathy, herbal medicines and acupuncture, *Without Sensation* (1995), the history of anaesthesia, *Lese Majesty* (1999), an account of Edward VII's appendicitis and *1361* (2001), the story of magistrates, of which he was one for many years. Denis Robertson died in 2005.

The last un-Mad Doctor to join the Club is the present Tyrannus, Michael Toseland, a retired General Practitioner. *No Orchids* (2001) comprised an uncomfortable treatise, at least for listeners, on castratos and their operations. *1886 And All That, By Jingo* followed in 2003, recounting the lives of Edward Elgar and Rudyard Kipling. *The Little White Wonder* (2005) dealt with aspirin and its sometimes turbulent history. With *A Simple Mechanism* in 2008 Toseland explored execution by guillotine and the same year substituted for Godfrey at the last moment, one of the perils accompanying Tyrannus' role, reading *Bubble Bubble*, a short dissertation on witchcraft in Northamptonshire. *The Full Monty* in 2011 gave the Club an insight into the life of M R James of Cambridge Chit Chat fame.

It is hoped there will be other medical men in the future brave enough to become Chatterers, only time will tell.

NOTES

1. *Northampton Herald* 26 February 1898.
2. Ib.
3. R Adkins *Our County.*
4. Northamptonshire Record Office. Medical Superintendent Diaries, Berry Wood.
5. Ib.
6. Ib.
7. *Raymond Or Life and Death: With Examples of the Evidence for Survival of Memory and Affection After Death*, published by Sir Oliver Lodge in 1916. His son was killed in WW1 and the book tells how contact was made and the solace it gave.
8. Second Sino-Japanese War 1937-45 in which bombing of civilians took place for the first time.
9. I am greatly indebted to Dr Kerith Trick for his book, with Arthur Foss *St Andrew's Hospital Northampton: The First One Hundred and Fifty Years (1838-1988)*.
10. Charles Stuart Calverley (1831-1900) was a Fellow at Christ's, Cambridge, his academical success remarkable considering his innate indolence. Famous for parodies and caricatures his examination paper on Pickwick at Christmas 1857 was printed in 'Fly Leaves'.
11. This could refer to the death of Joshua Bugg, killed in an explosion of fire damp at Warren Vale Colliery in 1851. Fifty one miners and lads succumbed. The Inverness Courier of 1864 reported a Mr Joshua

Bugg changed his name to Mr Norfolk Howard. There is no reference to any Joshua Bugg in common usage found around 1903, possibly it is a literary allusion. Perhaps there is a more obvious nickname for this man but it is not in the minutes.

12. In 1646 Sir John Gayer, Lord Mayor of London had founded a sermon to be preached annually at St Katharine Cree Church, Leadenhall Street in the City of London to commemorate his 'wonderful escape' from a lion which he met in the desert whilst travelling the wilds of Turkey.
13. Obituary, Northampton Chronicle & Echo July 11th 1989.
14. Remark attributed to author.
15. Google Chrome on Vortex theory.
16. Dr William Palmer used strychnine to murder John Cook and was hanged in 1856. It is probable he was a serial killer.
17. *Journal of the Chemical Society*. Obituary 1921.
18. Obituary. *Northampton Independent* January 28th 1928.
19. Peverell S Hichens MA MB Oxon MRCP Lond. *The Sanatorium Treatment of Pulmonary Tuberculosis with especial reference e to Nordrach Methods*, read to the South Midland branch of the British Medical Association, BMJ March 14, 1903.
20. Hichens and Percival have the distinction of being the two 'independent' doctors brought in to examine the poet James Kenneth Stephen at St Andrew's Hospital in 1891. JKS, cousin of Virginia

Woolf, was colleague and friend to many in the Cambridge Chit Chat Club. He later starved himself to death at the hospital.
21. Sir James Crichton-Browne MD FRS 1840-1938, psychiatrist.
22. This was already being done in some areas, including Birmingham, King's Heath, where the *Monyhull Colony*, Homes for Epileptics and Feeble Minded had been opened on April 11th 1908 and was to survive until the 1960s when there were over 1000 inmates at work on the farm.
23. *British Medical Journal* 13 April 2002.

11
Teachers

The teaching profession has been represented intermittently but well over the years. Canon Sanders, headmaster of Northampton Grammar School, was a Club founder whose life has already been considered. He presented three papers, *Protective mimicry in animal nature* (1886), *Cave explorations* (1888) and *Criminals* (1891), none of which are detailed although after the last *The discussion was most interesting: and the Members seemed inclined to "take sides"- more than usual.* Sanders left Northampton and the Club for Leicester in 1893.

The principal of Northampton's School for the Deaf since 1884, Hugh Neville Dixon, became a Chatterer in 1901 and over the next forty one years read twenty papers. In 1902 he presented *Alternating Personalities, a luminous exposition of the doctrine of the sub-liminal Self, associated with the name and work of F. W. H. Meyers* [Founding member of the Society for Psychical Research]..... *A good discussion followed, led by the Mad Doctors.* This subject must have been dear to Dixon's heart. In 1908 he talked on *Thought Transference* and in 1932 *Personality and Personalities* which was an extension of the 1902 paper treating on multiple distinct personalities being present in the same person at differing times but *Unfortunately the 'Mad Doctors' were not present to bring the sane logic of reason to bear on the subject, but an excellent paper was followed by an animated debate in which doctors, dreams and devil-possession were discussed together with madness, memory and mind.*

For his last treatise in 1942 under the title of *Which am I?* Dixon returned to the subject and this time *The Mad Doctors poured scorn on the idea of Multiple Personality: it was all pathological. The mind and the personality were perfectly good, simple things unless something went wrong with the cells of the brain. This was unfortunate for the patient, but gave him the great benefit of treatment by mental specialists.*

Dixon kept fighting and the other members of the Club hovered delightedly in the ring, occasionally offering a jab of their own and generally stimulating the major contestants. In fact everyone present took some part and that is what the Chit Chat is for.

Dixon, a Renaissance Man out of his time had interests and activities so varied the mere listing of them produces a sense of humility and wonder. *A medical practitioner of the 18th and 19th centuries* (1904) consisted of reminiscences of a doctor friend and *Education of the Deaf* (1906) was the only paper connected with his headmastership. In 1910 Dixon left the school and devoted his life to studying mosses, the science of bryology. He became a world expert, a fellow of the Linnean Society of London in 1885 and its Vice-President as well as a prolific author, his most important and best known book being *The Student's Handbook of British Mosses*, first published in 1896, still a classic on the subject. A quotation from his 1910 paper to the Club, *Some points of contact between Bryology and Humanity,* illustrates the driving force behind Hugh Dixon's passion.......*all over vast tracts of continent and country, these mosses, insignificant and unnoticed, which few pause to glance at, and all trample under heel, have been from age to age fashioning for us the very ground on which we live, and fight, and build, and buy and sell; and, without history themselves, have made history possible for mankind.*

Over the years Dixon produced five treatises on allied subjects, *How Trees Grow* (1915), *The Influence of Mind on Landscape* (1922), *How Flowers came to be* (1926) and *Plants as the Enemy of Man* (1935) in which *Poison plants, pampas grass, bramble, the rust of wheat, mildew of vine and the Upas tree came under his lash and made no defence. Our flesh crept at his figures. Seven million million spores from a single puff-ball, 1900 million bushels of wheat destroyed by rust! The fact that £5,000,000 of damage was done annually to the vine by mildew almost reconciled the members to the heavy cost of wine at the dinner.......*Another paper, *Mosses and Man* (1937) completes this section.

Dixon's travels to study his mosses generated three papers, *Portugal* (1912), *A Summer Holiday within the Arctic Circle* (1928) and *Sicily* (1930). Not all his travels were confined foreign parts, he climbed Snowden three times in one day looking for Welsh mosses and Skiddaw in Yorkshire at the age of eighty. His wide interests and knowledge can be judged by other papers, *The Arthurian Legend* (1916), *Class Distributions: good or evil* (1918), *Some Old Letters* (1919), *The Poet Cowper and Northampton* (1924) and *Reminiscences of a Would-be Octogenarian* (1940), in which *It was not surprising that he who possessed two careers, one who twice rode the winner of the Grand National and the other who was Skating Champion and who, himself, skated from Northampton to Wansford on the Nene, should have enjoyed a variety of experiences......he flitted from Cowper, the Chartist, to Todhunter, from Matthew Arnold to Hornby, from Philip Brooks to Kropotkin, from Chesterton to the Marquis of Healty and gave us witty verses or epigrams on Oscar Browning and Perowne.*

Hugh Dixon died in 1944. His successor at the School for the Deaf, by now situated in Cliftonville, was Frederick Ince-Jones.

*

If there is one name that recurs frequently in this history as Chatterer, reader, Tyrannus, and chronicler it is Ince-Jones. His minutes are a delight, full of wit and colour except when summarising his own papers.

Born in 1884 Frederick Ince Jones [sic] obtained a Science degree from London University and was called to the Bar at the Inner Temple but returned to his home town to teach at Cliftonville where he became headmaster in 1916, three years after he had been elected to the Club. After retirement Ince-Jones moved to Harpole, a village four miles from Northampton with his wife and two daughters. In his reign as Tyrannus the Club had some of its finest hours, fortunately recorded meticulously but in handwriting that at times became microscopic, containing words only interpretable by their context.

Within two years of being elected the new Tyrannus acquired a hyphen to his name and retained it throughout his life. At times he lapsed in its use, as did some others who wrote minutes and this accounts for several inconsistencies to be found among these pages.

All but three of his recorded papers, spanning at least 34 years, are in the Club archives, the first few hand written in students' notebooks from his school. They display a large range of subjects, starting with *Convention* in 1914, the year after he joined the Club. His opinions come through vividly in the original draft with crossings out, amendments and passages he apparently preferred not to include in the talk, such as extra marital relationships and comments on women's dress. Browne's minutes are formal; *Although conventions saved trouble they encouraged laziness and slavish adherence to them promoted narrow minded bitterness. The treatment accorded to Pre-Raphaelites and early women cyclists was cited as an example. After discussing a number of conventions, he pleaded for greater freedom in matters non-essential.* Ince-Jones was never conventional, at least at Club meetings, and in his second talk *The Law of Psychic Phenomena* (1916) he suggested psychic phenomena emanate more from the sub-consciousness of the living rather than the dead but nevertheless *argued for the existence in man of a soul, curiously dependent upon the mind and limited, but with amazing latent powers and probably persistent after physical death.*

When Browne came to write the minutes of *The Superman* (1918) he seemed to be out of his depth as many are when approaching Nietzsche. It is a paper of many parts including an analysis of selective breeding in humans. Ince-Jones had written an essay on this subject some seven years earlier and found himself, in the closing stages of the war against Germany, needing to rewrite some of the more contentious passages. With *Some possibilities of Northampton* (1920) Ince-Jones took on the mantle of town planner, remodelling *the ugly town* towards his idea of beauty with *a sort of super-citizen to manage the Town's affairs.* Browne's minutes enter into the spirit of the evening: *The speaker concluded by drawing a fanciful and hilarious picture of this Utopian fairy-land on May Day 2020, when the Civic Fathers would engage in sport in the gigantic Square of his imagination, amid grassy lawns and vistas fair, adorned with sculptured effigies, toga-clad, of local notables of a hundred years before.*

A travelogue, *Impressions of Central and Southern Europe* (1922) was followed by *Whom ought we to kill?* (1924). The original manuscript is unfortunately missing and the minute by Ince-Jones who had become Tyrannus in 1923 can only stimulate the imagination into realms perhaps best left unexplored: *Ince Jones read a blood-curdling paper on 'Whom ought we to kill?' At the end of his remarks there seemed to remain still some uncertainty in the minds of the members, but no casualties have yet been reported.*

At the Summer Meeting of 1926 *Ince Jones read a paper on "Luxury and Life" and his pious words were listened to with deep attention by the large number of clergy present.*

A lady was heard to say that she had never before seen so many handsome clergy at one meeting. This indeed was life and luxury.

Ince-Jones minutes regarding his own contributions could be terse, in 1926 *Ince-Jones read a paper on 'Provincialism' in which he tried to deal impartially with the advantages and disadvantages of Provincial Life.*

In 1930 he acknowledged criticism of his papers, ... *he had been accused of being too impartial,....* a view it is difficult to appreciate for anyone who had read his forthright words but *on this occasion he went the whole hog in an unsparing attack upon certain modern exponents of Art, Music, Sculpture and Literature.* With *Standards in Art and other matters* Ince-Jones produced a quintessential Chit Chat paper, a tirade against the swing to ugly modernism where the pendulum had swung too far from 'pretty-pretty'. The paper is beautifully written, even if labouring his point to excess, with wit and provocative but well researched references, ... *James Joyce in "Ulysses" devotes several pages to details of the thoughts and actions of his hero in the W.C.* This is followed by a section on *millions of women with ugly torsos* and sees Ince-Jones in typical fighting mode ....*ugly, stumpy figures with flopping breasts and obese stomachs beloved by modern artists may exist, but why paint them....There are plenty of ugly things in life, but why introduce them into Art except by way of contrast.* If the object of a reading is to provoke discussion as well as impart information Ince-Jones was a master..... *he inflicted great pain upon one of the visitors, Mr Travis, the Inspector of a large number of Art Schools, who pronounced the paper reader's mind to be chaotic and his hideous examples "spurious artists".*

After this promising beginning the meeting settled down comfortably to the prospect of a really good row, but was rather disappointed when the Leader of the Opposition tailed off into a very long and, not altogether to the point, History of Art from early times....and ultimately Mr Travis more or less committed himself to the following That nobody but a highly trained artist was qualified to express an opinion on Art – That exhibitions of Art were a mistake – That pictures should not be framed – That Artists painted for themselves alone and that Ince-Jones knew nothing whatever about it.

Nobody else gave enthusiastic support to any of these views except the last, but the discussion continued with animation until 11.20 and the paper-reader's chief regret was that even by that late hour there had been no opportunity to discuss and no doubt to condemn his heresies on modern music and literature. Regret indeed, there are problems for any Tyrannus when a lone voice, especially that of a guest, monopolises the Chat.

As a footnote Mr Travis, evidently not bearing a grudge against the Club over his previous reception, appeared again in 1933 when he deputised for H St John Browne, reading *Art and Utility*, defining Art as *the expression in any outward form of the Spirit of our civilisation*. He had a low opinion of the public and education where *Arts and Crafts were neglected in Secondary Schools and the Universities and the boys and girls of the lowest ability found their way into Art Schools*. This was not an opinion held by headmaster Cooke when it came to a vote of thanks. Mr Travis concluded with *the dogmatic assertion that the ordinary man had no more right to express an opinion on Art than had the layman to criticise a surgeon or a lawyer.* Tyrannus pointed out in the minute *if a man dies after an operation and a number of patients in succession die from the Knife of the same surgeon, nothing will prevent the public, however beautiful the technical skill of the operator, from expressing coarse opinions of the results.* There was *a prolonged discussion.*

*

Gronks is an unlikely paper title and annoyed a few members who *resented their inability to look the subject up beforehand in Encyclopaedia and Dictionary.* However after Ince-Jones *explained this was a name invented by himself to apply to "Gentlemen"* he regaled the Club with possible definitions and requirements. In the discussion among restrictions on behaviour *de Putron asserted that no gronk ever used the ancient ecclesiastic oath "By Our Lady". This was felt to be a little too exclusive.*

When considering Frederick Ince-Jones as Tyrannus his minutes are penetrating and thought provoking and as a writer of papers he stands out above most. Even with the subject *Thrift* Ince-Jones manages to infuse life into the minutes. *"A Dull Virtue"* (1936), *dreary both in subject and treatment* was certainly one of his less inspired productions but *As is often the case after a paper of less merit than usual, the discussion was very animated and continued until the late time of 11.20....The discussion closed on a depressing note for Shapland stated oracularly that Thrift was based upon the desire for Security, but Security was an illusion!*

Tyrannus was heard to murmur sadly "All the world smells of dead violets" and he went into the garden to eat worms.

In 1938 the minute .... *Ince-Jones read a paper on "Progress", which produced a considerable amount of discussion ....* was brief to the point of being useless, harking back to nineteenth century entries and quite rightly the next month earned a stern request *that if Tyrannus read another paper, the minutes on that occasion be written by another member, his minutes being unsatisfactory.* On studying the twenty eight typed sheets it is possible to see Ince-Jones' dilemma; as he puts it *It is not easy to review in half an hour the progress, past, present and future of humanity, and I am ill-equipped for the task, for my knowledge of History and Philosophy are far too meagre. And yet perhaps a plain man's attempt to express his views may have some value in eliciting from others, wiser than himself, their reactions to a complex question.* Essentially it is a rambling work, strolling through history as if through a minefield, taking three steps forward and two back, then going off at a tangent, acknowledging both the successes and failures achieved in the name of 'progress'. Whether the reader believed in attempting to progress as meaning *giving a purpose to life and making the inevitable struggle worth while* is not clear. He ends on thin ice when approving the Christian story, considering the Club's rule banning sectarian religion, but has hope for the future, slightly misquoting Arthur Clough,

Say not the struggle naught availeth......
For, though the tired waves idly breaking,
Seem here no patient inch to gain,
Far off by creek and inlet making
Comes silent, flooding in, the main.

Had Ince-Jones been entirely convinced that future *Progress* was for the good he might have included the last two lines

In front the sun climbs slow, how slowly!
But westward, look, the land is bright![1]
Fortunately for posterity Ince-Jones continued to minute his own readings. The Summer Meeting of 1940 was *at Dallington Vicarage, Perry being host. It was pleasant to meet there again and old members revived memories of Beasley and Streatfeild. In spite of the preoccupations of the war there was an unusually good muster.* With thirteen members and twenty two guests it was a memorable meeting *rendered the more pleasant by the kindness of the host and hostess and the beauty of their house and gardens.* Ince-Jones had prepared a talk on *The Weaker Sex* and nobly sat on the fence by discussing merits and demerits of both sexes, producing a discussion *longer and more animated than at most Summer Meetings.* Among the ladies' contributions *Mrs Hankinson put him in his place by saying emphatically that women dressed to please themselves and triumph over other women, not to attract men..... other ladies expressed regrets that women could not propose marriage.* Some of the men disputed the idea of women having a higher moral sense than men, but on the whole the male representatives sat rather tight (not it should be remarked by reason of the excellence of Perry's sherry and cider cup!) Overall the wise Tyrannus *left the decision as to which was the weaker to the judgement of the meeting and at the end came out by the same door wherein he went.*

As referred to earlier, in the middle of World War II *The Unpopularity of the Jews* (1942) might seem to have been an unfortunate choice of title but as has been seen Ince-Jones was never one to dodge controversy. *He tried to show some of the admirable qualities possessed by Hebrews, to whom the world owed much. He suggested that their less attractive characteristics were due mainly to their long history of persecution and oppression and* that inasmuch as this treatment reflected very considerably upon non-Jewish people, it was up to the latter to show more sympathy and understanding. The paper is a model of circumspection, giving both pros and cons of contemporary and historical views and this summary in the minutes by the reader does no justice to the paper. Like many wearing the mantle of Tyrannus, Ince-Jones was either over modest or not the best assessor of his own work, probably both. One point in particular had not been minuted, that the *less attractive characteristics* reported above appear equally in *non-Jewish people.* After the paper *The discussion was animated and prolonged. Shapland in the course of some well-thought-out comments, capped Hilaire Belloc's "How odd of God to choose the Jews" with "Of course, why not, He knows what's what".....Many other members and visitors made valuable contributions; in fact, everybody did his best to make up for the deficiencies of the paper.*

In 1944 Ince-Jones looked back at *The Victorians*, when he *drew attention to the extraordinary number of great men living in 1880 compared with 1944.* Having made his point the reader continued by contrasting the eras, not quite so favourably. This side of the coin is missing from the minutes, possibly due to *the reader's enthusiasm for these men of a bygone day.*

The archives only contain one more paper, *Where are the Outstanding Personalities?* (1948). This harks back like the previous reading to times gone by.....*Fifty years ago a book entitled Our County was published* [In 1893]. *It was written agreeably, though occasionally pungently, by one member of the Chit Chat Club, Sir Ryland Adkins, and illustrated with equal brilliance by another, W B Shoosmith, two bright blossoms of the naughty nineties.* It contained portraits of forty Northamptonshire personalities and in his paper Ince-Jones not only wonders if forty such could be found

in 1948 but extends Adkins' list by 22 or two cricket teams. He struggles to select a side for 1948 by including *Joan Wake who, though no gentleman, is an undoubted personality.* With *Heads of Colleges at Oxford and Cambridge have assured me of the superiority of the general run of undergraduates to those of fifty years ago and yet they deplore the insufficiency of men of highest rank* he develops ideas to account for this including *the decrease in the number of men with such large private incomes that they need not concern themselves with any profession or business* and the slightly more down to earth *Progressive breeding from the worst stocks may be another factor.* If any chronicler had only minutes to go by this treatise would not be considered worthy of being read. Ince-Jones shows little wit when recording his own paper and keeps his comments to the discussion where he manages to skilfully underline his thesis with *One member had the courage to confess that he found it pleasanter to play golf and cards than stand for the Council......Raynsford assured us that Victorian generals were contemptible.*
But not even those entrusted with the care of souls or of bodies could provide a remedy.
The last paper recorded as being written by Ince-Jones is *Awakened* (1951), two years after his minutes ceased and the Dark Age began. He died in 1954.

*

Edward Reynolds became Northampton Grammar School's headmaster in 1907 at the age of 33 and was elected to the Chit Chat two years later. His first paper, *Some problems on Education* (1912), was a comprehensive review of the history of schools and educational systems in England, comparing them with *the systems in France and Germany, in some respects to the advantage of the*

Continental nations. The indifference of many English parents, and the premature withdrawal of boys from School were referred to as accounting for much of the shortcomings. A travelogue, *Greece,* came in 1914 and *Classical and Modern Education* (1917) contained a plea for continuing teaching Classics in schools. Reynolds left Northampton in 1921 to become headmaster of Watford Grammar School.

Reynolds' successor was a Queen's Cambridge man, William Cyril Charles Cooke who joined the staff in 1910 at the age of 29 and remained there until 1944, having been headmaster for 23 years. His seven papers were divided between education and the lighter side of life, the former being *Choice of a Career* (1923), *What is an Educated Man?* (1927), in which *He began by giving the Club the benefit of some valuable opinions on the subject by various school-boys, entrusted to his care, presumably for the purposes of Education....*and *Some aspects of Education* (1934).

Cooke took it upon himself to compose words for a *School Song* with rousing chorus and four verses beginning with the lines *When Thomas Chipsey made this school in fifteen forty one*. He took this work seriously but with *Humorous Verse* (1925) introduced a side of his character not readily apparent to schoolboys. Cooke ... *passed from Swift to Swinburne by way of Barry Pain and Parodies to Lear, Lewis Carrol and Limericks.*

 At an early stage in his paper he quoted the lines –
>   *Whatever troubles Adam had,*
>   *Noone could make him sore*
>   *By saying when he told a joke,*
>   *"I've heard that one before".*

In 1929 *Cooke introduced his famous collection of performing birds under the guise of a paper on "Birds and the Poets". He produced melodies in praise of almost every feathered fowl – the nightingale, cuckoo, sky-lark, vulture, owl, aureole, raven, gold-finch, parrot, thrush, cock-pheasant, seagull, kingfisher, swallow, blackbird, duck and Perrine, a hen from sources ranging from Shakespeare, Milton, Wordsworth & Shelley to the Mikado, Edith Sitwell, Punch and the Sporting Times.*

For his paper Tea and Tattle (1932) Cooke gave *the history of tea from the 6th century, showed how heavily it had been taxed from early times and tried to prove some connection between the tattle of ladies' tea parties and the drinking of tea.*

A good discussion, largely on the value and dangers of stimulants, followed.

Cooke's last reading was on Humour (1937), a serious paper on the whole but ending with examples from *Hazlett, Leacock, G. Meredith, Chesterton, many others and some very amusing passages from "England Their England".* He resigned from the Club in 1938 and died in 1963.

Cooke introduced his second master to the Club as guest in 1931. Edward E Field, elected as member the following year, had served in the 1914-18 war in the Royal Engineers and latterly Intelligence. He became geography master at the Grammar School in 1927 and remained there until 1951. He read three papers, Problems of Progress (1933), claiming *Progress was not steady but by spasms and gave very interesting examples of desert and nomadic peoples conquering more cultured races.*

Trackway and Turnpike followed in 1935 and two years later Field tackled The Struggle for Population with opinions from Malthus and J M Keynes. His prophesy that *If present tendencies* [in birthrate] *were unchecked, the population* [of England] *would begin to decline in 1941 and by 2,000 might be reduced to about 20 millions* took no account of unexpected, war, prosperity and immigration. The ensuing Chat *covered a wide field but centred on two points (1) Was the fall in the birth-rate due to decreased fertility or modern methods of birth control? (2) Was a fall in population necessarily an evil? Shaw was learnedly gynaecological and L. Browne profoundly blood thirsty even for a Doctor of Divinity, but everybody enjoyed it.*

Field resigned from the Club in 1939 due to pressure of work and died in 1961.

Following Cooke's retirement in 1944 the post of headmaster was given to a young ex-flight lieutenant in the Intelligence branch, Martin Barnes Nettleton. An Oxford graduate Nettleton had taught at Repton before entering the Air Force and was looked upon as an ideal 34 year old to modernise a school in the post-war period. He joined the Club in 1949 and gave two recorded papers, *An Arctic Mystery* (1949) and *Education Act* (1952), both of which were after Ince-Jones minutes ended. Almost certainly he would have talked on other subjects, during the Club's Dark Age. Nettleton never lived long enough to achieve a …. *cherished ambition…* expressed during his last attendance as guest in January 1949 when Anthony Jackson spoke on *Mountaineering …. to retire from school mastering to run a hugely profitable Palace Hotel in Greenland from which he would sally during his frequent leisure to teach millionaires to climb Greenland's key mountains.* Martin Nettleton died in 1964 due to a drug overdose.

For over half a century there is no mention of the teaching profession until Dr David George joined the Club in 2007. One time Dean of the Faculty of Science and Associate Director at Nene College (now the University of Northampton) George is an educationalist and author of five books in the field. His first paper the year after he joined the Club, *Gifted is as Gifted Does*, dealt with *the educational needs of gifted and/or talented children* and his concern that these were not being met. The discussion afterwards came out in favour of the grammar school system. In January 2010 George read a paper designed to bring sunshine into winter blues, *A Merry Heart is like a Medicine.* Although a semi-serious discourse upon humour, *throughout the paper George threw off the mantle of pedagogism, replacing it with that of witty raconteur, verging on stand up comic*. During the Chat members were in jovial mood but fell short of the reader's wit. Later the same year George admitted to a lifelong fascination with woodlice in his treatise on *Isopods.*

NOTES

1. Clough A H, 1819-1861. *Say not the struggle naught availeth.*

12
Others

'Others', 'the remainder', 'rank and file' or even 'leftovers' are inadequate words to describe Chatterers who do not fall into one of the four previous pigeon holes. It is their diversity that contains their worth, members ready to read on subjects dear to their hearts, even sometimes daring to encroach into fields of church, law, medicine or teaching. From earliest days they provided a necessary counterpoint, with four of the original ten members coming into this category.

John Eunson, stalwart of Northampton's gas and water companies, only read one paper, *Roads, ancient and modern* (1886) and would appear to have resigned by the summer of 1889. Harrington Smith also read only once, on *Rating Areas in Northamptonshire* (1887). He left county and Club in the summer of 1888.

Some idea of Tom George's standing both in the Club and the town can be judged from the rather florid but entirely typical outpourings of Sir Ryland Adkins in the Northampton Independent[1] on the occasion of George's retirement in 1912 from Northampton Library.

Rarest of all is it, perhaps, that men devoted to public work, with the instinct of civic duty powerful, preserve and discharge their private duties well. The extravagances, the untidiness, the neglect of home and private affairs by persons immersed in the State, are the commonplaces of observation and of satire. It was not so with George. Home and friends were as much to him as if he had no sense of duty beyond the private circle.

Strangely, then, it happened that this man, so rich in inward possessions, had far more than seemed to be his share of outer misfortune and trial. His grandfather was a noted Huntingdonshire squire who did not find hospitality and electioneering and sport altogether good for his estate. His father, a famous agriculturist who farmed the estate when it had passed from their possession, died just as he was restoring the fortunes of the family. Then came agricultural depression and other injuries to prosperity; and young George left Cambridge in his second year and grappled with his difficulties.

...... And thus it happened that he who might have looked forward to a long life as a country gentleman came into Northampton in the early '80s with a young wife and two little children, and very, very slender private means.

After his paper on *Belemnites* (1885) George remained with his interest in archaeology with *Prehistoric Remains in Northamptonshire* (1887) when *...Weapons and Implements of Stone and Bronze were handed round; and a fine specimen of a Celtic Scabbard was produced*. This was followed by *The Old Pottery of Northamptonshire* in 1893, again with *numerous interesting specimens*. *Museums* was read in 1899 and *Who are the Celts?* in 1901, when *On the authority of George and Julius Caesar, it was generally conceded that certain peoples did exist who might, could, or should answer to the name of Celt, but that any such now survive having escaped the cauldron of mingled humanity, seemed to be received with varying degrees of doubt.*

The minutes note *Some interesting Old Books were produced and also a bundle of the Periodical Literature of the present day* when George spoke on *Northamptonshire Libraries* (1888).They continued somewhat ominously *specimens were carried off by some of the members for private study*. George read a paper on *Money* in 1891 and in 1903 *Edward Thring and the Classics* which turned out to be two papers, one on Thring, writer, and Uppingham Headmaster and the other on *various words* [in the Classics] *which have changed their meanings in English, such as "prevent", "tribulation"*. Reverting to his specialist interest George's last papers were *Recent finds of Saxon Remains at Kettering* (1904) and *The Arts in Britain 2000 Years Ago* (1906), the latter illustrated by Celtic artefacts and *several beautiful early gold coins.* History does not relate whether members carried off specimens for private study. George resigned from the Club in 1907 and died in 1920.

The last founder not detailed elsewhere is Richard Scriven, an active member of the Northamptonshire Natural History Society and its vice-president in 1932. He made many contributions to their literature and gave four papers to the Club, *The age of Trees* (1886), *Chaucer* (1889), *Farm Colonies* (1891) and *Agricultural Exodus* (1893) when *In the discussion Politics cropped up two or three times, but were* [sic] *speedily suppressed. At times the debate was animated.* Scriven resigned in the spring of 1897, not having attended any meetings that year.

Sir Hereward Wake was considered in chapter I and Thomas Jesson, who joined in 1890 only attended three meetings and *is believed to have left these parts* in 1891. It is unfortunate he managed to escape giving a paper as he was an inveterate collector of fossils from local quarries donated to local museums and bryazoa, aquatic invertebrate creatures whose remains were given to the British Museum. W H C Church has been difficult to trace and is assumed to be of the famous *'Church Shoes'* family. In 1894 he gave the rather long titled paper *Intellectual, not Moral, Agencies the dominant factors in the progression of Society.* George Eunson, son of founder member John, who it will be remembered married Sanders' eldest daughter, only lasted one season in the Club without taking any part in the proceedings. It may well have been that at the tender age of twenty three he felt unable to cope with more senior members. Another bird of passage was J Hardy, elected in 1891. In December *The Secretary reported that Hardy could not read his Paper on Spiders as he would be in Germany when his turn came.* Hardy is not mentioned again and must be assumed he let his membership lapse.

Henry Butterfield became a member of the Club in 1892 at the age of 52. He had moved in literary circles and among his claims to fame was meeting Charles Dickens. He bought the *Northampton Herald* in the early 70s, later to be renamed the *Chronicle*. Henry became mayor of the town in 1909. He is remembered locally as being in charge of an Empire Day parade on June 28th 1910 when 14,000 children marched from the Market Square along the Kettering Road to the old Racecourse. Butterfield's great interest was social welfare but only gave one paper, *The forward movement in Social Reform* (1892) which *was unusually lengthy but the reader twice asked leave to curtail it, but was pressed by the meeting to read it to the end. On its conclusion an unusual expression of approval burst from every part of the room and an active and interesting discussion – the major half of which was contributed by Adkins – followed.*

Sanders proposed and somebody else seconded a motion that Butterfield's paper be printed in the first Volume of the Transactions, and this was unanimously passed. Butterfield consented. These comments are of particular interest as they show not only the way in which a specific member of the Club, in this case Ryland Adkins, tended to take over the Chat but also the intention to publish papers, a consummation devoutly to be wished but sadly never materialised. Butterfield resigned in 1894.

Eighteen ninety two also saw the arrival of Harry Manfield, a director of another well-known Northampton firm of shoe makers. Harry gave two readings, *The various forms of Gambling* (1895) and *Mars and its marvels* (1898), neither of which brought forth any pertinent comments from the Secretary. In 1896 Harry was joined by his brother James, another director of the family firm. James read two papers, *Italy* (1897) and *Our Umbrellas* (1899), after which *the Club entered upon a very facetious discussion of the subject* although no details were recorded. Harry Manfield became Member of Parliament for mid-Northamptonshire from 1906-9 and James, having been mayor of the county town in 1905 held the post of High Sheriff in 1916.

In the nineteenth century Northampton was synonymous with shoes. William Hickson, head of Hickson and Son, shoe manufacturers, joined the Club in 1899 and with his papers demonstrated the social awareness of so many industrialists at this time. *Socialism in business* (1900) was followed, as a sort of light interlude, by *The Cat* (1903)..... *not the gentle companion of one domestic aide, but the wholesome and cherished instrument of correction.....it did nathless too painfully reflect the humanitarian mind of the reader, who had nothing nice to say about the "harmless necessary Cat". The members, not to mention the visitors, were for the most part grieved at the low esteem in which the reader evidently held an Institution justly and almost universally valued. Unfortunately the information on the subject was all second hand, there being no habitual criminal present to narrate his experiences.*

Back to social reality. *How we make paupers* (1905) *shewed clearly that though the "poor" must always be with us, the "pauper" need not and should not have any place in our social system.* In 1909 *Poor Law Report* gave *rise to an interesting discussion.*

In 1899 the manager of the Northamptonshire Union Bank, Percy Page, a grammar school lad, became a member and showed his wide education by talking about *Alfred the Great* the same year.

*

The Phipps family is well known in Northampton for building St Matthew's Church and the Brewery but it was Albert Edward, director of Northampton Gaslight Company who joined the Chatterers in 1901. He read no papers even though he remained a member until 1910. How he escaped is not minuted.

George Abbott JP gave two papers, *Old Age Pensions* (1908) and *Edmund Spenser* (1910), both of which were apparently factual.

Bruce Muscott became a Chatterer at the age of 40 in 1907. The managing director of the B&S (boot and shoe) and leather firm William Sylvester and Son, Muscott was summed up by Tyrannus Ince-Jones in 1933 as *highly esteemed, very regular in attendance, a genial host, a reader of papers of unusual ability and catholic taste, one who took a stimulating and well-informed part in discussion, and had left many friends but no enemies.*

Muscott senior read nine papers, the first three, *The marriage of Philip of Spain with our Queen Mary* (1908), *A trip to Brittany and Normandy* (1909) and *Is the national character deteriorating?* (1910), all being recorded by title only. With *Questions to be faced after the War* (1917) more details are given, *The main points of the paper, which were fully discussed, were:- Greater Production, Piece Work, Capital and Labour, Agriculture.* With each successive paper it is possible to understand Ince-Jones enthusiasm for Bruce Muscott as a reader. In 1923 *Bruce Muscott read an excellent paper entitled "The King's Business", this being the name given to the various proceedings taken by Henry VIII to obtain a divorce from Katherine of Aragon. The paper showed wide historical knowledge and contained many interesting details.* When it came to *Problems of Population* (1926) there was a factual and statistical approach rather than one of problem solving. *Muscott discoursed on the Population of England and other countries from early times, showing how the numbers have varied owing to The Black Death and other accidental causes. He showed how over-population produced lack of labour in this country and underpopulation in France produced lack of man-power.* Ince-Jones adds feelingly *A competent accountant would be required to appreciate some of the niceties of this paper.*

When Muscott came to talk about *the origins of civilisation, which he placed on the banks of the Nile some 6000 years B.C* in *Downland Man* (1929) *Cooke, abandoning the flippancy, which not infrequently camouflages the inner profundity of his thoughts, showed a charming and disarming surprise that scholarship was not the monopoly of headmasters and said unreservedly that the paper was a remarkably good one.* In addition [Dr] *Hayes without a blush, confessed to robbing graves, whereupon Hankinson left rather early, but there may have been no connection between the two events.*

A travelogue, *Jottings from Spain* (1931) proved to be Bruce Muscott's last paper, he died in 1933. His son Guy who became a Chatterer in 1923 continued the Spanish theme with three treatises, *Spain* (1937), *More about Spain* (1942) and *More notes on Spain* (1949), preceded by an introductory *The Balearic Islands* (1929) extolling *the charm of these Isles of the Blessed, where sunshine for 200 days of the year mellows the inhabitants to the most ingenuous honesty and beautifies the earth.* Not all Guy's talks were so matter of fact although his first, *English Monumental Brasses* two years after he joined the Club in 1924, threatened to be so. However *The windows of Dixon's room presented an unusually festive and decorative appearance. Hanging from the curtain poles were representations of Knights in shining armour.* These however were not scalps of the host's earlier and more riotous days, still hanging to adorn his wigwam, but rubbings of English Monumental Brasses made by Guy Muscott during a youth that obviously was spent in an ecclesiastical atmosphere or at any rate, so far as holidays were concerned, in ecclesiastical buildings. The paper turned into an audiovisual presentation when *The proceedings were further enlivened by brilliant acrobatic feats performed on step ladders by father and son with occasional assistance by the host.*

In *A Good Tune* (1932) Muscott suggested music appreciation should go beyond just a memorable tune but *hinted that even the pleasure taken in the Merry Widow by the austere members of the Club was produced largely by the association with shapely legs and the enjoyment of a comfortable seat after a good alcoholic dinner.* Comments by the austere members were not recorded.

The Fens (1934) proved to be rather more factual as was *The Staple Trade* (1942), a dissertation on leather, *full of illuminating detail and illustrated by specimens.* The last year of the Second World War included *Wine* (1945), a subject that went down well with Chatterers and *brought memories of far off things and dinners long ago.* Muscott looked ahead and *warned that after the war fine burgundy and claret would be rare and expensive, but our hopes were raised by the favourable prospect of port sherry and madeira.* The following year Muscott travelled across the Channel bringing back *The Continent Revisited, a tale of discomfort, scarcity, poor food, poverty, high prices coupled with efficient and widespread black markets. Of intolerable delays on frontiers slow dirty and overcrowded trains and buses a lack of taxis. Cold and cheerless* hotels. *His account gave little encouragement to those who are longing to go abroad again for holidays as they used to do.* It would appear to have been quite a Grand Tour, taking in Switzerland and Spain, *Havana cigars at 1/8* (8p) *and sherry at 6/8* (33p) *a bottle,* as well as war torn France and Italy where he *found great quantities of luxury goods and good restaurants* although *Northern Italy rather cheaper, many luxury goods, much real and distressing poverty and largest black market.* Whether Guy Muscott remained a member during the Dark Age must remain a mystery but it is highly likely he was elevated to honorary status. He died in 1965.

Betty Moore Fullerton, elected in 1915 read two papers, *Environment as a factor in Evolution* (1915), apparently a somewhat complicated treatise and *Personality* (1917), another detailed talk including *a comparison.......between English and German Personalities, and the Educational Environments of both countries contrasted, to the decided advantage of the former.* Browne, as Tyrannus, ended the discussion part of his minute in philosophical mode, *mention was made of the value of religion and its teaching, and the proposal was made to welcome new knowledge as definitely more divine than any untruth however venerable.* Fullerton resigned in 1921.

William Waite Hadley, born in 1867, held the post of Editor of the *Northampton Mercury* when elected in 1919. During his short ordinary membership he contributed several papers with interesting titles including *What is wrong with the Middle Classes?* In 1920 in which *he accused the middle classes of apathy towards public interests. They are more prosperous, more self-indulgent, less inclined to listen to the calls for public service. A great moral revival is badly needed. If it comes the middle classes may save the nation.*

After reviewing *Northampton's Great Days* (1922) Hadley went on to ask the question *How can we improve Town Government?* (1923) and gave as possible answers *development of intelligent Public Opinion, extension of private contract for work now undertaken by the Public Authority, Further co-option of those peculiarly qualified for special work.* As ever there is the feeling things change little over the years.

Parliament and Empire came in 1924, after which Hadley was elected to honorary status due to his imminent departure to London as parliamentary correspondent of the *Daily Chronicle*. He remained a member and frequent reader until at least 1951, when records cease. In a comparison of *Life in Northampton and Life in London* given at the Summer Meeting 1932, the year Hadley became editor of the *Sunday Times*, Ince-Jones writes *As usual he succeeded with consummate skill in not treading upon any tender corns and gave the impression of an urbane metropolitan who still loved provincial lanes.* Another six years went by before Hadley addressed the Club again with *A Rural Revolution Fifty Years Ago* in 1938, recounting factors leading up to *the astonishing change in the control of County Affairs, until fifty years ago in the hands of the aristocracy...In the spring of 1880 came an election in which Hadley played a part.....The Red Earl* [5th Earl Spencer 1835-1910] *diluted the benches of magistrates by appointing business men of standing. Their reception was cold...*

Hadley's last three recorded papers were political but escaped by a hairsbreadth from having the party tag attached. 1943 marked the midway point of the Second World War and Hadley travelled to Humfrey's house in Dallington for the Summer Meeting where he talked on *No. 10 Downing Street,* answering questions on Winston Churchill, *Mr Neville Chamberlain at Munich and the working of the*

Censorship in war time. It is probably just as well this was a private meeting and no outside reporters were present.

Although there are no minutes extant *Recollections of Ten Prime Ministers* (1950) and *The Crown and the Cabinet* (1951) were undoubtedly highlights of the Club years. Hadley died in December 1961.

*

At this time three members are mentioned only briefly. Marshall Heanley managed to read only one paper, *Gibraltar* (1921), in his eight years of membership from 1919. Thomas Collier was elected in 1922, attended one meeting and disappeared from the records.

T G Carter entered the Chit Chat Club in 1933, attending regularly but never reading, up to the Jubilee Dinner of 1935, after which he disappeared from the records until his resignation letter was read out in February 1936, the occasion when Trevor Lewis voted against accepting it, no reason given.

*

Born in 1878 Henry Percival Shapland was elected to the Club in June 1936. The previous month, technically as a guest speaker, he had given a reading on *Fakes* when *In a witty introduction he professed a nervousness that was by no means apparent, he stated that the rarer or scarcer a thing was, the more men wanted to buy it and the greater the motive for fakery.* Although originally an architect by profession Shapland was a brilliant speaker and raconteur on many subjects, giving ten recorded papers as a member, starting with *Fleet Street* (1936) from an insider viewpoint, followed by *Architecture* (1937), a comprehensive history with high hopes for the future. This was the only dissertation connected with his calling and he never talked about his magnum opus, *The Practical Decoration of Furniture*, a three volume work published in

1926. Possibly Shapland was at his best in 1940 with *Food and Drink.....a subject obviously dear to his heart and comforting to an organ rather lower in the body.*

It rippled with fun, sparkled with jest and epigram and moreover was full of the best Chit Chat to lead to further Chat to follow. Ince-Jones produced one of his longer narratives as Tyrannus the recorder, including *....With mock solemnity he showed the importance of the subject as exemplified by literature, art and proverb, history nursery rhyme and legend......He gave us a description, poetic and aesthetic of the eating of a luscious peach and then for a change described the same process coldly and scientifically. He showed himself a gourmet and an enthusiast when he proclaimed that greater is he that invents a new dish than he that discovers a new star... And yet, lyric though he was, a touch of cynicism would occasionally break through, as for example when he doubted how long love would survive constant meals of dried herbs instead of stalled oxen and when he reminded us that "It is easier to eat caviar on impulse than baked beans on principle"*

….. some of the clergy seemed very expert on wine. In fact it was a tasty discussion. A surprising interest was exhibited by some members in questions framed to discover what was the best form of food to neutralise some of the less happy effects of drink. It became clear that though the universe may have a spiritual basis, part of it has a spirituous bias..

The following year Shapland addressed the Summer Meeting on *Colour*. Ince-Jones again....*It was a brilliant effort, scintillating with prismatic flashes as from cut diamonds and full of gems of pleasure as rich as rubies, emeralds and sapphires. The purple patches cannot be reproduced in the limited space of the Minutes.......Seeing so many ladies present, he trailed his wit on "Women's use of colour for adornment"* with the result that the discussion was definitely more animated than is usual at a summer meeting out of doors. 1943 produced *Summum Bonum*, another *brilliant paper, full of humour, wit and wisdom* including towards the end *He urged the living of the life to the full, for the Highest Good was Life itself.* An insight into Shapland's character comes with the comment *One of the high lights of the paper was an early poem by Shapland, written at a time when he was practically untouched by cynicism.*

Two years later Shapland read *Conversation Piece*, a history of the art of conversation, or Chit Chat. 1948 brought forth *Revolt*, notably French and Russian varieties and including the assertion *revolt was not against individual tyrants but was directed to the overthrow of the existing form of society.*

At the Summer Meeting in 1949 Shapland spoke on *Personality and Possessions*. This proved to be more philosophical than usual and included the suggestion that *Possessions provided a means by which a man expressed and developed his personality. Far from despising the man with the muck-rake, Shapland thought too many people were obsessed by envy of those whose rich personalities enabled them to enjoy a variety of possessions.*

Only two more papers are recorded, but being in the Dark Age are not minuted, *The Press 1900-1951* in 1951 and *Conversational Opening* (1956). When skeleton minutes were resumed in 1964 Shapland is not present at meetings and it must be assumed he resigned some time during the missing years. He died in 1968.

*

Northampton's County Librarian Geoffrey Ellison gave a paper in 1936, the year he joined the Club. *Atmosphere in Fiction* analysed the way factual settings of fictional works added to their credibility, ending with *probably towns got the literature they deserved*. It was *rather depressing to think the home of the Chit Chat Club had produced no immortal literature save the papers of its members and that the County itself had given little beyond Whyte Melville.* This is illuminating as Whyte Melville, considered earlier, had been dead for nearly sixty years, twenty years before Ellison was born and would appear to be still a best seller. The local best seller, H E Bates, with at least twenty four works published by 1936 was not truly recognised until the collection of stories, *My Uncle Silas,* appeared in 1939.

Two years later Ellison posed the question *Should I rather have lived in the 18th Century?* Neither speaker nor guests came to a definite decision, as possibly *there was neither more nor less safety in the 18th Century because, then as now liberty existed in England, there was less noise, more spaciousness, less mass-suggestion, but also fewer conveniences, more snobbishness, a less sound view of sin and less relief of poverty.*

In a learned treatise in 1940 entitled Some *Lessons from Ancient Greece* Ellison *wished to apply to modern times the following lessons from the Greeks.*

(1) An essential quality in affairs is intelligence, everybody except the secretary being highly intelligent, this was agreed nem. Con.

(2) Though highly intelligent, the Greeks did not regard peace as an end in itself. It was not quite clear whether this was a proof of intelligence.

(3) They were insincere and did not appreciate the value of service. In this they may have been too intelligent.

(4) Their history, which he illustrated suggestively from their three great wars, showed the supreme value of sea power. This comforted us all not a little.

This last remark must be taken in the context of the United Kingdom being at war and relying greatly on the Royal Navy.

Ellison's last paper, *The Village Community* (1942), centred on Great Brington where he had been living for seven years. The following year he moved to Yorkshire.

*

Richard Montague Raynsford came to the Club with a long history of army service in the South African War and the 1914-18 war in which he gained the rank of Lieutenant Colonel and was awarded the Distinguished Service Order. He appeared as guest speaker in 1936 when he posed the question *Francophile or Francophobe.* Pros and cons were aired and with *A warm feeling for France, engendered perhaps by the French connections of his wife and fostered by pleasant sojourns in that country....* it was clear in which camp the speaker resided.

Raynsford joined Club ranks the following year and may well have remained a member until his death in 1965. His papers mirrored his background. In *The Territorial Army* (1938) he gave the meeting a history lesson and *described the Northamptonshire Assn. and discussed the function of the Territorials should another war break out and wondered whether they would do their work well. He pointed out that their main work would be Anti-Aircraft Defence.*

When it came to *The Future of England* in 1941 there was no question of which side would win the war but rather a list of reforms in the fields of *Unemployment reduction by Government control, removal of snobbery, paying the clergy better, abolition of slums* with *improvement of the Poor Law System* and, rather surprisingly, *supersession of the Party System in politics.* Ince-Jones, in a rare note of understatement added *Though he professed himself a Conservative, he revealed himself a Radical.*

Later in the war, April 1943, a discussion was started with *Leadership or Linoleum*, when Raynsford talked on *the way of distinguishing between the few.... ready to lead and the many who were only too willing to be trodden on.*

He emphasised the need for leaders in the future, involving a levelling of the classes and thought *we had much to learn from Russia*. It was felt by the Club the process should be one of levelling up rather than down and *the advantages of the Public School system should be extended to a larger section of the people, rather than that the system should be abolished.*

The last two recorded papers by Raynsford were on politico-economics in *Greece* (1948) and *A Visit to USA and Canada* (1950).

John Alan Turner became Clerk to the Northamptonshire County Council in 1938 and from 1939-45 Air Raid Precautions Controller for which he was awarded the Order of the British Empire in 1943. On being elected to the Club in 1945 Turner spoke on *Local Government,* its history going back to the 16th century. He ended with high hopes for the future, tinged with a prophetic warning …. *The serious danger ahead is the usurpation of the functions of local authorities by the central government. It is probable that members of local authorities will in future be paid for their services in England and Wales as they are in Scotland. Politics should play no part in local government.*

A paper directed mainly at those legal practitioners present, *Crime and Sentence* (1948) produced controversy early on with *it lies with the High Court Judge, the Recorder, or the magistrate, to pronounce sentence. Turner's view was that many such sentences show a lack of wisdom in dealing with offenders.* Types of crime, criminal and sentence were discussed in detail and the meeting ended on a philosophical note *The professional man or business man of* standing was broken utterly by the disgrace of a term in prison, the habitual criminal took it as a matter of course.

Turner's other two recorded papers, *Martyrs* (1950) and *Holidays – Active or Idle?* (1956) were given in the Dark Age. He remained a member, perhaps a reader, until moving away in 1966 and becoming an honorary member.

After obtaining his degree at Balliol College Oxford the Hon. Michael Francis Eden served in the Life Guards as Captain during the 1939-45 war. He became a Chatterer in 1948 and gave at least two talks, *Beards* (1950) and *Agriculture and Land Tenure Today* (1952) both of which came after Ince-Jones' minutes ceased. This is a misfortune, Eden lived an interesting life and his early opinions would be worthy of record. It was in 1962 he succeeded his father as 7th Baron Henley of Chardstock, County Dorset and 5th Baron Northington of Watford, County Northampton, and later became President of the Liberal Party 1966-7 and Chairman of the CPRE (Council for the Protection of Rural England) in 1973. He died in 1977.

The manager of Barclay's Bank in Northampton, Cecil Garnham, read three titles following his election in 1949, *Retribution* (1951), *Can it Work?* (1953) and *Fashionable Delusions* (1955).

*

Whether Stanley Hill should be included among medical men is a point verging on the moot, he was with them, not of them. Stan, as he was known to all, came to Northampton as superintendent of the General Hospital in 1945, having been deputy superintendent at Birmingham Infirmary from 1937-40 and involved with the rehabilitation of refugees and relief organisations during the war, working with General Frederick Morgan, Chief of Staff to General Eisenhower. A Club stalwart, he contributed twelve recorded papers, ten of which are held in the archives. *Out of Bondage* is listed in the programme for 1952-3 and is likely to be his first. The second reference to Hill is the manuscript of *Committeemanship* (1962) a comprehensive assessment containing generalisations ....*a committee is as infinite and varied, as good or as bad, as bright or as dull, as are human beings themselves.....* and a heartfelt .....*certain types of persons do seem to crop up with fair regularity.....people who collect committees as redskins* (do) *scalps or schoolboys collect conkers.*

Criticism (1967) appears in the sparse pages of Jackson's reign as Tyrannus, although hand written by Lee. This is not unusual, when Tyrannus was unavoidably absent a substitute, often Tyrannus elect, took over. In this case Jackson is recorded as being present and Lee's notes are dated April 28th, three months after the meeting. No reason is given for Jackson's memory lapse. As with many of Hill's papers *Criticism* is very much to the point, *It* [criticism] *should be factual and on matters of general or public concern and should be without malice.*

A travelogue manuscript, comparing his private visit to Italy with Lee's professional travels in *Jordan Revisited* the month before, appeared as *Fragments of Calabria* in 1980.

N. S. E. & Centre (1983) described a trip around England examining management structures, a heady subject but fortunately for the Club *this paper has no particular theme or serious message for posterity: rather a light-weight description of a few visits to interesting places.....a supermarket at Newcastle on Tyne, the Royal Naval Hospital, Portsmouth, The U S Airforce Base hospital at Lakenheath, the Cromwell private hospital London, National Children's Homes in London and Luton Airport.* This reading was during Hill's tenure as Tyrannus which lasted until mid-1985.

Fortunately a new volume of minutes were started in January that year with the result some of his excellent entries are available, previous entries during his reign as Tyrannus being lost. *The Strike* in April gave a detailed analysis of the miners' strike the previous winter, headed by Arthur Scargill.

Chance followed in 1987, ...*an abbreviation of: "The influence of chance upon historical events".... how chance continually influenced our daily lives, how trivialities such as blocked roads or delayed journeys could sometimes make all the difference between success and failure, safety and catastrophe.* He concluded *with passing reference to Pocahontas, Sigmund Freud, King William III, Socrates, and Fidel Castro – a motley crew if ever there was one; but all, like the rest of us, equally subject to the whims and vagaries of chance.*

I.O.M. in 1989 proved to be more a history of the Isle of Man than a travelogue. During *Irritations* (1990) Hill bared his soul describing *irritating things from spilt sugar and coffee, breadcrumbs and blunt scissorstojunk mail and animal activists who so love animals that they poison human food to prove it.*

After giving a survey and examples from history in *Humour* (1993) Hill told some characteristically short but pertinent samples by way of illustration and finished.....*enjoy humour wherever you meet it, expect the twist to be unexpected and if you are the raconteur, don't fluff the punch line.*

In February 1995 Hill read a moving tribute to Heygate Senior who had died recently.

Hill gave his last paper on *The Workhouse*, a history of workhouses and their masters from the Elizabethan Act of 1601 until the National Health Service erupted in 1948. Hill defended the retention of the 'master' title with *Of course there was a strong element of sentiment involved: I was after all a third generation workhouse master, and as such, a workhouse master's son, widely regarded in the trade as the most obnoxious creature on earth. Of course I cannot comment on that opinion......*

The script is undated but internal evidence would suggest late 1996 or early 1997, the year Hill died.

*

The name of Heygate, together with the village of Bugbrooke, means flour milling to Northamptonshire folk. The family has farmed locally since 1562 and since the early 18th century been involved with milling. In 1900 Mr Arthur Robert Heygate started the present business now run by his grandchildren. It was sometime before 1955 when his son Arthur Robert, known to members as Bob Senior joined the Chit Chat and read many papers during his forty year membership. *Our Daily Bread* appears for 1956 and *An Assortment of British Grain and Cereal Processing* is minuted in 1964. This latter, unlikely to be the exact title was ... *although lucid a little too technical for Tyrannus* [A Jackson] *and some members to comprehend fully*. Undated but from internal evidence between these two talks was *Country Life and Agriculture*, the first Heygate paper in the archives. It is typically profound, starting with repeal of the Corn Laws and changes in land ownership during the second half of the nineteenth century leading to decline in farming only stemmed by an overwhelming need for food production in World War I. Changes due to mechanisation and application of science to farming were succinctly outlined. Heygate viewed the impending 1958 Agriculture Act as possibly *the thin end of the wedge so far as agricultural stability in Britain is concerned.* By 1966 Robert had moved on to *Capital Gains*, another topical subject. There is a gap of fifteen years when *The Common Agricultural Policy and the Green Pound* (1981) saw a shift from countryside and agricultural subjects to the wider economy. This erudite paper questioning some of the applications of the Common Agricultural Policy of the European Union brought forth no comments in Lee's notes of the evening.

Mergers and Management of 1988 started well …. *Mergers have been in existence for as long as mankind. Possibly one would accept that Eve and Adam was the earliest merger ….. Whilst accepting the very first merger has been beneficial, I doubt if many of the others have improved society generally.* Having gained his audience's attention Tyrannus Tasker remarks on … *a paper…. Which proved to be a stimulating critical review of Britain's business practices and prospects.*

In October 1989 Heygate Senior gave his last recorded paper, unfortunately not in the archives. Fortunately Tyrannus Fincham proved as always an informative recorder. In *The Countryside* the speaker gave an optimistic view of the future in spite of EEC policies on pesticides, 'The Greens', the Common Agricultural policy, movements of population, leisure facilities and high land values.

Heygate died in December 1994 and was given a tribute by Stanley Hill at the January meeting of 1995. He concluded … *A man of many parts, ranging from jet-hopping, globe-commuting business tycoon and Government advisor, through country squire, Deputy Lieutenant, and Magistrate, to family man, modest friend and companion. …. A humble, gentle, loyal and charming man who we are all proud to have known as member of the Chit Chat Club.*

Let the last comment come from Bob Senior himself over thirty years previously: *Perhaps the greatest value the countryman gives to the Nation is his ability …. To disregard the temptation which most men fall into of being led away by genius. Men of genius have given us everything that is beautiful and good but also everything that is hideous and vile. It isn't their fault. Genius is something quite incomprehensible to the common man. The fault is with us...... The fault, dear Brutus, is not in our stars but in ourselves, that we are underlings.*

With two members having identical names overlapping for over twenty years there could well have been some confusion in attributing papers but fortunately the present Bob Heygate was able to help the author unravel records.

Arthur Robert Heygate Junior, an Oxford St Edmund's Hall graduate joined the Club in 1975 and gave his maiden paper in 1977 on *John Maynard Keynes*. This proved not only to be a biography of the great economist but also a history of British economics and a discussion on Keynes' General Theory.

It is typical of Heygate Junior that one paper moved seamlessly into the next, *International Debt* (1979) being followed by *Boom or Gloom* (1980). *Chips* (1982) dealt with the burgeoning microchip and computer revolution and its effect on the world, particularly the rise of Japan regarding automation. *Economic Waves* (1986) and *Work* (1989) continued the trend whilst *Green* in 1992 cast doubts on the policy of *environmental improvements* being made *"regardless of cost"*. Heygate concluded ... *The Doom situation is still with us*, having pointed out a minute earlier ... *A decision to invest in a cleaner environment is a decision not to invest in something else.... Boffins who spend their days working out better ways to get rid of toxic waste do not invest in money making and perhaps life-saving drugs.*

Democracy and Capitalism (1994) produced a wide ranging paper starting with ... *the collapse of communism in Eastern Europe and the former Soviet Union and the spread of market economies in the third world*. Heygate dealt with the separation of politics and economics in democracies and problems with which third world leaders were faced, *the same challenges which politicians of western nations dealt with 180-200 years ago* ….

Heygate reviewed Britain's economic place in Europe and the world with *The Right Market* (1996) and *1-01-99 (In with the Euro and Out with the Pound)* (1998). *Doom* (2002) became a prelude to economic collapse in *Bubbles* (2004) and *A Small World* (2006) dealt with the IMF and global banking. *Change* (2007) and *Crunch* (2009) have explored years of recession and the Club eagerly awaits the next foray into current economics.

With nearly eighty years of combined membership the Heygates provided a plethora of thought provoking papers and a delightful venue for many Summer Meetings at their home.

*

Another family, Jackson-Stops, provided two members, Timothy who joined in 1989 and his father Anthony. Regrettably the latter is only credited with one paper, *Manners* (1969) in the twenty one years of his membership. Tim has two papers in the archives, *Liverish* (1994), an account of the Livery companies of the city of London and *The Paint Box* (2003), where *after starting off in the realms of physics and wave lengths far beyond the comprehension of Tyrannus* (Cornelius), he moved on to *philosophical questions about the existence of light and colour* and the history of paint. Tim Jackson Stops is credited with two more readings in the minutes. In *Preservation of Country Houses* (1991) he discussed buildings that could no longer be maintained as family homes and the various ways they could be converted to other uses whilst preserving their architecture and interior decoration and *The Lords of the Ring* (2004) proved to be a history of the Nurnberg Motor Racing Circuit in Germany. A further paper on Navigation and Longitude was given but there are no details.

*

John Robert Riggall joined the Club in about 1970. Farm Director for Heygate Industries he was a Board member of Moulton Agricultural College. After *Wildlife and Farming* (1971), of which there are no details there is a gap until *Lost Villages* (1980), a treatise on the ways in which villages had disappeared in the Northamptonshire countryside by means of plague, landlords and enclosures. *The ways of water* (1985), subtitled *How to manipulate rivers* gave a detailed account of fenland drainage. When Riggall talked on *Wild life at home* in 1987 he recalled the earlier paper read sixteen years before as including *widespread anxiety that modern scientific farming methods were banishing wild life from the land. The depressing effect of organophosphorous insecticides on the breeding capacity of birds of prey was a case in point.* Having reported improvements in the situation he continued *But if agriculture must learn to support wild life, so too must horticulture, for the gardens of Britain cover no less than ¾ million acres.* There followed an analysis of birds in his own garden, sparking off a lively discussion where *Opinions polarised into two opposing views. Heygate (junior) thought that in years to come farmland would be increasingly threatened and violated by town-dwellers. Hill on the other hand felt that we had now reached a stable balance between agriculture and the leisure activities of the great British public.* Riggall died in January 1989.

Douglas Atkinson, known to all as Peter, joined the Club in 1979. He served as a major in the Royal Artillery, and the Education Corps in the 1939-45 war when he was wounded in North Africa. When elected to the Club he held the position of manager of Lloyds Bank in Northampton. Copies of three papers are in the Club archives by courtesy of his widow Mary. *Mons Calpe* (1981) dealt with the turbulent history of Gibraltar from 3000 BC and *Camellia*

Sinensis(1986), identified as *an evergreen plant with elliptical serrated leaves, indigenous to S. E. Asia* presented the rise and fall of china tea in great detail. Atkinson's third paper, *England Confides*, set out to answer the question *What sort of man was Nelson?*, working backwards from his body arriving *at Gibraltar in a cask of brandy lashed to the mizzen.*

Cecil Featherstone, a leading Northampton architect from 1963 became a Chatterer in 1979. Responsible for several local landmarks he always maintained his best, at least his favourite was the *Chronicle and Echo* building on Northampton's Upper Mounts, built in 1978 at a cost of £5.5m. Featherstone has five papers in the archives. The evolution of the English country house was considered in *Upstairs Downstairs* (1982), containing *in a review of the 19th century......the effect upon the country house of the newly rich from the industrial revolution which led to the idea of the romantic house with ever greater opportunities for the house party and the way upwards in the society world...*

With *Sitting Pretty* (1984) Featherstone pondered on *one of the oddest things about man is the length of time he will put up with appalling discomfort* and reviewed the history of furniture, notably relatively recent times when it had become more comfortable. In *Customs* (1985) examples were, among many, many others *the Furry Dance of Helston, the Horn Dance of Abbot's Bromley, the Glove Fair of Honiton, the Mop Fair of Stratford, the Goose Fair of Nottingham, and the Wardmote of the Woodmen of Arden.* In *Boats* (1988) Featherstone *traced the history of sailing ship design from Ancient Egypt to the present.* Having gone into design difficulties experienced by boat architects he ended with *their boats have extraordinary beauty and purity. No wonder they are ranked as feminine, for are they not lovely to behold, difficult to control, and expensive to maintain?* Featherstone's 1990 paper, *Nil Desperandum* tackled the problem of town planning with particular emphasis on architecture, present and future, ending on an optimistic note....*I believe we have turned the corner, the man in the street is up on his feet demanding a better life in a better surrounding.* Featherstone died in 1993.

*

Lionel Hadden, retired BOAC and British Airways captain and 'Pip' to his friends, read his first paper *1997 and After* in 1985. This *dealt with the agreement reached between China and UK upon the future of Hong-Kong when the 99 year lease expires in 1997,* and produced a somewhat surprisingly hopeful view among members. *What Price Speed* (1987) considered the history of supersonic flight and environmentalists' concerns for the future. Concorde had been flying for 11 years by then and already travel to Australia in 90 minutes was being considered. *To the Club's relief the reader felt that such speeds could not be justified. It would be far better to use the money to increase the safety, comfort, and cost-effectiveness of subsonic jets.* Hadden produced *Communication* in 1988, which the Club found very complicated. *Even with the benefit of re-reading the paper Tyrannus* (Fincham) *found it so detailed and explicit that it was difficult to epitomize.* With characteristic lateral thoughts the meeting discussed *the pecadillos* [sic] *of the animal kingdom when the club was regaled with details of the goose which "Biffed" a Boeing 707 on the nose and of the poodle in a microwave oven.* The last paper recorded was *Arteries of an Empire* (1991), being a review of British maritime history, ending with future commercial transport of goods by air. Pip Hadden resigned from the Club in 1992.

*

In 1970 Clifford Ellison, an established picture restorer in London was given 'A Royal Appointment as Picture Restorer to Her Majesty the Queen'. A Club member from 1985 Clifford has five papers in the archives. *The Decline of the English Country House* (1987) traced its history from Tudor times to the houses' heyday in the pre-war era of the early 1900s. The decline that set in after 1918 produced mixed feelings *but The Club felt that, though the life for which these houses were built is past, somehow they must be saved.*

The Olympic Games, their history and background from fourteen centuries BC to the twentieth century AD provided Ellison with the subject of his next paper, *Play* (1989). The following year *Nor all, that glisters, gold* told the story of fakes, in particular those by Han Van Meegeren and Tom Keating. *A near run thing* (1996) referred to a remark made by the Duke of Wellington after he defeated Napoleon at Waterloo, a battle recounted in detail by Ellison.

Ellison's last paper in the archives is a heartfelt personal account of *Then and Now* (2001), changes that took place in Britain during the twentieth century. Improvements in education, health and material goods along with affluence had to be set against *Visually there can be hardly any room for doubt that Britain is a much uglier place than it used to be.......The few get wealthy on the destruction of natural beauty and the break up of communities all in the cause of faster growth. Will society one day say, "Hold! That is enough".* Clifford Ellison moved south in 2001.

Anthony Rickett combines a thriving practice as an architect with farming of pedigree cattle. Two years after his election to the Club in 1987 he talked about *Rates of Change*, a history of the Poor Rate from 1698 to the, then proposed, Community Charge. The history of *Whisky* (1991) gave the Club time to mull over-

"Here's to good old whisky
So amber and so clear
'tis not so sweet as women's lips
But a damned sight more sincere."
After describing agricultural shows and the responsibility of judges, Rickett explained the way in which breeders assess animals and also the title of his paper *BLUP* (1993) – Best Linear Unbiased Prediction – whereby ancestry is used to ensure the best beast. In *Equity and Law* (1995) Rickett considered the adversarial nature of English courts and the desire to win cases winning over the establishment of truth. Once again the Club illustrated its essential nature when *the members became involved in a wide ranging discussion covering Roman and Napoleonic law, the Nuremberg trials, America and O J Simpson and so on....*

There is a gap of records until 2003 when Rickett, in *Officious Secrets*, talked about restrictions of information due to the Official Secrets Act and *restraints on discussion and publication of matters relating to the livestock epidemic of recent years.* Two years later his thoughts about official red tape in the European Union, particularly with reference to agriculture were expressed in *Negativity*. Ranging from household to nuclear waste Rickett explored worldwide rubbish in *This is all Rubbish* in 2006. As Tyrannus Peter Hardingham recorded *it was a gloomy picture for the future of the planet. Rickett sought to cheer us up by ending on a light note with tales of rubbish masquerading as art.*

Rickett *extrapolated porcine competitive spirit when feeding to human individuals* in *Trotters and Troughs* (2009), suggesting *this was basically a desirable feature, only becoming unacceptable when poorly regulated or completely unregulated.* Overpaid personnel in the public sector produced the final question *What, as taxpayers, do we make of all this?* There appeared to be no answer, at least none that could be written down. Slightly less contentious was *Tunes of Glory*, a treatise on National Anthems in 2011, which produced a discussion ranging from *What is truth?* to the suggestion *the Furry Dance should be translated into Cornish,* thereby showing the Club still maintains its capacity for lateral thought.

*

A Major in the Northamptonshire Regiment 1939-46 and mentioned in despatches Neil Soutar joined the Club in 1989 at which time he was managing director of the Odell Leather Company in Bedfordshire. His first paper *Justice* (1991) dealt more with the history of Justices from earliest times than Justice itself according to the minutes. His second reading, *The Last Frontier* (1994), dealt with the story of Alaska in detail, including the sale by Russia to America in 1867 for $7.2 million, about two cents an acre. For his last recorded paper Soutar followed the habit of disguising paper titles and produced *In a Persian Market* (1996), an in depth study of leather, its manufacture and uses.

Trevor Underwood, founder partner of a large Northamptonshire property agency, gave his first paper in 1993, the year after he joined the Club. *Any Volunteers* described Voluntary Housing Associations with their charitable status and the speaker considered their efforts one of the greatest exercises in social realism. The discussion ranged wide from slum clearance to rebuilding the centre of Northampton. *Chaos and Cavaliers* in 1995 was all about the Scilly Isles where *Underwood's enthusiasm for the place was evident. It may have been the one policeman or the limited tourism or the abundance of flowers. The poor water supply....didn't bother him and clearly there were alternatives.*

An enigmatic *Watch This Space* (1998) proved to be an analysis of land use for development and planning, a presentation of both sides in this difficult problem for Local Authorities on the one hand and environmentalists on the other. The next year Underwood gave the name of his paper *A Giant on Its Back* and explained to the Club *"The Canals of England" would have been a more forthright and obvious title but would have lacked imagination and deprived members of the opportunity to exercise their curiosity.*

A Novel Experience followed in 2003 when Underwood presented a life of Charles Dickens, concentrating on the man rather than his books. The last paper, *The Long and the Short of it* (2005) centred on problems associated with *depletion of natural resources and increasing demand for energy and the means of producing it*. Underwood resigned from the Club later that year.

Francis Sitwell became a member in 1993, the year in which he gave his maiden paper *A Portrait of Edith Sitwell*. As nephew and literary executor to one of the most colourful and eccentric poets of the age Sitwell was able to recount Aunt Edith's life better than anyone. As he told a host's wife quietly in the kitchen, "I used to ask my aunt Edith not to wear her funny clothes and hats because my school friends would laugh at her". Her apparel was part of her wonderfully memorable eccentricity. *A Notable Disappearance* (1996) took listeners back to 1974 when the professional gambler Lord Lucan disappeared after the murder of Sandra Rivers, his children's nanny. Speculation was rife, not only from the speaker but also Club members, Ellison, as Tyrannus, noting *Even the Loch Ness monster came into it – I can't remember quite how.* For his last paper Sitwell gave the Club no doubt of his subject. *Our National Hero and the Georgian Navy* (2002) meant just that, *the first part devoted to Nelson's extraordinary campaign in the Mediterranean from 1797-1805 and the second on the Georgian Navy and its principal ships.* The meeting was enlivened by the presence of Simon Nelson

Douglas Preston, a direct descendant and author of a learned paper to the *International Colloquium on Naval History* at Venice in 1996.

Francis Sitwell died at the early age of 69 in 2004. The crowded church at his funeral service was well supported by fellow Chatterers saying their last goodbyes.

John Gale occupied the post of Bandmaster at RAF Hereford from 1953-6, followed by a managerial position with the music publishers Boosey and Hawkes until 1961. In 1965 he became an independent music publisher and joined the Chit Chat in 2001. In the first of two papers, *OO7* (2002) the story was told, not of a modern spy and womaniser but the eighteenth century *Charming, Dangerous, Debonair, Energetic, Handsome, Romantic, Seductive* – and many more – Lorenzo Da Ponte, librettist of three of Mozart's operas, *The Marriage of Figaro, Don Giovanni* and *Cosi fan Tutti*. For his other talk, *Strike up the Band* (2004), Gale regaled the Club with bands and symphony orchestras, back as far as primitive man and the music he made with *sticks, stones and possibly bones*. He ended on a sombre note asking *if computers can produce accurate sounds of real instruments....no need for an orchestra or is there?* Gale resigned from the Club later in 2004.

Michael Reed, accountant, read his first paper, *Five letters and it's a puzzle....perhaps an enigma?* in 2004, two years after joining the Club. This comprehensive study of Bletchley Park and the Enigma coding machine was followed two years later by *A Good Shepherd Should Shear His Flock Not Skin It*, a brief history of taxation from Roman times to the present day. The Club was pleased to hear *penalties are, happily, now less severe than under....Rome where the penalty for failure to pay taxes was death;* Reed went on to say, with some relish, that *the same punishment was visited upon tax collectors who failed to collect.*

Kathmandu – Derring Do in 2009 presented a picture of Nepal and the Gurkhas, the name coming from Sanskrit meaning cow-protector, who have a unique relationship with the British Army going back to 1816. *Plus ca change* (2011) centred around changes in the English language over the years. He gave the Club plenty to think about when it came *to the possible decline of handwriting with the introduction of the keyboard..... i-pad and Kindle.* (The) *paper divided the Club in two, those who could and would use them and those whose feelings towards the heirs of Gutenberg and Caxton were expressed in no uncertain terms.* Following a successful September 2012 meeting in Malta, Reed recounted the history of Mediterranean corsairs, both Christian and Moslem, in *Valletta to Mogadishu via Baltimore in 400 years*.

Peter Nock, a well-known jeweller and gold valuer in Northampton came to the Club in 2004. His first paper given the following year, *Does Charity begin at Home?* showed Peter's other side, committee member and key worker at the Cynthia Spencer Hospice in Northampton. Nock answered his own question by pointing out the decreasing role of the National Health Service in funding hospices. *Diamonds are Forever* in 2005 gave a detailed account of a particular crystalline form of carbon and paved the way for *Valuation, a question of Opinion?* (2008) when the Club was treated to an account of the valuation process and learned the difference between probate value and insurance value.

Although records are incomplete in all probability Gary Shaeffer is the only United States citizen to have become a Chatterer. With his position of *Popperfoto,* a commercial photographic library Shaeffer was able to present *Beautiful Tragedies* (2006), an illustrated talk about Herbert Ponting, photographer to Captain Scott's ill-fated South Pole expedition. The unique pictures *showed that Ponting's technical and compositional talents were "superb, which....rise to the heights of true photographic greatness"*. In 2008 Shaeffer presented *UH,* being a history of the American Upper House, or Senate. Two years later, staying across the pond for his subject, *From the 18th to the 21st .... How Do You Look When I'm Sober* Shaeffer dealt with Prohibition Years in the USA, including biographies of Carrie Nation, hatchet lady of the Temperance Movement and Al "Scarface" Capone, protectionist gangster. Reading *Third Time Lucky – Again?* Shaeffer *proceeded to enlighten the Club in his own way and enthuse with 'stories full of quirks and foibles and coincidences and drama'*, telling the sometimes chaotic history of London hosted Olympic Games in 1908 and 1948, a topical subject for 2012.

Two years after becoming a Chatterer Peter Talbot, a Fellow of the Royal Institute of Chartered Surveyors showed his interest in heritage with his paper *Lost Souls* (2010). He limited himself to years prior to the middle of the 16th century, describing 84 villages that had been deserted in Northamptonshire. In 2012 Talbot had wished to consider the relationship between philanthropy and bureaucracy but in fear of drifting into politics took a sideways leap into the subject of bridges with *Ways and Means.* A history of bridges was combined with the means of financing their construction and produced a discussion that went off at a tangent involving three-seater loos.

Ian Lowery, chartered surveyor and estate management consultant became a Chatterer in 2009 and presented his first paper *The birthplace of civilisation?* in 2011. Members who had always considered the Euphrates river area to be where it all started were fascinated to learn about the Tryptillian race in the Ukraine where recent Russian research had uncovered a peaceful civilisation existing some 7000 years ago.

An engineer, Chairman of the European standard for Aluminium from 1983-90 and a Trustee of the Dyslectic Society 2009-11, Derek Bull became a member in 2010. His first paper, *Time* (2012), dealing with the measurement of this elusive product, gave the Club an insight into the workings of clocks through the ages.

*

Throughout this history of Chit Chat in Northampton has run a thread of outsiders, guest speakers from many walks of life. At first they tended to be substitutes for members but gradually became almost exclusively attractions imported as bait to entice members, families and friends to gather for Summer Meetings. A few, a very few, have been described in the text where they seem relevant. This has meant that many have been omitted who deserve fuller mention. It would be a Herculean task to trace every guest speaker and an even greater problem to unravel their talks. Only two, Isobel Tasker in 1981 and the Marquis de Piro in 2012 have papers in the archives. They have been recorded however, where possible with their credentials, in Appendix 2. They deserve more than this.

Epilogue

Tyrannus XVII, possibly XVIII or XIX, sat at his desk on Easter Saturday. A bright frosty morning but with prospect of snow showers. It had been a long journey. Three years or more delving into not only his Northampton Club's history but also that of Cambridge University. He had been privileged to enter the lives of so many men, writers, politicians, professionals, academics, local and national figures, all gifted with an ability to hold forth on subjects so varied it was impossible to categorise them. Some were household names in the past, others destined to become mere footnotes in the book of ages, if mentioned at all.

Had it been all worthwhile? Certainly the journey was, but the result, that remained another question. Would anyone be interested enough to read about it? Possibly one or two members of the Club.

What started off as a list, a very long and boring list, of names and titles of papers has been expanded to a slightly less tedious account of a group whose sole function was, at least on the surface, to meet infrequently and discuss topics that might or might not be of interest. It was, and is, more than that. However hard you try it is never possible to improve upon those words of the fifth Tyrannus, Frederick Ince-Jones in 1951 …. *It is not a mean achievement in a somewhat prosaic provincial town, where things of the mind are none too prominent, for these men of widely differing tastes, professions, political and religious views to have preserved in a friendly spirit for sixty seven years a gathering for the discussion of intellectual matters.* How much more true today, another sixty two years on.

The Club still has status today although perhaps not in the public eye. A few years ago a priest in Northampton was heard to remark …. *If you are invited to a meeting of the Chit Chat you do not hesitate, you go ….*

Back to the present. As Tyrannus there is much to do, minutes to send out together with notice of meetings, the membership list to be updated, correlating members' ideas to share and complaints to calm. A sort of non-religious mediator and advocate. Easier these days with the internet but still needing words, lots of words. Like the writer of the lyrics to *Land of Hope and Glory* whose diary ran to over 4 million words, the Master of King's who wrote the best ghost stories ever and the mayor of Rye who created Dodo, Mapp and Lucia, all members of that other, Cambridge Club, Tyrannus also suffers from logorrhoea. He is not penitent. Now, to get on with recounting that other Club…..The Great Beginning of it all at Cambridge University.

APPENDIX 1
Guest Speakers

Year		Speaker	Details	Topic
1888		Mr A J Gotch	Kettering.	The Renaissance in Northamptonshire.
1889		Mr C Burdett		Pre-Christian Hospitals.
1890		Dr William Harding	Assistant Medical Officer Northampton Lunatic Asylum. Subsequently a member.	The Balance of Nature.
1892		Dr Clifton		Sir J. Crichton Brown's Oration on Sex in Education.
1895		Rev H A Boys		Earthquakes.
1902		Dr Peverell Smythe Hichens	Physician Northampton. Subsequently a member.	Sir Thomas Browne
1902		Mr S Lee		Shakespeare in Oral Tradition (In Association with The Moot).
1905		Prof. S J Hickson	D Sc, FRS	Mendelism.
1905		Mr Arthur Sleight BA		Origin and Growth of English Towns.
1906		Professor Reynolds Green		The British Association in South Africa.
1907		Mr M A Browne BA	Son of E M Browne.	Combustion.
1907		Mr Conrad Thies		A Hospital in the suburbs of Hamburgh.
1909	S	Mr H C Crockett		Egypt.
1910		Mr Blake Odgers MCH. (Ox)	Demonstrator and Examiner Anatomy Oxford	Miracle Plays.
1911		Dr John Bain		Telepathy.
1911		Mr T Bosworth BA BSc FGS	Oil Prospector.	Travels in Trinidad
1911		Mr Harold St John Browne	Son of E M Browne.	Proverbs.
1912		Mr Wyman Abbott		New phases of the Neolithic Period.
1913		Rev C E Simpson		The problem of the future government of the British Empire.

1913		Mr William Arthur Walker	Subsequently a member.	Scouts.
1915		Rev Basil Henry Davies	Ex Member. Vicar St Sepulchres Northampton.	The War and After.
1917	S	Mrs Chamberlain		Woman in the Home.
1918	S	Miss Schooley		The New Spirit in Education.
1919	S	Lt Col J J Abrahams DSO	Medical Officer RAMC.	The Palestine Campaign.
1919		Mr E F Bowman		The Government of India.
1919		Mr A Millington		The Influence of Mountains.
1920		Mr Guy Bruce Muscott	Son of member and subsequently a member.	Experiences of the Prisoners' Camp at Ruhleben.
1920		Mr Mervyn L Posten	Queen's University Belfast.	Anglo-Irish Literature.
1920		Mr Thomas Wright	Olney.	John Payne.
1921		Mr William Charles Cyril Cooke	Northampton Grammar School.	Empire.
1921		Rev Alfred A Fawkes	Vicar Ashby St Ledgers.	Fogazzaro as Novelist and Religious Thinker.
1921		Lt Col P Hichens	Medical Officer RAMC. Served France. Ex member.	Casualty Clearing Stations.
1922	S	Rev S Wathen Wigg	HM Inspector of Schools.	Reminiscences as an Inspector of Schools.
1923		Rev B E Evans	Rector of Milton, Northamptonshire.	Rights of Sanctuary.
1923	S	Mr Bertram Faulkner		Music.
1924		Mr F R Parnell	Late of Indian Civil Service.	A Christmas Camp in the Jungle.
1925		Mr Harold St John Browne	Son of E M Browne.	Transportation.
1926		Mr E E Field	Deputy Head Northampton Grammar School. Subsequently a member.	The Northampton Town Planning Scheme.
1926		Dr D T Hayes		Vienna Today.
1926		Mr Meredith Jackson	Son of James Jackson.	Buildings.

Year	S	Speaker	Role	Topic
1927	S	Sir Edward Penton	Industrialist and Explorer	Overland from India to Russia.
1927		Mr Beeby Thompson		The Evolution of Corn Mills.
1928	S	Dr Stephen Rowland	Medical Officer of Health.	Down to the Sea in Ships.
1930	S	Mr J L Holland	British Association.	South Africa.
1933	S	Mr King	Senior Master Oundle School.	Oundle, an Old Market Town.
1933		Mr Walter Travis		Art and Utility
1934	S	Dr John M Mackintosh	Medical Officer of Health Northamptonshire.	Comedy without Laughter.
1935	S	Dr H Travers Jones	Ex Member. Currently Medical Superintendent Cambridge County Mental Hospital.	The English Village.
1935		Mr Henry Percival Shapland	ARIBA.	Fakes.
1936		Lt Col Richard Montague Raynsford	DSO. Subsequently a member.	Francophile or Francophobe?
1938		Mr John Blakeman		The Mysterious Universe.
1939	S	Rev James Lawrence Cartwright	Ex Member. Vicar Christ's Church, Northampton.	Mountain Walks in Wales.
1940		Mr Blakeman		The Spiritual Basis of Life.
1941		Surgeon Commander Hopkins RN		Reminiscences of the Royal Navy.
1942	S	Miss Joan Wake	Local Historian.	What Next?
1944		Mr William Charles Cyril Cooke	Ex Member. Headmaster Northampton Grammar school.	Hopes & Fears.
1944		Dr H G Thornton	FRS.	On Pure & Applied Science.
1945		Lt Col H A Burne	DSO.	Marlborough and Montgomery.
1945	S	Dr John M Mackintosh	Ex Member. Currently Chief Medical Officer of Health Edinburgh.	New Houses for Old.
1946	S	Mrs Raynsford	Wife of Lt Col Raynsford.	How to be happy though Educated.

Year		Name	Details	Topic
1947	S	Lady Henley		Should the Unfittest Survive?
1948		Dr R M Jackson	Secretary Royal Commission.	Royal Commissions.
1948		Mr Barry Pemberton		Let Europe bring back her Kings
1952	S	Lady Henley		Is it fight or heil Fuhrer Alcohol.
1953		Mr Nicholas Horsfield		Modern Paintings: to admire and to laugh?
1969		Sir Joseph Hutchinson	FRS. Draper vProfessor Agriculture Cambridge University.	World Agricultural Policy.
1970 (?)		Sir Sacheverell Sitwell		Air Travel.
1979	S	Admiral Martin Lucy	CB DSC RN.	The Eel.
1980	S	Professor B Spencer		Our Daily Bread.
1981		Mr Gervase Jackson Stops	MA. Consultant to National Trust.	Canons Ashby.
1981	S	Miss Isobel Tasker	Daughter of Dr Tony Tasker. 2 years in China on British Council Scholarship.	East is East and West is West. (Impressions of a foreigner in CChina)*.
1982	S	Mr Clifford Ellison	Restorer of pictures to HM the Queen. Subsequently a member.	Some aspects to the cleaning and restoration of Easel Paintings.
1985	S	Mr Henry Bird	Artist, together with actor wife Freda Jackson.	My Life and the Theatre.
1986	S	Mr W J A Lockhart	Past President Association of Foresters.	Forestry and Conservation.
1987	S	Mr Stephen Drew	Head of English Department Rugby School.	Rupert Brooke.
1988	S	Sir Gordon Roberts	Chairman Oxford Regional Health Authority.	The NHS – 40 years on.
1989	S	Mr Bruce Bailey		The Changing Styles of the English Garden.
1990	S	Mr Eric Roberts	Writer on Natural History	Armchair Naturalist.
1991	S	Sir Terence Streeton	KBE CMG late High Commissioner Bangladesh.	Modern British Diplomacy.

1992	S	Miss Barbara Young	Chief Executive Royal Society for the Protection of Birds.	RSPB.
1993	S	Mr Gervase Jackson-Stops	Architectural Advisor to National Trust.	Restoration of the great gardens of Stowe.
1994	S	Unknown		The other Grand Tour.
1995	S	Dame Jill Knight	Baroness Knight of Collingtree. MP for Birmingham Edgbaston. MBE DBE.	Experiences as a Conservative MP in Birmingham.
1996	S	Sir Wilfred Cockcroft		Experiences as Vice-Chancellor and Government Advisor.
2002	S	Lord Lawson.	Nigel Lawson, Baron Lawson of Blaby. Politician and ex Chancellor of Exchequer 1983-89.	Economics.
2004	S	Mr Rupert Litherland		Work of the Trust.
2005	S	Rev David Saint		Some interesting incidents and people in the history of the Town and County.
2006	S	Rt Rev Peter Hullah	Principal Northampton Academy. Formerly Suffragen Bishop of Ramsbury (See diocese - Salisbury).	Northampton Academy.
2007	S	Mr Peter Lawson	Notary Public, Liverpool.	A Dickens' Letter?
2009	S	Professor Alison Liebling	PhD. Professor of Criminology and Criminal Justice Cambridge University. Director Prison Research Centre. Author.	Private Prisons.
2010	S	Dr Twigs Way	Garden Historian, broadcaster, author.	Women and the Garden in the 18th Century.
2011	S	Mrs Judith Allnatt	Author (Inter alia 'The Poet's Wife'). Lecturer and broadcaster.	John Clare.
2012	S	Giles Cole	Actor, Author and Researcher.	Terence Rattigan
2012	S	Marquis Nicholas de Piro		The Domestic

Arrangements of Grand Masters*.

S denotes guest speaker for a Summer Meeting.
* Paper in archive.

Regulations, carried 28th July, 1887.

1.—That the members meet at seven p.m. for seven-thirty, on the third Thursdays of the months of September, October, November, January, February, March, and April.

2.—That the arrangements for the Summer Meetings be made at the April Meetings.

3.—That the discussions close at nine-fifteen p.m.

4.—That the Meetings end at ten-thirty p.m., but that the host for the time being may ask the guests to stay until midnight. (If such invitation be not given, no member is to feel agrieved.)

5.—That refreshments be limited to the following:—
Sandwiches, Coffee, Tea, Jellies, and Fruit.

Any two, but not more than two of the following wines:—
Port, Sherry, Claret, Hock.

Brandy or Whisky and Aerated waters may be offered.

That members send in the titles of their papers not later than the 1st September.

Northampton Chit-Chat Club Rules 1887

APPENDIX 2
Rules

The first Rules of the Club were laid down at the preliminary meeting in 1885, probably in May. It is a series of resolutions, presumably carried.

It was resolved to form a club for the purpose of discussing subjects other than of a political or religious nature.
It was resolved to limit the number to eight members for 6 months
It was resolved that each member be allowed to bring a friend to the meetings
It was resolved that each member in turn bring forward a subject for discussion
that the member appointed to open the discussion be permitted to choose a substitute
that all business be transacted before the discussion
that the meetings be held on the last Monday in January, March, May, July, September & November.

In February 1887 the rules were expanded considerably

RULES

1. *This Club is formed for the purpose of discussing subjects other than of a religious or political nature.*
2. *Each Member is allowed, with due notice, to introduce a friend at the Meetings.*
3. *Each Member is expected in turn to bring forward a subject*

for discussion.
4. The Member appointed to open the discussion is allowed to choose a substitute, not necessarily a Member of the Society.
5. All business to be transacted before the discussion.
6. New Members to be chosen by post-card ballot, one black ball to exclude.
7. The Meetings to be held in the last week in September, October, November, January, February, March and April; and a Summer Meeting at the discretion of the Secretary. The Meetings to be held on Monday, Tuesday, Wednesday, Thursday and Friday, in rotation.
8. Any Member not attending at least two Meetings during the year ceases to be a Member of the Club, unless excused on application.

Later that year

CHIT-CHAT CLUB
*
Regulations, carried 28th July 1887
*

1.—That the members meet at seven p.m. for seven-thirty, on the third Thursdays of the months of September, October, November, January, February, March, and April.
2.—That the arrangements for the Summer Meetings be made at the April Meetings.
3.—That the discussions close at nine-fifteen p.m.

4.—That the Meetings end at ten-thirty p.m., but that the host for the time being may ask the guests to stay until midnight. (If such invitation be not given, no member is to feel agrieved.)
5 —That refreshments be limited to the following:- Sandwiches, Coffee, Tea, Jellies, and Fruit.
Any two, but not more than two of the following wines :— Port, Sherry, Claret, Hock.
Brandy or Whisky and Aerated waters may be offered.

*

That members send in the titles of their papers not later than the 1st September.

About 1890 another printed set appeared although there is no mention in the minutes and it is not identified in accounts.. The Club now had an object.

October 1892 saw the next set with sweets being substituted for jellies. There would be no limitation to the number of guests the host might invite providing of course it was not his wife. There is no trace of this edition of the rules but that of April 1896 is unlikely to be very different.

RULES

1. This Club is formed for the purpose of discussing subjects other than of a religious or political nature.
2. The number of members is limited to 18, and they shall entertain the Club in rotation, where practicable.
3. Each member is allowed, with due notice, to introduce a friend at the meetings.

4. Each member is expected in turn to bring forward a subject for discussion.

5. The member appointed to open the discussion is allowed to provide a substitute, not necessarily a member of the Society.

6. All business to be transacted before the discussion.

7. Every new member must be proposed and seconded at a meeting of the Club, and his election—which is by post-card ballot—shall not proceed till after the meeting next following. One black ball shall exclude, and the ballot shall be kept open seven days.

8. New members pay an entrance fee of half-a-crown.

9. The Club shall meet on the Second Monday in September, October, November, December, January, February, March, and April, at 7 p.m. for 7.30 p.m.

10. The discussion shall be declared closed at 9.15 and the meeting shall end at 10.30. The host for the time being may ask the guests to stay until midnight. (If such invitation be not given, no member is to feel aggrieved).

11. The Refreshments are limited to the following:- Sandwiches, Coffee, Tea, Fruit, and Sweets. Any two, but not more than two, of the following wines:- Port, Sherry, Claret, Hock. Brandy or Whiskey and Aerated Waters may be offered.

12. One or more extra Summer meetings shall be arranged at the April meeting.

13. Any member not attending at least two meetings during the year ceases to be a number of the Club, unless excused on application. The reading of a paper to be held equivalent to two attendances.

14. Ten clear days' notice of each meeting is to be given to the members.

15. Members not answering the intimation cards before the

morning of the day of meeting are fined sixpence each.
16. The expenses of the Club will be met by a call made by the Secretary when necessary.
17. No alteration is to be made in these rules without notice being given at one meeting and a resolution duly passed at the next.

1901 produced an amendment, to rule 16, otherwise the list remained the same.

16A. Honorary members may be elected from among past members, to shew recognition of distinguished services, but that such members be asked to contribute a paper to the Club in person, at least once in two years, as a condition of such Honorary membership.
16B. The election of Honorary members shall be at the meeting of the Club next following that at which the nomination takes place, and it shall be by show of hands.

There is a gap until October 1950 when there are only minor alterations, *sectarian* **religion and** *party* **politics are now specified. This rule had been amended in 1917.**

RULES OF THE CHIT CHAT CLUB.
*

1. This Club is formed for the purpose of discussing subjects other than those dealing with sectarian religion or party politics.

2. The number of members is limited to 18, and they shall entertain the Club in rotation, where practicable.

3. Each member is allowed, with due notice, to introduce a friend at the meetings. At the summer meeting a lady may be invited.

4. Each member is expected in turn to read a paper.

5. The member appointed to read a paper is allowed to provide a substitute, not necessarily a member of the Society.

6. All business to be transacted before the discussion.

7. All remarks by members or visitors during discussion must be addressed to Tyrannus and should not exceed ten minutes at a time.

8. Every new member must be proposed and seconded at a meeting of the Club, and his election - which is by postcard ballot - shall not proceed till after the meeting next following. One black ball shall exclude, and the ballot shall be kept open seven days.

9. New members pay an entrance fee of five shillings.

10. The Club shall meet on the last Friday in September, October, November, January, February, March and April, at 8 p.m. for 8.20 p.m.

11. The discussion shall be closed by Tyrannus at such hour as he thinks fit and the meetings should end not later than 11.0 p.m.

12. The Refreshments are limited to the following:- Cake, Sandwiches, Coffee and Tea. Any two, but not more than two, of the following wines:-Port, Sherry, Claret, Hock. Spirits, Beer and Soft Drinks may be offered.

13. One or more extra Summer meetings shall be arranged.

14. Any member not attending at least two meetings during the year ceases to be a member of the Club, unless excused on application. The reading of a paper to be held equivalent to two attendances.

15. Ten clear days' notice of each meeting is to be given to the members.

16. A member, whose reply to the intimation card does not reach the host at the latest on the day preceding the day of meeting, will be fined sixpence.

17. The expenses of the Club will be met by a call made by Tyrannus when necessary.

18. No alteration is to be made in these rules without notice being given at one meeting and a resolution duly passed at the next.

Advancing now to March 1984 the rules have become more complicated, some would say top heavy.

1. This Club is formed for the purpose of discussing subjects other than of a religious or political nature.

2. The number of members is limited to 18, and they shall entertain the Club in rotation, where practicable.

3. Each member is allowed, with due notice, to introduce a friend at the meetings.

4. Each member is expected in turn to bring forward a subject for discussion.

5. The member appointed to open the discussion is allowed to provide a substitute, not necessarily a member of the Society.

6. All business to be transacted before the discussion.

7. Every new member must be proposed and seconded at a meeting

of the Club, and his election - which is by post-card ballot - shall not proceed till after the meeting next following. One black ball shall exclude, and the ballot shall be kept open seven days.

8. New members pay an entrance fee of half-a-crown.

9. The Club shall meet on the Second Monday in September, October, November, December, January, February, March, and April, at 7 p.m. for 7.30 p.m.

10. The discussion shall be declared closed at 9.15 and the meeting shall end at 10.30. The host for the time being may ask the guests to stay until midnight. (If such invitation be not given, no member is to feel aggrieved).

11. The Refreshments are limited to the following:- Sandwiches, Coffee, Tea, Fruit, and Sweets. Any two, but not more than two, of the following wines:- Port, Sherry, Claret, Hock. Brandy or Whiskey and Aerated Waters may be offered

12. One or more extra Summer meetings shall be arranged at the April meeting.

13. Any member not attending at least two meetings during the year ceases to be a number of the Club, unless excused on application. The reading of a paper to be held equivalent to two attendances.

14. Ten clear days' notice of each meeting is to be given to the members.

15. Members not answering the intimation cards before the morning of the day of meeting are fined sixpence each.

16. The expenses of the Club will be met by a call made by the Secretary when necessary.

17. No alteration is to be made in these rules without notice being given at one meeting and a resolution duly passed at the next.

Following problems with the expression 'black ball' the rules were amended in 2004.

Chit Chat Club rules [rev Nov. 2004]
1. The club is for the discussion of subjects other than party politics or sectarian religion.
2. Membership is limited to 18 and members shall entertain the club in rotation where possible.
3. A member may, with due notice, introduce a guest to meetings. A lady may be invited to the summer meeting.
4. Each member, in turn, is expected to read a paper.
5. The member appointed to read a paper may provide a substitute, not necessarily a member.
6. All business to be transacted before the paper is read.
7. During the discussion period following the paper one member (including the reader) or guest shall speak continuously for not more than five minutes.
8. New members shall be appointed in the following manner:
    1. The candidate should attend at least three meetings as a guest of his sponsor, who shall advise Tyrannus that he considers the candidate suitable for club membership.
    2. Tyrannus shall informally canvass each and every member's opinion of the candidate.
    3. If opinion is at all unfavourable (that is to say if any one or more of the members expresses an unfavourable opinion), Tyrannus shall advise the sponsor not to proceed and the sponsor shall accept that decision.
    4. If opinion is favourable (that is to say if each and

every member is in favour of, or expressly does not oppose, the admission of the candidate to membership) Tyrannus shall ask the sponsor to ascertain the candidates interest in membership.

5. If the candidate declines, nothing further is to be done.

6. If the candidate accepts, then at the next club meeting (unless at or before the commencement of the business part of that meeting the sponsor withdraws his support or any one or more members objects to the candidate becoming a member whereupon rule 8.3 shall apply) Tyrannus shall declare that the candidate is and the candidate shall thereupon become a member of the club.

9. Tyrannus shall be elected as follows:

1. By members for a 3 year term, followed by 3 years ineligibility for re-election.

2. During his final year, Tyrannus shall ensure that the nomination of his successor reflects members' wishes.

10. The club shall meet in October, November, January, February, March and April at 7.30 pm.

11. Tyrannus shall close the discussion at such time as he thinks fit, but no later than 10.30 pm.

12. Modest refreshments shall be provided at the host's discretion and shall be so consumed

as to permit business to commence at 9.00 pm.

13. One or more summer meetings may be arranged.

14. Membership shall continue for as long as the member both wishes and is able to satisfy membership requirements. Tyrannus shall exercise discretion in individual circumstances.

15. Membership obligations shall be regarded as a whole and no minimum number of attendances is prescribed. Tyrannus shall exercise discretion in individual circumstances.

16. When a member appears to depart from membership obligations, Tyrannus shall seek from him some assurance as to his future intentions. If that assurance is not given or is not honoured, Tyrannus may suggest that member's resignation. If no satisfactory conclusion eventuates, the club shall decide the outcome.

17. When possible, 10 days' notice shall be given of each meeting.

18. Any member who fails to notify the host of his attendance intentions by the day preceding the meeting shall be liable to a fine of sixpence.

19. The expenses of the club shall be met by a call from Tyrannus when necessary.

20. No alteration shall be made to these rules except by notice given at one meeting and a resolution supported by at least two thirds of the total club membership at a subsequent meeting.

In 2010 the then Tyrannus was anxious to resurrect the Honorary Membership category and managed to persuade members to that effect. This meant redrafting by a legal mind.

CHIT CHAT CLUB
Founded in Northampton
in the year 1885
RULES

1. The Club is for the discussion of subjects other than party politics or sectarian religion.
2. Membership is limited to eighteen ordinary members and members shall entertain the Club in rotation where possible.
3. A member may, with due notice, introduce a guest to meetings. A lady may be invited to the summer meeting.
4. Each member, in turn, is expected to read a paper.
5. The member appointed to read a paper may provide a substitute, not necessarily a member.
6. All business to be transacted before the paper is read.
7. During the discussion period following the paper no one member (including the reader) or guest shall speak continuously for more than five minutes.
8. New members shall be appointed in the following manner:
8.1 The candidate should attend at least three meetings as a guest of his sponsor, who shall advise Tyrannus that he considers the candidate suitable for Club membership.
8.2 Tyrannus shall informally canvass each and every member's opinion of the candidate.
8.3 If opinion is at all unfavourable (that is to say if any one or more of the members expresses an unfavourable opinion), Tyrannus shall advise the sponsor not to proceed and the sponsor shall accept that decision.

8.4 If opinion is favourable (that is to say if each and every member is in favour of, or expressly does not oppose, the admission of the candidate to membership), Tyrannus shall ask the sponsor to ascertain the candidate's interest in membership.

8.5 If the candidate declines, nothing further is to be done.

8.6 If the candidate accepts, then at the next Club meeting (unless at or before the commencement of the business part of that meeting the sponsor withdraws his support or any one or more members objects to the candidate becoming a member whereupon Rule 8.3 shall apply) Tyrannus shall declare that the candidate is and the candidate shall thereupon become a member of the Club.

9. Honorary membership of the Club shall be as follows:

9.1 Any member who has been an ordinary member for not less than 5 years is eligible for Honorary membership if unable to fulfil his obligations of membership by reason of change of location, infirmity of himself or his partner, financial constraints or any other reason considered sufficient by other ordinary members.

9.2 The number of Honorary Members shall be limited to four at any one time.

9.3 Honorary members shall be permitted to attend two ordinary meetings, without guests, during any one year in addition to the Summer Meeting when a guest may be allowed.

9.4 Honorary members shall not take part in the management or decision making of the Club but may attend business meetings

9.5   Honorary members shall be elected unanimously by ordinary members, excluding the candidate himself.
9.6   Honorary Members may at their discretion contribute to the funds of the Club as they think fit.
10.   Tyrannus shall be elected as follows:
10.1 By members for a three-year term, followed by three years ineligibility for re-election.
10.2 During his final year, Tyrannus shall ensure that the 9.2 nomination of his successor reflects members' wishes.
11.   The Club shall meet in October, November, January, February, March and April at 7.30 p.m.
12.   Tyrannus shall close the discussion at such time as he thinks fit, but no later than 10.30 p.m.
13.   Modest refreshments shall be provided at the host's discretion and shall be so consumed as to permit business to commence at 9.00 p.m.
14.   One or more summer meetings may be arranged.
15.   Membership shall continue for as long as the member both wishes and is able to satisfy membership requirements. Tyrannus shall exercise discretion in individual circumstances.
16.   Membership obligations shall be regarded as a whole and no minimum number of attendances is prescribed. Tyrannus shall exercise discretion in individual circumstances.
17.   When a member appears to depart from membership obligations, Tyrannus shall seek from him some assurance as to his future intentions. If that assurance is not given or is not honoured, Tyrannus may suggest that member's

	resignation. If no satisfactory conclusion eventuates, the Club shall decide the outcome.
18.	*When possible, ten days' notice shall be given of each meeting.*
19.	*Any member who fails to notify the host of his attendance intentions by the day preceding the meeting shall be liable to a fine of sixpence.*
20.	*The expenses of the Club shall be met by a call from Tyrannus when necessary.*
21.	*No alteration shall be made to these Rules except by notice given at one meeting and a resolution supported by at least two-thirds of the total Club membership at a subsequent meeting.*

Over 125 years the rules of the Club, including the heading, have increased from 148 to 789 words.

Appendix 3
Tyranni

1885-87	Hooper
1887-92	R Greene
1892-1901	A H Jones
1901-23	E M Browne
1923-?	Ince-Jones
?	
? – 1971	Jackson
1971-82	Lee
1982-85	Hill
1985-88	Tasker
1988-91	Fincham
1991-93	Featherstone
1993-96	Ellison
1996-99	Rickett
1999-2002	Saint
2002-05	Cornelius
2005-08	Hardingham
2008-	Toseland

Appendix 4

Awake, Northamptonshire
A ballad for the time

From where St. Peter's Minster
Beholds across the Fen
The ruined tower of Crowland,:
And the homes of Cromwell's men,
To that fair Cherwell valley,
Where springs Kings Sutton spire
From town and tilth and woodland,
Awake, Northamptonshire!

The battle of the nations
Is ringing in your ears,
And German will brings German skill
To vent the hate of years.
On a11 who live beneath the flag
The days of crisis break;
Show that you dare to take your share
Northamptonshire, awake !

Gone are the gallant gentlemen
The Pytchley pastures know;
For they who rode to hunt the fox
Now ride to hunt the foe.
And you who throng the football field,
Look not for those best known,
For they have had the manliness
To drill with Mobbs' Own.

God save those gone already,
The pioneers of right;
God save the old great houses
Whose heirs are in the fight.
From lawns of ducal Wakefield,
From Althorp's stately trees,
From Wicken Park to Stamford Town,
Their scions have crossed the seas.

Come, follow their example!
Your tools and trades lay down,
And foremost in the cause be you,
Sons of Northampton town.
[Northampton, where the ages
Heard loud the lapstone ring;
The town of banded freemen,
No Lord beside the King]
In many a famed election,
Your vigour carried far;
The force you gave to politics
Now give to righteous war.

And you from farm and country!
Let women tend the kine,
Come forth from fold and byre and plough,
From quarry, pit, and mine.
You men of strength and sinew,
Hark to the great appeal;
You who have worked the iron,
Go! learn to thrust the steel.
High on the Naseby uplands,
Whose steeple stabs the sky,
For Church and Cause, for King and Laws,
Your fathers went to die.
If then, in civil conflict,

Such doughty deeds were done,
How much the more you now can do,
When England all is one.

The regiments of your county
Have records void of fleck;
They stormed Gibraltar's arid height,
And triumphed o'er Quebec.
Firm in the shell-swept trenches
The gallant Steelbacks stand;
Up, Men! and take your fitting place,
To fight at their right hand.

For you are of the centre,
By England's heart you dwell;
To none can come with clearer note
The call to serve her well.
Six thousand of your comrades
Are gone from field and street;
Your King asks twice six thousand more
To make your tale complete.

What though by foreign hamlets
The lines of war are set.
Though down the valley of the Nene
To cannon thunder yet.
By Scheldt and Aisne, by Meuse and Rhine,
The battles must be won,
If you would keep Northamptonshire
Unblasted by the Hun.

Begirt by armoured millions,
Your mighty foeman lies;
Equipped with deadly science,
And served by swarms of spies,

Keen in his foul ambition
To outrage and to kill,
No limit to his lust of power,
His only law - his will.

Or if his brutal menace
Need more to make it plain,
Ask them who hear his cursed yoke,
Alsatian, Pole, and Dane.
Think of the fields of Flanders,
Red where his hoofs have trod:
A madman for his Kaiser
And Moloch for his God.

Go! and our hopes go with you!
For you our hearts will burn,
And there shall be a better land
To greet your glad return.
Or, if in duty's pathway,
On honour's field you fall,
With Him who gave His life for men
Meet the great Judge of all.

By all the things men care for,
Wealth, fame, success, or ease,
The love of wife and mother,
The children round the knees;
For all the things men pray for,
For happiness and peace,
Rise up, Northamptonshire, and strike,
Till all the horrors cease.

W. Ryland D. Adkins
From an unnamed periodical in
Northamptonshire Central Library

INDEX

In the interest of clarity only names have been included in this index. Name exclusively in chapter notes have not been included.

ABBOTT George Edward, 277.
ADKINS, Sir William Ryland Dent, 27, 29-30, 31, 38-39, 42, 43, 44, 47, 48, 53, 54, 57, 59, 66, 71, 72, 139, 161, 163-166, 167, 198, 202, 203, 206, 218, 265, 272, 275.
ALDRED Cyril Clowes, 125.
ALMENT, Sir Edward Anthony John, 86, 90, 246-248.
ATKINSON Douglas Mason (Peter), 295-296.
BAKER, Rev Robert Sibley, 27.
BATES, H E, 285.
BEASLEY, Rev Thomas Calvert, 39, 48, 49, 50, 60, 121-123, 161, 205, 206, 218, 264.
BEVIR Anthony, 130.
BIRK, Rev A H, 65.
BLAKEMAN John, 79.
BLYTH, Dr Alexander Wynter, 44, 202, 225-226.
BROWN, Sir James Crichton, 37-38, 229.
BROWNE Edward Montague, 21, 23, 27, 38, 46, 50, 55, 57-68, 70-71, 72, 77, 124, 157, 161, 162-163, 167, 174, 177, 203, 206, 226, 228, 229, 258, 259, 280.
BROWNE Harold St John, 71, 77, 83, 150, 158, 182-184, 261.
BROWNE, Rev Laurence Edward, 77, 80, 132, 150-152, 269.
BROWNE, Eustace, 77.
BULL, Derek James, 305.
BURDETT, Sir Henry C, 32.
BURY, The Rev Canon William, 27, 139-140, 161, 164, 198, 200.
BUTTERFIELD Henry, 275.
CARTER Thomas G F, 132, 282.
CARTWRIGHT, Rev James Lawrence, 73, 149.

CHAMBERLAIN James Thomas, 173.
CHAMBERLAIN, Mrs, 66.
CHAMBERLAIN Russell, 172.
CHURCH W H C, 39, 218, 274.
CLIFTON, Dr, 37-38.
CLOUGH Arthur, 263.
COLES, Dr Richard Bertram, 86, 248.
COLLIER Thomas L, 282.
COOCH Peter, 189.
COOKE William Charles Cyril, 71, 169, 183, 210, 212, 261, 267-268, 269, 278.
CORNELIUS Michael, 190-191, 294.
COX, Rev John Charles, 53-54, 138-139.
CROOKSHANK, Dr Francis Graham, 48, 49, 207.
CROPLEY, Dr Henry, 155, 223.
CUNNINGHAM, Rev John, 38, 143, 217-220.
DALGLEISH, Dr Peter Gordon, 87, 241-242.
DAVIES, Rev Basil Henry, 65, 145.
DAVIES, Dr E Meredith, 230.
De PIRO, Marquis Nicholas, 135, 305.
De PUTRON, Mrs, 73, 149.
De PUTRON, Rev John Percy, 73, 136-137, 262.
DIXON Hugh Neville, 59, 68, 70, 79, 133, 138, 179, 233, 255-257, 279.
DOCKRELL, Dr T Hayes, 86, 240-241,
DOLLAR, Rev Joseph Bartholomew, 148-149.
EAMES, Dr Peter 223.
EDEN, Hon. Michael Francis, 288.
ELLISON Clifford James, 189, 190, 298, 301.
ELLISON Geoffrey Walker, 79, 172, 212, 284-286.
EUNSON George, 18, 274-275.
EUNSON, John, 6-9, 14, 18, 272.

335

EWART, Rev L A, 131-132.
EWEN, Rev Alfred, 62-4, 65, 72, 167, 174-176,
FAULKER John Joseph, 29, 46, 163.
FEATHERSTONE Cecil, 296-297.
FIELD, Dr Ernest E, 71, 268-269.
FINCHAM Thomas George, 87, 187-188, 292, 297.
FORBES, Judge, 186.
FULLERTON Moore Betty, 280.
GALE John, 302.
GARNHAM Cecil John, 288.
GASKELL, Ernest, 122, 142.
GEORGE, Dr David Rodney, 269-270.
GEORGE Thomas John, 6, 14, 17, 18, 272-274.
GILL, Rev Anthony Clarke, 153.
GODFREY, The Rev Canon Simon Henry Martin, 134-135.
GOMPERTZ, The Rev Canon Peter Alan Martin, 152-153.
GORDON Rev Charles James, 8, 19.
GRAHAM, Dr Andrew Noble, 222-223.
GRAY Charles, 25, 42.
GREEN Thomas, 8, 18, 25, 43, 155-156, 200, 203.
GREENE Dr Richard, 14, 19, 20, 21, 23-33, 36, 37, 39, 43, 44, 47, 50, 55, 57, 66, 72, 142, 155, 157, 159, 164, 197-204, 206, 225.
HADDEN, Lionel Truss (Pip), 297.
HADLEY William Waite, 67, 280-282.
HALL, Rev W C, 70.
HAMMOND Rev Charles Edward, 6-9, 14, 18, 121, 138.
HANKINSON, Mrs, 264.
HARDING, Dr William, 29, 42, 43, 58, 159, 204-207.
HARDINGHAM Peter Alan, 191-193.
HARDY J, 275.
HARPER, Rev Alfred Mussendine, 49, 144-145, 155.
HAVILAND John, 24, 31, 46, 162, 163.

HAYES, Dr Edmund Duncan Tranchell, 213-216, 278.
HEANLEY Marshall, 282.
HEYGATE Arthur Robert, 293-294.
HEYGATE Arthur Robert (Sen.), 86, 290, 291-293.
HICHENS, Dr Peverell Smythe 66,167, 227-228.
HICKS Gilbert, 184.
HICKSON William, 59, 167, 276-277.
HILL Stanley, 86-87, 288-291, 292.
HOOPER Rev George Brereton, 3-9, 12-14, 15, 20, 21, 23, 32, 66, 121, 126, 138, 155, 197.
HORSFALL-CARTER, 187.
HUMFREY, Dr Stuart Harold Guise, 86, 235-237, 281.
HUTCHINSON, Sir Joseph, 86.
HUTTON, Rev Frederick Robert Chapman, 121.
INCE-JONES Frederick, 10, 30, 53, 65, 67, 68, 70-84, 86, 88, 99, 133, 148, 149, 156, 158, 169, 205, 208, 211, 232, 233, 236, 257-266, 277, 278, 281, 283, 306.
JACKSON Antony H, 86-87, 185-186, 238, 269, 288, 289, 291.
JACKSON James, 42, 58, 66, 81, 83, 130, 132, 167-173, 177, 216, 234.
JACKSON -STOPS Anthony, 294.
JACKSON-STOPS Timothy William Ashworth, 294.
JENNINGS, Dr Alan Maurice Charles, 90, 248-250.
JESSON Thomas, 274.
JONES Dr Arthur Henry, 19, 23, 24, 26, 27, 29, 33, 35-55, 72, 136, 140, 202, 203, 204, 224.
JONES, Dr Henry Travers, 213.
JONES Owen Meurig, 187.
KEYSELL, Rev Folliott Sandford, 145-147.
LAVER, Dr Basil, 214, 230-231.
LAWSON, Rev Frederick Pyke, 145.
LEE Julia, 239, 240.

LEE, Dr Ralph Owen, 86-87,127, 237-240, 247, 289.
LEE, Sir Sidney, 60.
LEWIS Rev John Trevor, 127, 130-134, 150, 171, 172, 212, 288.
LINEY, Rev A A, 153.
LOWERY Thomas Ian, 304.
LOWICK Geoffrey Heygate, 86, 186-187.
LUNT, Rev Geoffrey Charles Lester, 128-130.
MACKINTOSH, Dr John M 83,131, 171, 234-235.
MANFIELD Harry, 48, 276.
MANFIELD James, 276.
MARKHAM Christopher Alexander, 25, 43,, 48, 50, 58, 64, 67, 71, 74, 129, 156-162, 181, 210, 213.
MARKHAM Henry William Kennedy, 25, 156.
MILLET, S, 13-14.
MILLIGAN Dr Robert Arthur OBE, 24, 72, 226-227.
MONIE Peter Ralph
MORGAN, Rev Grenville, 128.
MUSCOTT Bruce Beckwith, 66, 71, 136, 161, 277-278.
MUSCOTT Guy Bruce,68, 278-280.
NETTLETON Martin Barnes, 269.
NOCK Peter John, 303.
ORTON-JONES Michael, 194.
PAGE E Murray
PAGE, Percy Hawkins, 48, 49, 277.
PARKER Henry Nichols, 79.
PENTON, Sir Edward, 72-73.
PERCIVAL, Dr George Henry OBE, 227.
PERCIVAL, Mrs, 42.
PERRY, Rev Thomas Hattam, 78, 79, 125-127, 134, 264.
PHIPPS Albert Edward, 277.
RAYNSFORD, Lt. Col. Richard Montague, 77, 78, 80, 81, 83, 234, 266, 286-287.
REED Michael, 302-303.
REYNOLDS Edward, 266-267.

RICKETT Anthony, 298-300.
RIGGALL John Robert, 295.
ROBERTS, The Rev Canon J L, 41, 201.
ROBERTSON, Dr Denis Wilson, 251.
SAINT Jerome P, 188-189.
SANDERS Canon Dr Samuel John Woodhouse, 5-9, 11-12, 18, 23, 26,-27, 30, 35, 67, 121, 138, 197, 201, 255, 275.
SANDERS Millicent, 18, 274.
SCRIVEN, Mrs, 42.
SCRIVEN Richard George, 6, 14, 25, 27, 155, 161, 274.
SEAMAN, Owen, 149.
SHAEFFER Gary William, 61, 303-304.
SHAPLAND Henry Percival, 83-84, 172, 232, 262, 265, 282-284.
SHAW, Dr Eric Hemingway, 81,86, 127, 130, 215, 231-234, 269.
SHEPHERD, Rev Dr Arthur Pearce, 147-148, 233.
SHEPPARD, Dr Robin, 247.
SHOOSMITH Fanny Violet, 181.
SHOOSMITH Thurston Laidlaw, 181.
SHOOSMITH William Buxton, 61, 66, 161, 164, 179-181, 182,265.
SITWELL Francis Trajan Sacheverell, 301.
SKINNER A F, OBE, 187.
SLEIGHT, Rev William Blomefield, 50, 72, 142-143.
SMITH Harrington, 272.
SOUTAR Neil, 300.
STONE, Dr Noel, 238.
STREATFEILD, Rev Leonard Champion, 123-125, 147, 178, 264.
STUART, Dr Frederick Joshua, 79, 167, 207-213.
STURDEE Robert James, 123.
TALBOT Peter Lindsay, 304.
TASKER, Dr John Rendel (Tony), 86, 188, 242-246, 249, 292.
TASKER Isobel, 305.
TASKER Matthew Howard, 193-194.
TENNENT, Dr Thomas, 127, 220-222.

TERRY, Rev George Russell, 51-53, 173-174.
THOMAS, David, 13.
THOMSON, Sir Basil Home, 53-55.
TOM, Mrs, 142.
TOM, Rev Edward Nicholls, 29, 50, 58, 140-142, 201.
TOSELAND, Dr Michael Anthony, 192, 250-251.
TRAVIS, Mr, 261-262.
TURNER Charles Simkin, 176-177.
TURNER John Alan, 86,287-288.
TUSON, Rev Edward Luxmoore, 135-136.
UNDERWOOD Trevor, 300-301.
VAUGHAN Christopher James, 193.
WAGSTAFF, Dr Frank Alexander, 66, 211, 228-230.
WAKE, Sir Hereward, 20-21, 25, 155, 274.
WAKE Joan, 80, 266,
WALKER William Arthur, 65, 181-182.
WHYTE-MELVILLE, George John, 164-165, 285.
WILLIAMSON John, 221.
WILSON, Rev William, 138.
WOOD, Rev Francis Henry, 143-144, 167.